BUG
MAKING

Books by C. Boyd Pfeiffer

Tackle Craft (1974)

Shad Fishing (1975)

Field Guide to Outdoor Photography (1976)

The Practical Fisherman (with Irv Swope) (1981)

Angler's Guide to Plug and Bait Casting (1985)

The Orvis Guide to Outdoor Photography (1986)

Tackle Care (1988)

The Compleat Surfcaster (1989)

Modern Tackle Craft (1992)

Bug Making (1993)

BUG
MAKING

C. BOYD PFEIFFER

LYONS & BURFORD, PUBLISHERS

To Jackie, again, for her patience and understanding as yet another book comes into being.

To Cody, our first grandchild, and our family's future, who hopefully will have some of the chances that I have had to feel throbbing fish on the end of a line, to view a sunset at the end of a spring day while throwing a long line and a well-crafted bass bug for one last chance for an explosive surface strike, to experience the pleasures of tackle making and rod building and tying up surface fly-rod bugs, but most of all to enjoy the bounties of nature. After all, there is more to fishing than the fish.

Copyright © 1993 by C. Boyd Pfeiffer

Printed in the United States of America

Design by M.R.P. Design.

10 9 8 7 6 5 4 3 2 1

Library of Congress Cataloging-in-Publication Data

Pfeiffer, C. Boyd.
Bug making : a thorough guide to making and tying floating bugs for all gamefish—bluegill to billfish / C. Boyd Pfeiffer.
p. cm.
Includes bibliographical references
ISBN 1-55821-258-2
1. Fly tying. 2. Flies, Artificial. I. Title.
SH451.P48 1993
688.7′9—dc20   93-21220
                                          CIP

Contents

Acknowledgments   *vii*

Introduction   *xi*

Note to the Reader   *xv*

1 Tools and Materials   *1*

2 Terrestrials—Designs and Tying Styles   *23*

3 Tying Hair-Bodied Bugs   *49*

4 Hair-Bodied Bug Designs   *77*

5 Cork Bug Construction   *85*

6 Balsa and Wood Bug Construction   *99*

7 Molded Bug Construction   *119*

8 Soft-Foam Bug Construction   *131*

9 Tying and Finishing Methods for Hard-Bodied Bugs   *147*

10 Hard-Bug Design and Styles   *171*

11 Painting and Finishing Bugs   *201*

12 Rigging Bugs and Bug-Fishing Tackle   *221*

13 Fishing Methods, Retrieves, and Manipulation of Bugs   *235*

APPENDIX

A Suppliers   *247*

B Manufacturers   *251*

C Bibliography   *255*

D Videos on Bug Making   *259*

E Record-Keeping Organizations   *261*

F Tips on Fly Tying and Using Foam   *263*

Index   *269*

Acknowledgments

This book was born out of my frustration about not being able to find a single source for a wide variety of bug designs and construction methods. To be sure, bug making in all its various styles, and for different types of fly fishing, has been touched upon in a number of fly-tying and fly-fishing books. Most of these books are listed in the bibliography, and my debt to their authors is gratefully acknowledged.

Many others have helped directly and indirectly with this book, through information and samples of their bugs, through samples of supplies for the tying photos, and through tips and techniques they have shared with me. In no particular order, they include:

Professional fly tyer Chris Helm, for his tips in tying hair-bodied bugs, and for samples for photography.

Jason Shiba, of EdgeWater Fishing Products, for time spent with me at the Fly Tackle Dealer Show in Denver in 1992, helping to fill in my gaps of knowledge on soft foams, the appropriate glues and construction methods, and other tips in working with foam.

Roy Hilts, of Hilts Molds, for first alerting me to the idea of foam bodies for bugs (as well as fishing plugs), and his subsequent help in working with two-part foam to mold bugs.

Joe Messinger, Jr., of Morgantown, West Virginia, for demonstrating to me, and in allowing me to photograph, the intricate and specialized method of tying beautiful hair-bodied bugs that he learned from his father.

Chuck Edghill, for his suggestions regarding and additions to the bibliography and appendices, for the specialized aluminum jigs that he made for me as an aid in making the Potomac River popper—a simple and effective bug for this shallow smallmouth river—and for his unwavering friendship and constant offers to assist in any of my projects.

Norm Bartlett, for sharing his ideas on bug construction, for his help with the appendices and bibliography, and for his innovative, no-frills methods of making bugs that are fish-takers.

Jack Goellner, for general help and for the loan of some bugs to photograph; Irv Swope, for his help and ideas on making jigs to make bugs, for samples of jigs to photograph, and for his tips in general on bug making; Lefty Kreh, for his wisdom, general advice, counsel and tips on all phases of fly fishing, bug fishing, and bug making—particularly on some phases of big-game fishing and bugs; fly tyer Rod Yerger, for his help with his McMurray ant and other terrestrial patterns, for materials, and for photo samples.

Rainy Riding, of Rainy's Flies and Supplies, for her help, photo samples, and permission to reprint her foam fly-tying instructions; Fly tyer Floyd Franke, who first alerted me to the fly-tying wing cutters that work even better as foam-sheet punches for making ant and beetle bodies; Cam Sigler, for information on his new billfish popper heads; Jack Samson, record holder and saltwater fly-fishing writer, for his help in better understanding big-game bugs; Billy Pate, big-game fly rodder and record holder, for information on big-game popping bugs.

Walter Knapp, for his tips on foam bugs; Lou Caronna, for his ideas on bugs, and for loaning bugs for photography; Rocky Mountain Dubbing, and Steve Kennerk, for materials for fleece-silicone and deer-hair bugs, and permission to reprint their tips on choosing and using body hair in making bugs; King Neptune Flies, and Greg Snyder, for samples of the Ethafoam that Greg uses for saltwater bugs, and sells as a component; Bob Popovics, for his time spent instructing me on proper construction of his silicone-coated floating bugs.

Phil Camera, of Phil's Tackle, for help and materials; Jeff Hahner, of Mystic Bay, for his help, suggestions, and ideas on foam and working with foam bugs; Mustad, and Skip Mortensen, for information and samples of Mustad's bug hooks; Tom Schmuecker, of Wapsi, for information,

and samples of his hard foam-body bugs; Vern Kirby, an expert on old tackle and lures, for the loan of his collection of surface bugs for photography and for sharing his knowledge of old patterns and styles.

Randy Swanberg, of Flycraft, for his help, samples for photography, samples of his Flycraft products, and permission to print his instructions on making bugs from his products; Tiemco, and Ken Menard, for samples of Tiemco hooks; Daiichi, and Bill Chase, for hook samples and ideas; Eagle Claw, for their ideas on hooks and popping bugs; Owner American, for hook samples for surface bugs.

Nick Skirkanish, for his help in understanding the chemistry of foam, and glues for foam, and for information on cutters, deer-hair trimmers, and foam products; Hackle-Back, and Tom Thomason, for samples of his product for photography; Chuck Furimsky, developer (with Phil Camera) of Bug Skin, for his ideas, and samples for photography of Bug Skin-covered bass bugs; Matt Hodgson, for his ideas on surface bugs and poppers, and for his suggestions.

Bill Skilton of Bill Skilton's USA Flies for samples of his products and sample flies for photography. Alex Suescan for information and for the loan of bugs for photos.

Finally, and certainly not the least of these debts, is to my publisher, Lyons & Burford, all the fine people of their staff, and especially Nick Lyons—who has stuck with me through publishing efforts since my first book in 1974, when I knew little or nothing about writing books, and only had an idea. Fortunately for me, Nick was willing to take a chance on it and on me. This book might not have come to pass had not that first one been accepted and successful.

Introduction

I t would be easy—but a mistake—to call this a book on bass bugs or popping bugs. But when describing the work in progress to friends, other fly tyers, suppliers, and manufacturers, I would often slip and do just that. The fact is that this book has a far broader base—one that covers any type of floating bug, from tiny terrestrials for trout to #7/0 billfish poppers.

The subject of this book is anything that can be used on a fly rod that, when pushed underwater, will pop back up to the surface. It is not intended to include those surface bugs that are really works of art—for instance, the ties and patterns of Tim England, Bob Mead, and Yas Yamashita, among others. These are true art forms that I hope will be covered someday in another book.

This book *does* cover practical fishing bugs made of any type of cork, balsa, other woods, hard molded foam, EVA foam, PVC foam, Ethafoam, Live Body EVA/PVC foams, sheet or rod foam, deer hair, elk hair, other hollow hair, hollow wing quills, hollow plastic or aluminum tubing, you name it—provided that it floats and that the resultant bug can be cast with a fly rod.

Examples of the first bugs known - Jamison Coaxers in both the bass and trout size. These were cork bodied bugs with feather tails.

And, unlike the initial mindset of myself and others, this is not just a book on popping bugs, but one on terrestrials of all types (ants, crickets, hoppers, beetles, jassids, termites, caterpillars, inchworms, dragonflies, damselflies, ladybugs, leaf hoppers, tree hoppers, spiders, cicadas, bees, yellow jackets), poppers, sliders, skippers, pencil poppers, a design that I call a splider, pencil minnows, quill minnows, fly/cylinder body combinations, surface minnows, jointed-hook bugs, jointed-tail bugs, tube bugs and tails, extended-hook bugs, hair-bodied bugs of all types. . . .

In short, bug making has come a long way since the Peckinpaugh cork bug and commercially made Jamison wood-bodied bug—perhaps the first that can really be considered bass bugs—were developed around 1910, or the clipped deer-hair style that was developed by Dr. James Henshall, probably in the late 1800's. And since these basic bug materials and styles were developed for bass, perhaps bugs still suffer from being plugged into that narrow field.

They shouldn't be. Bugs of the appropriate style are just as at home on the south-central Pennsylvania trout stream where many terrestrials were developed. They are also used today on offshore big-game boats, where an ever-increasing number of fly rodders are trying for—and taking—big game such as marlin, sailfish, dolphin, and others. They are used for stripers and snook, bass and bluefish, trout and tarpon, pike and perch. They are used everywhere for everything that will hit a lure on the surface. And they should be.

This book does exclude some flies and ties. For example, some trout and salmon flies have clipped deer-hair bodies: the Green Machine, Bomber, and Buck Butt would be examples of salmon patterns; the Irresistible and Rat-Faced McDougall examples of trout flies with clipped deer-hair bodies. The methods for spinning and stacking the hair for making bodies on these trout and salmon flies are covered (Chapter 3, Tying Hair-Bodied Bugs), but specific patterns or details of this facet of tying are not, as they are more in the realm of traditional fly tying, not bug making.

But there is a lot of et cetera, and there are some gray areas. In researching this book (even after forty years of making various types of basic freshwater and saltwater bugs), I discovered and developed a lot of alternative methods of making bugs, and a lot of possible variations, and was helped by others with their own revelations, tips, and techniques. Some of the non-traditional forms of bugs and bug construction include: various minnows that use straws or plastic tubing to form a hollow, floating body; using quills for the same purpose; methods of boring holes through a cylindrical popper face to make a bubbling head for big game; making floating bugs from fleece-coated silicone; covering bugs with various foils and sheeting materials; gluing materials onto bodies instead of tying them onto the hook shank; jointed-hook styles; methods of folding deer hair instead of clipping it to shape; weedless hook styles (about a dozen methods); methods of shaping foam; and more.

If there is a point to all this rambling, it is that experimentation in patterns, designs, styles, materials, and techniques continues to be the forte of the fly tyer in developing effective patterns, and that fly tying and bug making remain in a constant state of evolution.

That evolution continues with you. I hope some of the enclosed ideas spur you to reach farther, to tie differently, to try harder—to experiment with some yet-untried materials, or to design a yet-unseen pattern in a continued effort to take more fish and have more fun with surface fly-rod bugs. After all, that's what it's all about, with the bug making simply the forerunner of the fly fishing—the anticipation of surface strikes yet to be and catches still to come.

—C. Boyd Pfeiffer
November, 1993

Note to the Reader

This book describes a variety of ways to make and finish bugs. Special note should be taken of some aspects of the book. I mention painting with or using materials that are glow-in-the-dark, and many anglers find these an advantage in night fishing. However, check local regulations, since some states may prohibit or restrict their use.

Also, some states—primarily on trout waters—may prohibit the use of any flies (or bugs) with more than one hook. Thus, the descriptions of double and multiple hook arrangements are out for these waters. Finally, some areas (Pennsylvania has bounced back and forth on this) do not allow the use of cork bugs that are plain (no dressing) and are made to resemble anything other than natural foods.

Thus, bugs that would be made to resemble mulberries, cheese or marshmallows would not be allowed, while those resembling caterpillars, dragonflies, and leaf hoppers would be. Check first on this if at all in doubt.

Naturally, other regulations of which we are not aware may be in effect in some areas. Check first, since in no way is this book approving or authorizing the use of any bug or bug design where not permitted.

Also, the author is planning a book of bug and terrestrial patterns and would welcome any standard or unusual patterns or information on bug patterns. Please feel free to write to:

C. Boyd Pfeiffer
14303 Robcaste Rd.
Phoenix, MD 21131

CHAPTER 1

Tools and Materials

I f you are a fly tyer, you undoubtedly have most of the tools that you need for making and tying bugs. There will be some additional tools and materials you might want that are readily available at your local tackle shop, fly shop, or through mail-order catalogs.

Tools for making bugs include:

Vises

Any fly-tying vise can be used, provided it is sturdy and has jaws that will take the size hook you plan to use. Vises are not used for gluing the bug, but for tying tails and hackle, adding skirts, and the many parts added to closed-cell foam terrestrials. They are a must for tying hair-bodied bugs. For this, you can use any strong, standard vise.

Almost any fly tying-vise can be used for the tying part of making bugs. Those used by the author include the spring-loaded Regal, which allows rotary movement of the jaws (although not a rotary vise) and the Griffin Superior 3A, which has an offset jaw. Both allow angular adjustment of the jaws for different tasks, such as vertical jaws for using the Messinger hair-body tying methods.

You might wish to consider using a vise that can be positioned vertically, as does Joe Messinger, Jr., who follows the lead of his father by using a vertical vise for tying his bugs. Many vise models can be positioned vertically, pivoting them at a point between the post and jaws. Possibilities include models by D. H. Thompson, Griffin, Regal, and others. For tying tube flies, and some types of bodies and tails on slip-on tubes, both Perry Designs and Dyna-King have good vises.

Rotary vises are also useful for some tying, particularly for wrapping hackle around the hook shank in back of a bug body, or hackling on terrestrials or cork bugs. Excellent models are available from Renzetti, Norlander, and others.

Most vises come with a choice of pedestal or clamp base. I prefer a clamp base when tying deer hair, or with any technique where some force must be used.

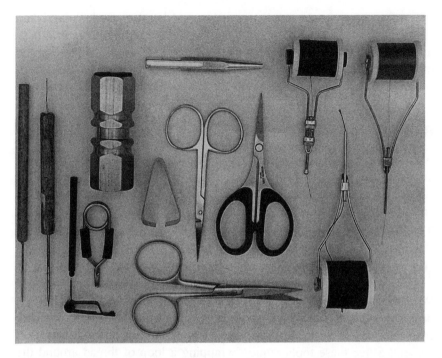

Assortment of bug-making fly-tying tools includes: *(left to right)* bodkins, hackle pliers (two types), stacker, Brassie for compressing hair on hair-bodied bugs, scissors, half-hitch tool, and bobbins.

Bobbins

Bobbins come in different sizes to fit mini spools (such as steel sewing-machine spools), standard size (thread spools), larger spools (bobbins such as those by Griffin and Gudebrod). Bobbins are available with short or long, stainless or ceramic tubes or with ceramic ends (the ceramic designs are meant to minimize breakage and grooving). I like those with the longer tubes, since they are easier to use when tying the tail of a bug.

Scissors

The best scissors for making bugs are the larger styles, preferably those with finely serrated blades that will prevent slippage with coarser materials (deer hair) or the many synthetics used today. Both curved and straight styles are available, with the curved preferred by many for shaping the curved bodies of hair bugs. Fine scissors are also ideal for the more delicate tying tasks of tying terrestrials. Squizzors is a new spring-operated style that should be good for hair-bodied bugs.

Bodkins

A bodkin is nothing more than a sharp needle with a handle. Many are available, but you can make one by inserting a large sewing needle eye-first into a short wooden dowel. They are useful for picking out hackle and fibers after tying hackle onto a bug, working glue into a slot or hole in a bug body, or depositing head cement onto a wrapped and finished head.

Whip-Finishers

Whip-finishers come in a wide variety of sizes and styles, but all are designed to do one thing—make wraps around the head or hook shank over the end of the thread to secure it for cutting and sealing with head cement. Since these tools require wrapping a loop of thread around the body of the fly or bug, they are most useful for flies or bugs that are finished at the end (such as hair-bodied bugs or terrestrials). Special long-reach whip-finishers are made to clear bug bodies on each turn. It is also possible to use your fingers to make a whip-finish (or half-hitch) when finishing any bug.

Half-Hitch Tools

While you can do half-hitches on any bug at any position (tying off or securing thread while tying) it is possible to use half-hitch tools only with bugs that are finished at the head, directly behind the hook eye. I also use half-hitches when wrapping thread around a hook shank for better purchase when gluing into a bug body.

Hair Packers

Many forms of hair packers are available, all with the purpose of packing bug-body hair tightly so as to make a dense, good-looking, and high-floating hair bug. Most are simply a tool with a hole that slips over the

4

hook eye and shank to pack the hair. The Brassie is similar to ice tongs, with two gaps that fit over the hook shank and pack the hair. An ideal homemade tool can be made from the end of a screw-apart ballpoint pen, the hole enlarged if required to fit over large hook eyes. The advantage here is that all the force used is directed at the base of the hair for tight packing.

Hair Stackers

Hair stackers are nothing more than tubes that fit into a heavy base; hair is dropped into the stacker, then the stacker is hammered several times to even the fiber lengths. Removing the cylinder from the base makes it easy to grab the materials. Stackers can be used with any length fur or synthetic material for a variety of applications, including tails, whiskers, throats, and legs.

Hackle Pliers

Hackle pliers are small spring-loaded pliers used for holding hackle and winding it around the hook shank when making collars on bass bugs (or hackle on dry flies). Different sizes and jaw materials are available, and Griffin makes a neat one that rotates on a small handle to prevent twisting the hackle.

Saws

Saws are useful for cutting face angles on cork, balsa, and other wood bodies, slotting all types of bodies for insertion of the hook, cutting slots for insertion of rubber hackle, and fur or feather "wings." The best saw that I have found is a hacksaw blade. (The regular hacksaw handles are too unwieldy, so just use the blade.) Blades with eighteen or twenty-four teeth per inch seem best—coarser blades tend to chew up cork and finer blades take too long to cut.

For some bug work, I like to cut wide slots in bodies to hold hook shanks wrapped with lead wire (used to weight the bug for lower flotation), with a glass rattle glued on the hook shank, or with a wrap of chenille to increase the surface gluing area for strength. For this, I bind several blades together. I reverse the tooth direction on alternate blades for easier cutting and less binding or "chewing" of the material. Use enough blades to make the desired slot width.

5

Rasps and Files

Fine rasps make it easy to remove material from bug cylinders to form them into tapered bodies. Since the bug is small and the rasp large, I like to fasten the rasp in a workbench vise (using wood strips to protect the rasp) and work the bug against the rasp, rather than the other way around. Control is much easier this way. Files for finer work, and saws, can be used the same way.

Sanders

You can use electric sanders, but I don't recommend it. I have used a small vertical belt sander to shape cork, balsa, other wood, and foam bodies (only before the hooks are added!) but there are still risks of the sander "grabbing" the bug body and ruining it, or sanding your fingers when the bug flips out of your grasp. *Never use sanders or any electric tool on a bug body with the hook attached; if the bug slips or is pulled from your grasp, you can end up with a hook deep in your finger.*

Sandpaper

Sandpaper comes in a wide variety of grades. The best are those that are medium to fine, since the sanding for any bug is slight and the materials easily worked. Fingernail emery boards are also ideal, since they are stiff enough to work on only one section of a bug body, and most have both fine and coarse sides. Consider the larger salon or professional style. I just learned about sanding sticks, which are spring-loaded plastic "sticks" that hold a one-quarter-inch-wide sanding belt. Various grades of sanding belt are available.

Shaping and Sawing Jigs

Shaping jigs are not available commercially, but are easily made. One of the best is a simple jig for sawing slots in the base of bug bodies for insertion of the hook shank. To make one, you will need only scrap wood, metal, or acrylic plastic and some precise sawing. What you will be making is a simple miter box that will hold any diameter body along with guides for sawing straight down lengthwise to cut the slot. For this, make a base of scrap wood about four inches wide by six inches long. Cut a

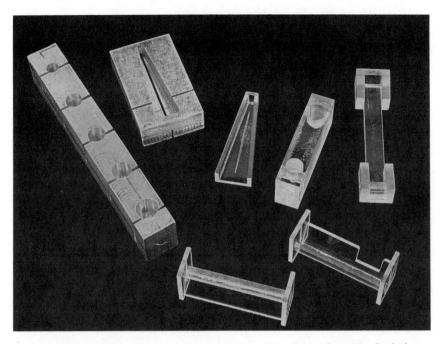

Two types of jigs used to shape balsa and cork bodies—both of these for cutting hook slots and making the Potomac River popper. The set on the upper left by master machinist and fly-angler/fly-tyer Chuck Edghill is of aluminum; the one in the lower right, by Irv Swope, is of acrylic plastic for cutting slots and shaping bug bodies. Similar jigs can be make for cutting face angles, flattening bellies, and similar tasks for any bug design.

second six-inch scrap in half lengthwise, using a table saw or hand saw to cut on a forty-five-degree angle. Turn one of these strips over so that the two edges when meeting make a "V" and mount (screw and glue) to the base board. Cut two additional scraps of wood (four inches wide by two inches long) and cut each strip almost completely in half along the wider edge. Screw and glue the uncut edge along each end of the base to make vertical guides for the saw blade. Make sure the vertical slot through these two ends is just barely wide enough for the saw.

To use, place the cork body in the "V" of the miter box and the saw into the slots at both ends. Hold the bug body with a finger and thumb on each side of the saw blade and use gentle pressure to saw a slot just deep enough to hold the hook.

A similar open-end miter box can be used to cut the face angle of popping bugs. For this, you do not use the vertical end supports, but

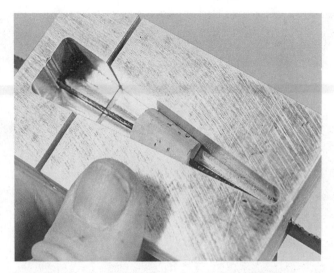

Tapered cork bug in the Edghill aluminum jig holds the cork in place while a slot underneath allows proper and accurate slotting of the cork.

instead cut the "V" blocks at a precise angle, or cut through the "V" blocks at an angle after they are mounted on a base board. Then hold the bug body manually in place in the "V" groove and use a fine-tooth saw or razor blade to follow the slot or end of the "V" block to angle the bug face. Similar sawing jigs can be made of aluminum or acrylic plastic.

My friend Chuck Edghill, a master machinist, made me two aluminum shaping jigs from a design by friend Irv Swope to make the Lefty Kreh Potomac Popper. One of these is a block with holes of different sizes drilled into it, each with a tangential slot designed to cut the bottom flat. The second is a smaller block with a tapered opening to take the tapered bug body with a slot at the proper angle to cut the sloping front face. The bottom of this block also has a partially cut groove for cutting the slot into the base of the bug for the humped-shanked hook.

Cylinder Cutters

Cylinder cutters are nothing more than tubes by which cork or foam cylinders are cut out for making round bugs. Generally they are made of metal tubing, sharpened at one end (but not serrated—this would tear the

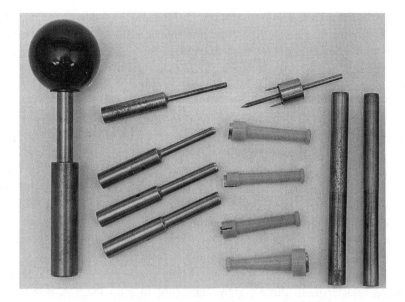

Various cutters are available or can be made for cutting either foam for various types of bug bodies or balsa wood for pencil poppers. These include *(left to right)* cutters by Nick Skirkanish of Fins 'N Needles, shaping tool by EdgeWater, beetle cutters from Floyd Franke, and fly-tyer Irv Swope's homemade tubing cutters for forming balsa cylinders for pencil poppers.

foam as you cut), and rotated to punch through a block of foam to form a cylinder. The best materials, in order, are stainless steel, steel, brass or copper, and aluminum. (The harder steel and brass retain a sharp edge best.) Sharpen by using a countersink or similar tool to grind the inside edge, touching up the outside with a file or belt sander. Punch out the foam with a wood dowel smaller than the interior diameter of the tubing.

You can also plug the tubing cutter so that it is not as deep as the thickness of the foam block you are cutting. For example, you would want a 1 and three-quarter-inch-deep tube to cut through two- inch foam. That way, the foam will compress as it is cut and when you remove the cutting tube, the foam will expand to stick out enough to be pulled free.

An alternative to a cutter with a permanent plug is to make one with adjustments; it's ideal if you are punching out blocks of various thickness. To do this, use a long tubing cutter and drill small holes transversely through the tubing at any interval you wish (half-inch intervals are good).

Then drill through the side of a one-inch-long piece of dowel that will fit into the tubing. Use a small bolt and nut to fasten the wood dowel into the tubing at the desired spot for each thickness of foam, realizing that the end of the dowel will be one-half-inch closer than the bolt to the cutting edge. Changing the dowel position allows changing the depth of cut for different thicknesses of foam.

While you can cut foam by hand, working carefully against a firm base, it is also possible to mount these tubing cutters with shafts for a drill. For this, accurately center-drill a hole through the end of a short dowel that will fit the tubing cutter. Use a nut to fasten a three-sixteenths- or one-quarter-inch bolt into this hole, then glue and screw the dowel into the end of the tubing cutter. The extended bolt allows attachment into a drill for quick cutting at slow (800–1,000) rpm.

An easy alternative to this is to buy small hobby-style sanding drums. The long sanding drums (about two inches long) are best, since they will hold the tubing better and straighter. Many diameters are available, including quarter-inch, three-eighths-inch (not in long lengths, however), and two-inch lengths with diameters of half-inch, three-quarter-inch, one-inch, one-and-a-half-inch, and two-inch. With a set of these, it is possible to make a foam cylinder of any diameter by securing cutting tubes with the expansion drum.

Another type of cutting jig is suggested by Greg Snyder of King Neptune Flies, who sells the round-diameter Ethafoam for making big saltwater poppers. Greg suggests a short length of PVC or other plastic tubing of a size to take the Ethafoam, the ends of the tube cut exactly square to make square cuts in the Ethafoam. That way, you can insert the foam rod and make a perfect square cut with a razor blade or sharp fillet knife. I have further modified this idea by mounting the tubing in an adjustable, right-angle wood bracket so that the distance between the wood "stop" and the edge of the tube can be changed. Then it is easy to feed the Ethafoam through the tubing to the stop and cut with a razor blade or fillet knife, remove the section, and feed more foam. The same technique can be used to cut foam at an angle.

Foam Shapers

EdgeWater makes a foam shaper that fits into a drill or Dremel tool. It consists of a shaft for the drill and a point on which the foam cylinder is impaled. Annular rings keep the foam from coming off, while two "outrigger" spikes keep the foam turning without binding against the sandpaper. In use, the shaper is placed in a drill and inserted in the center of the foam, then carefully turned at an angle against sandpaper to shape the bug body.

A shaper can also be made from the same tubing used for making the cutters mentioned earlier. The cutter must have a shaft for holding in a drill. Do not sharpen the edge, but insert the foam into the shaper and then—with the drill on—turn against a flat sheet of sandpaper. Because there is no center support, this does not work well with long popper bodies, but is fine for short, bullet-shaped bodies.

Power Tools

About the only power tool that I can recommend (other than the possible use of an electric sander mentioned previously and a drill for cutting foam as above) are the small rotary hobby tools such as the Dremel Moto Tool.

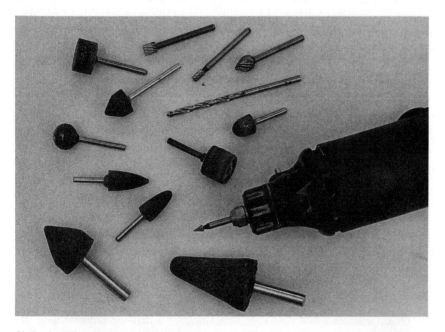

Various grinders, routers, and drum sanders in small sizes are ideal for use in drills and hobby rotary tools for shaping, cutting, making leg and tail socket holes, and cupping faces for hard-bodied bugs.

11

These high-rpm tools will take small-size drills, drum sanders, routers, rasps, and various other bits that make it possible to shape both concave and convex surfaces for a variety of bug shapes. Models with fixed and variable speeds are available, along with accessories such as holders (ideal for working the bug against the bit for better control) and small-drill press fittings.

Curing Motor

A curing motor (used to rotate hard bugs while paint dries) is not a necessity, but will make life easier and paint results better on any bug. They are commericially available (Flex Coat makes one) but can be easily made with any low-rpm motor. I use a slow AC motor mounted on a stand, with the split end of a short length of PVC pipe hose-clamped to the motor gear. The other end of the pipe (it can be made any length) is supported by a "U"-shaped bracket on another stand. Regular pipe-insulation sleeve material slipped over the PVC pipe is ideal to hold the bugs, stuck into the foam insulation as the motor turns. If the PVC pipe is too thin in diameter for the interior diameter of the pipe insulation, build it up with several spiral wraps of heavy cord for a snug but adjustable fit. When the foam becomes too frayed from too many bugs, it is easy and

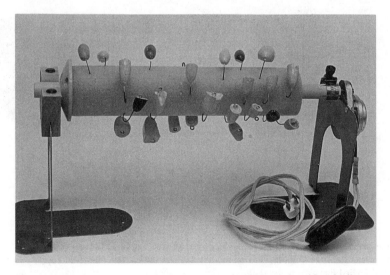

Homemade slow-rpm dryer made by the author for drying painted bug bodies. Directions in the text describe how to make this tool.

inexpensive to replace. I find that a one-foot length is ample for several dozen bugs at a time.

Another possibility is a motor-mounted wheel holding a series of alligator clamps to which the bug hooks can be clipped.

Glues

The basic requirement for making bugs is that a glue be easy to work, waterproof, and suitable for the task. The most common task is in gluing a hook into a bug body, but glues are also used to glue eyes to bugs, glue legs into sockets in bugs, seal thread while working on hair-bodied bugs, and glue materials together.

Some suggestions and their possible uses:

- As my friend Norm Bartlett continues to remind me, glue guns have a great place in a lot of fly-tying tasks. He uses them for everything, although I like hot-melt glue best for adding eyes, legs into holes in bug bodies, and similar tasks. The glues are now available in color, so that a dot of glue can be placed on a bug as an eye.

- **Twenty-four-hour epoxy glues.** These take the longest to dry but are the strongest, according to glue experts. They will run, but the curing motor will help prevent this.

- **Twenty-four-hour epoxy gels.** While gels are never quite as strong as the less viscous glues (they have less wetting capability, and thus about five to fifteen percent less strength), they are still ideal—perhaps the best choice—for gluing hooks into bug slots to form the bug bodies.

- **Five-minute epoxy glues and gels.** These are the same as the above, but with a formulation that causes them to set up and dry rapidly. They are not quite as strong, but certainly strong enough for any bug making.

- **Cyanoacrylates.** These are the "super glues" (sometimes called by their initials—CA glues) and will glue your fingers together if you are not careful. They come in a glue formulation (runny) and also gels (medium viscosity) and pastes (high viscosity), so you can pick the right glue for the job. They are ideal for sealing thread when making bug bodies, with the medium, or gel, viscosity best. Thin glues will run too much, although their wicking properties are valuable when applied to one end of a hook in a foam bug to bond the hook in place.

You may want some special glues for working with foam. Jason Shiba of EdgeWater suggests Borden's Aron Alpha Ethyl Type #232 bonding adhesive for bonding thread to the hook, and Borden's Aron Alpha Ethyl Slow Type #202 for bonding the foam to the thread-wrapped hook. Both are available from Vigor (address in Appendix A.)

Clamps

If working with any glue other than those that bond in seconds (such as the CA types), you might want to use clamps to hold the material together. These are easily made from spring-type clothespins. If the opening is not exactly right for the bug you are making, widen it by using a Dremel router bit or small sanding drum between the jaws. Make enough of several different sizes for different size bugs. For tiny bugs, doll-size spring clothespins are available from craft stores.

Thread

In most cases, you can use your favorite fly-tying thread for making bugs. Since bugs (as defined by this book) cover a wide range of artificials and sizes, these threads can vary from fine 6/0 and 8/0 sizes for tying tiny foam-body terrestrials on up to heavy rod-wrapping threads for tying big saltwater poppers. Every tyer has his favorites. Chris Helm likes a German-made Dynacord in 3/0 size; its very strong for tying his excellent deer-hair bugs. Joe Messinger, Jr., likes a cotton-covered polyester thread (available in sewing stores) for tying his Messinger frogs and bugs, but insists that it must be waxed to work properly. Size A rod-wrap thread is often used for heavier wrapping of legs on hair-bodied frogs—some tyers even go to size D or E. William McIntyre, of Corkers, likes silk thread, since sealers penetrate it better and there is less likelihood of the thread unraveling should it be cut by a fish.

Kevlar thread, available from Gudebrod, is extremely strong (as strong as size D thread, or eight-pound-test) for its fine size (3/0), but some tyers do not like it because it dulls scissors. One answer for using Kevlar is to keep a pair of old scissors for cutting it.

Flat thread is often better than round, twisted thread for tying hair-bodied bugs, since it will be less likely cut through the hair under the pressures of spinning and stacking. (Round thread can be untwisted.)

Other fly-tying threads from Gudebrod, Danville, Kreinik, and others are all good. Often several threads will have to be used on one bug. For example, it helps to have a coarse thread to wrap around the shank of a hook to be glued into the slot on a foam, cork, or balsa body, since the heavy thread provides greater bulk and aids in bonding. With these exceptions, it helps to have a fine thread where possible, provided it has sufficient strength for the purpose.

Cork Bodies

Cork bodies are available in a variety of shapes and sizes from many tackle shops, all fly-tying shops, and most fly-tying mail-order catalogs. They come in cylinders (use as they are or shape them into tapered bodies), bottle-cork shapes (tapered, but with flat, parallel surfaces at both ends), short and elongated forms of tapered bodies, rounded and tapered bodies, straight-sided tapered bodies, slim pencil-popper styles, and round balls that are ideal for floating mulberry bugs and in small sizes as float pods for nymphs. Sizes can range from about one-eighth to three-sixteenths of an inch up to about one-inch diameter, with lengths proportional to diameter and shape and up to about three inches long. Some larger diameter corks are sometimes available, and used for the larger slider heads for big-game fishing.

Wine and bottle corks can also be used and shaped. Tapered cork-float "blanks" are good, since they can be cut in half at an angle to form two poppers, skippers, or sliders. Many companies sell cork in basic shapes. Gaines has two cork bug assortments available (one panfish size, one bass size) that include painted and unpainted bugs either mounted on hooks or slotted to be glued.

Balsa Bodies

Balsa bugs are sometimes available, cylinders generally available, but they are less common than cork bodies. The advantages are a different flotation effect and the lack of pits, which makes them easier to finish and paint.

Closed-Cell Soft Foam Bodies

Closed-cell foam also makes for an ideal bug. Finished closed-cell foam bodies and stock foam in a variety of colors are manufactured by Edge-Water, Live Body cylinders and blocks from Dale Clemens and others, in rod form from Rainy's Flies, in sheet and cut-sheet form from Phil's

Various types of soft closed-cell foam for making bugs include Larva Lace foam, foam from Flies-USA, Rainy Riding, Flycraft, Live Body, EdgeWater, King Neptune, and others.

Tackle, in cylinders of Ethafoam from King Neptune's Flies, and in die-cut form from Flycraft. The term "soft foam" as used in this book does not indicate that these materials are soft and squishy like a sponge, but only to differentiate them from the hard-foam bodies available molded on hooks or for gluing on hooks, or those polyurethane bodies made with Hilts Molds kits. These soft-foam materials can be worked by sanding and sawing, just as with cork and wood. The foam is also available in square chunks for individual shaping and many types of foam are available.

See Chapter 2 and Chapter 8 for more details on appropriate foams.

Hackle

Hackle is a must for many bugs, since it is standard for some tails on cork and foam bass and saltwater bugs. Saddle hackle, because of its length, is best. If you are into big-game poppers, you will need a lot of it—some

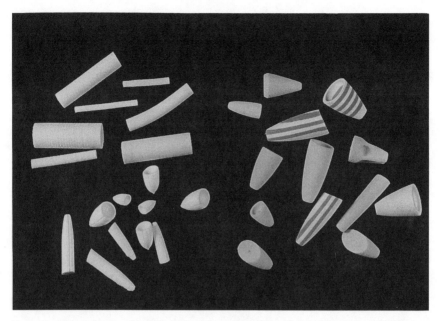

Examples of both hard and soft foam used for making bugs. To left, Live Body cylinders in all sizes. Bottom left, hard body molded foam shapes available from Wapsi include pencil and standard poppers. Right, solid and banded color foam bodies available from EdgeWater.

billfish bugs take up to forty saddle hackles in one tail. Standard hackle or saddle hackle is also used for winding around the hook shank to form the hackle skirt that hides the tie-down point of the tail on freshwater bugs.

Fur

Fur is a must for some types of bug tails. This is *not* the body fur such as body hair from deer, moose, antelope, or elk that is used for hair bodies. This is bucktail, kip, impala, or anything else that will tie down without flaring and spinning. It can be used with or without a hackle skirt.

Deer Hair and Other Hair

This is the body hair from deer, but fur from moose, antelope, elk, caribou, and other animals can be used if it is hollow. Fur varies with the

17

animal. Moose is very coarse, often used for mouse whiskers, but also long enough for big bugs. Elk is softer than deer; it is a little more difficult to tie, but makes the most durable bugs. Caribou is often fine and difficult to spin, while antelope is coarse but sometimes brittle. Hair from different parts of an animal will vary in length. See Chapter 3 for details.

Synthetics

Synthetics such as Mylar, Ultra Hair, FisHair, Mystic Bay Fish Fur, Gehrke's Fish-Fuzz, Krystal Flash, Flashabou, Kreinik Metallic Flash, and craft hair are all useful in tying bugs. Kreinik has three weights (diameters) of Hi Luster braids that, while really designed for fly bodies, are also ideal for tails and skirts on large bugs. Most of these long materials are best for the tails, legs, and wings of various bug ties or added in small quantities to natural furs and feathers for added flash and sparkle. Most are available from fly-tying sources; craft hair or fur, braids, and other stranded materials are also available from craft and hobby shops.

Eyes

Eyes for bugs are available from a wide variety of sources. Movable glue-on doll eyes are ideal for many solid-material bodies, although they can be used in hair-bodied bugs as well. Many different types of eyes are available (see Chapter 11 for details and types of eyes available).

Other Materials

While the above materials will make most simple bugs, other materials are required for more complex bugs. For example, in tying various terrestrials, beetles, jassids, ants, cicadas, hoppers, crickets, and the like, you will need various standard fly-tying materials such as black hackle for around the ant thorax, mottled turkey wings for cricket wings, and green-dyed wing quills for hopper wings. Chenilles can be used to wrap around the hook shank between the tail and the body, or glued down as a covering over a simple cork bug to make it "furry."

Other feathers and fly-tying materials can be used in making bugs. Traditional patterns of years ago had wide hackle feathers tied to the cork bugs to make moth patterns. Your only limit to any of this is the tradition of the past in reproducing such patterns, or the materials of the future and your imagination to develop new styles and patterns. Rubber legs or thin rubber bands are useful as legs and feelers on bugs, and can be glued into slots or pulled through holes punched into the bug material. Special rubber is available from fly-tying sources, or the Living Rubber from spinnerbait skirts can be used, or thin rubber bands cut and dyed. Lumaflex is a new Spandex DuPont material that makes great tails that won't rot or mildew.

Small preformed foam and cork bodies are also available for making specific ant (such as the McMurray ant pattern), jassid, cricket, hopper, beetle, ladybug, and similar terrestrial patterns.

Paints

Paints are generally not used on soft-foam bugs, but are used on cork, balsa, and hard-foam bodies. Any durable waterproof paint will do, but I particularly like the epoxy paints in Roy's Benchmark Paint Set (available from Hilts Molds and retail outlets), along with the small bottles of acrylic paints, lacquers, and enamels available from fly-tying, lure-making, and hobby shops. Even nail polish will work well and dry fast. Sealers should be used first on cork or balsa.

Most of these are best if they are covered with a clear finish coat compatible with the paint used. Another possibility is the fabric paints that can be brushed onto bug bodies—particularly good for EVA, PVC, and Ethafoam bodies. Some of the soft-foam bugs come in colors (Live Body comes in eight colors) and are not generally painted. The hard-foam bugs molded in Hilts molds can be painted or can be molded with the color mixed in with the foam. (See Chapter 11 for details.)

Other Tools

Eye-painting tools are nothing more than nails, tacks, and pins inserted into a handle (a dowel works well) for painting eyes by dabbing the paint from the tool onto the bug body. Another handy tool for making eyes is some sort of burner. Wood burners and soldering irons are used to burn sockets into clipped hair-bodied bugs for gluing in plastic-stem or doll eyes. Rainy's E-Z Leg Tool is a latch-hook tool in two sizes that makes it easy to form bends (joints) in all types of leg materials.

This homemade stand made by the author will support the fibers when glued into sockets in the back of a popping face. These tail skirt materials will make the attached fly (to make the complete bug) bulkier and thus more attractive for large game fish.

Hooks

Good hooks are available from most manufacturers, and from most retail and mail-order companies. For some bugs such as those with deer-hair bodies, terrestrials, and similar styles, you will want a hook with a straight shank. For gluing into bug bodies you will need hump-shanked or similarly kinked hooks to prevent the hook from twisting once molded into the body. Currently, kink-shank hooks are made by Eagle Claw, O. Mustad, Tiemco, and Mystic Bay. Lacking a hump-shank hook, there are ways to prevent hook twisting that we'll cover later.

You can also make your own kink-shank hooks, although it is a nuisance unless you absolutely must have a kinked shank in a specific hook style. To do this, use two pieces of angle steel or aluminum that will fit onto your work-bench vise. Cut a slot near one end of one piece of the angled material. Place the angles into the vise jaws. Bend a nail of the size desired for the kink so that it will hang onto the vise jaw. Place the nail directly opposite the cut groove and place a straight-shank, straight-eye hook between them, making sure that the bend and point are out of the jaws. Tighten the jaws. **Since tempers vary with all hook styles and brands, wear safety goggles in case the hook should snap.**

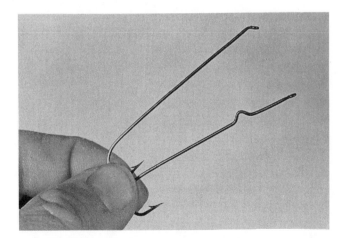

Long shank hooks like this can be made into kink-shank hooks for bugs. This one made by the author has the same kink as commercially available hooks. See text for details.

21

Molded Bodies

Molded plastic bodies are available with grooves for inserting the hook, and with the hook molded into the body. These include both popper and slider styles, often in colors so that painting is not necessary. Those with the hook molded into the body just need tail materials added before fishing. Many styles, designs, and some different materials are available from manufacturers such as Mystic Bay and Wapsi.

CHAPTER 2

Terrestrials—Designs and Tying Methods

T errestrials are made of deer hair, foam, and sometimes cork or balsa (the latter used most notably in the McMurray ant patterns). As such, they do not lend themselves to inclusion in the specific chapters on making cork, balsa, or foam bugs, and since they often involve more intricate fly-tying techniques, are better covered in a separate chapter.

Terrestrials by definition are those (generally) small insects that include ants, bees, wasps, spiders (actually arachnids), jassids, beetles, leaf hoppers, tree hoppers, crickets, grasshoppers, caterpillars, hornets, ladybugs, roaches, butterflies, moths, and cicadas. Dragonflies and damselflies are not land based, but because the construction of their imitations is most like those of terrestrials, they are included here.

It would be possible to write an entire book on terrestrials, and some writers have. For details on both fishing and tying them, see Ed Koch's *Terrestrial Fishing* (Stackpole Books, Harrisburg, Pennsylvania, 1990; more on fishing and history than tying) or Gerald Almy's *Tying & Fishing Terrestrials* (Stackpole Books, 1978; lots on tying, patterns, and fishing).

Naturally, not all terrestrial patterns are floaters, and not even all those that float fall into our somewhat arbitrary definition of surface bugs. Even those that do fall into the realm of this book range widely in patterns, tying methods, hackle, wings, tails, wing case, or legs.

Unlike most other bugs (other than hair-bodied bugs), which involve a little gluing and a little tying, terrestrials require a good bit more knowledge of basic fly-tying procedures. This does not mean that they are hard to tie—in fact, some are downright simple—but only that you have more possibilities for variations in style, tying methods, and patterns with terrestrials than with other types of bugs covered in this book.

Foams for Terrestrials

Terrestrial bodies of foam fall into four general categories: preformed bug bodies, rods, plugs, and strips. The preformed bug bodies are those small closed-cell foam shapes that are available from most suppliers in various basic beetle, ant, and jassid shapes; they are easy to tie down and use as they are. The rods are typified by the cylindrical rod material from Rainy's Flies and Supplies. Cylinders in many colors and sizes as small as one thirty-second of an inch are available in Live Body from Dale Clemens and others. Flycraft has some neat cylinders of foam pre-punched in a block of closed-cell foam that are easily pushed out for making ants, hoppers, crickets, and other terrestrials; they're all available in several sizes and colors. Larger-shaped sizes are available for making frogs, with legs to match. Phil Camera, of Phil's Tackle, has both sheet and sliced forms of closed-cell foam sheeting in various colors for making terrestrials. The strips come precut on sheets of foam and are easy to cut out for use. Bill Skilton's Flies USA has similar foam strips, with dots of bright color that aid in spotting the terrestrial while fishing. No doubt there are other sources, and there is no attempt here to ignore them or slight their products' effectiveness—only to emphasize various types.

Ants made from various types of foam material available for making terrestrial patterns. In these cases, the ends have been rounded by using a flame to melt and form the ends.

Some "found" foam materials (thong beach shoes, lobster- and crab-trap floats, scrap pieces of Ethafoam packing material) also used for making bugs are equally appropriate for making terrestrials, along with some of the sheet foams available from craft and hobby shops.

Many of the supply houses also sell sponge bodies for making spiders and bugs, often offered in both underwater (open-cell foam) and top water (closed-cell) styles. While the tying methods are similar, be sure to order the closed-cell foam for top-water bugs.

Balsa and Cork Terrestrial Bodies

Rod Yerger sells balsa cylinders that can be used for making dragonfly and damselfly abdomens, inchworms, caterpillars, (as well as cut for other bug bodies), and various bug bodies, including those for McMurray ants, ladybugs, wasps, and bees. Some of these, such as the bee bodies, are essentially McMurray styles (two parts joined by mono) but with a yellow/black finish resembling a bee or yellow jacket. Other ant bodies include the single-balsa form or abdomen, on mono for easy tying to the hook. Similar bodies in different shapes are made to resemble beetles, ladybugs, and other insects. All these are available in different sizes matched to standard hook sizes.

William McIntyre sells cork bodies, in addition to his finished "Corkers" bugs, that can be used for terrestrials as well as larger surface bugs for panfish and bass. His straight cylinders in one-eighth- through three-eighths-inch sizes are ideal for making caterpillars, inchworms, damselfly, and dragonfly bodies. Pointed cylinders are similar to the bullet shapes for bass bugs but also suitable for some terrestrials.

Hooks for Terrestrials

Fly hooks in standard styles and sizes are appropriate for terrestrials. For example, a slightly long-shank hook (2X to 3X long) is best for cricket, hopper, caterpillar, inchworm, dragonfly, damselfly, and hopper patterns, while a regular-length hook is used for ants, beetles, wasps, bees, yellow jackets and leafhoppers. A short-shank hook is usually used only for ladybug or spider patterns.

The buoyancy of foam, cork, and balsa allow floating any type and style of good fly hook, but you might want to consider going to a fine-wire hook for some of the sparse deer-hair or small terrestrial patterns to aid in flotation. Good hooks are available from Mustad, Eagle Claw, Daiichi, Tiemco, Partridge, VMC, Kamasan, and others.

Cutting and Shaping Foam for Terrestrials

Cutting and shaping foam for terrestrials will vary with the type of foam. In all cases, you can easily cut the foam with scissors, a razor blade, or any sharp cutting tool. Many tyers like to round off the edges of a foam body once it is cut so they have a more realistic body shape rather than a cube of foam (as with the sheet or shaped forms) or a cylinder (as with the rod or punched plugs).

Some outlets sell FTM Wing Cutters, originally designed for cutting mayfly wings for dry flies, but better for punching out elliptical bodies from sheet foam for making beetles, jassids, and ants. To use, lay the foam on a firm backing sheet and punch firmly with the cutter, rocking back and forth slightly to assure that all edges are cut.

Example of the cutters found by Floyd Franke and used for cutting beetle bodies. Originally designed for cutting mayfly wings, they are ideal for cutting beetle shapes in thin closed-cell foam.

Heat from an open flame can be used with all foams to round off the corners for a more realistic shape. For the very lightweight sheet foam (such as that from Phil Camera, the pre-punched plugs from Flycraft, and scraps of Ethafoam), a very light touch with the flame from an alcohol lamp or butane lighter is a must. Too much flame, too close, or for too long will melt the foam to a cinder. In contrast, more heat (through contact or length of time) is required when working the denser rod-like foam from Rainy's Flies.

I generally like to use fine scissors to roughly shape the end of the cylindrical foam, and then heat it for final shaping. It is also easier to shape after heating if you rapidly rotate the heated end with your fingers—just be careful doing this, since the foam is hot.

Boiling, suggested by Randy Swanberg of Flycraft for their products and Dick French of Dale Clemens for their Live Body foam cylinders, also works. Dick French also suggests that foam placed in a microwave at full heat for two and one-half to three minutes will work to soften and shape Live Body (this might work on other foams as well). Dipping in cold water holds the shape desired.

Another method Randy Swanberg recommends for shaping the Flycraft foam is to use a hot soldering iron held close to (but not touching) the foam to bend it into an arc. This is effective on inchworm bodies.

During all cutting and shaping steps, check the developing body against the hook size that you plan to use for any necessary adjustments.

Cutting and Shaping Cork and Balsa for Terrestrials

Cork and balsa are both handled the same way for cutting and shaping. If you have a block of either material, you can use a punch or thin-diameter tube sharpened at one end to punch or drill out cylinders. This is easier with balsa than with cork, since cork tends to compress, making accurate shaping difficult. Using a drill is best, but the disadvantage is that you will have to remove the tubing from the drill chuck after several punches and then push out the formed cylinders with a narrow dowel or nail.

Other methods of rough shaping include sawing, cutting, or splitting (generally balsa) the material into square cross-section blocks long enough for the bodies being made. The squared corners can be rounded off with a file or sandpaper to make the bodies cylindrical for further cutting and shaping. Emery boards or sanding sticks (available in hardware stores and hobby shops) are ideal for this.

Further shaping is best with sandpaper, emery boards, or sanding sticks to round the ends to make them more lifelike. Since these bodies are much smaller than standard cork or balsa bug bodies for bass, panfish, and saltwater species, they do require more care in handling.

Painting Terrestrial Bodies

For full details on painting, see Chapter 11. Some tips specifically for terrestrials are as follows:

First, many terrestrials are not painted at all. Those that are often perform better with a painted finish that will resemble their body parts, such as the hard shell of a beetle, exoskeleton of an ant, wings of a leafhopper, or body of a caterpillar. As with any bug body, when you paint them is a function of the pattern and how the bug is tied and made. Most often, terrestrials have only part of their bodies painted and most often are painted after the pattern is completed. Examples would be some cork or balsa patterns of beetles, ladybugs, caterpillars, dragonflies, damselflies, and leafhoppers. Examples of those that would be painted first would be

McMurray ant bodies and bee bodies, some beetle bodies, and ladybug bodies tied down in McMurray style (such as those supplied, already painted, by Rod Yerger).

The best paints for balsa and cork bodies are any of the good water-proof epoxy paints, lacquers, enamels, lure paints, and sometimes even nail polish. Use sealer first for an even coat and to prevent water absorption. Standard paints will not adhere to most foam bodies, and almost never to Ethafoam. For these, the fabric paints are best; squeeze the paint out of the bottle and onto a sheet where it can be spread and then brushed onto the terrestrial body. These paints have the best adherence and will remain flexible on soft foam.

Many beetles, ladybugs, and caterpillars have spots on their bodies. These are easily duplicated by dotting a pin or nail head into the paint and then touching it to the body. This method is described in more detail in Chapter 11.

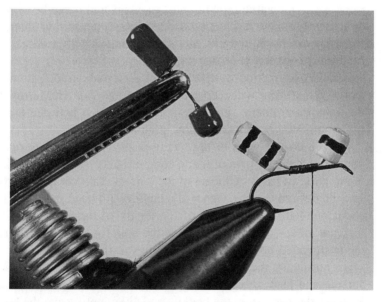

Various types and sizes of McMurray bodies are available—these from Rod Yerger in both ant and wasp patterns.

Tying Terrestrials

Terrestrials are made of deer hair, soft closed-cell foam, and hard materials such as hard foam, cork, or balsa. Both finished bodies of foam, cork, and balsa are available, along with the raw materials for cutting and shaping as described above.

Some sample ties—certainly not the only way to tie any of the terrestrial styles or imitations—are as follows:

- **Ant.** Most floating ant patterns involve only tying down the body material on, or slightly forward, of the center of the hook, and then making the legs. For this, balsa bodies for McMurray ants, foam cylinders, foam sheet, foam rod, or other materials can be used. The McMurray ant bodies are pre-strung on mono so that all you have to do is attach the thread to the hook, then wrap the mono in place to form the abdomen and thorax. Foam in any form can be used the same way. One variation with most foams is that it can be trimmed to a slightly rounded shape on the ends, and then further shaped to resemble an insect body by slightly burning it with a flame, then rotating it between your fingers.

  The key to making an effective ant is to make a long thorax or waist so that trout will recognize it as an ant. For McMurray ants this is not a problem, since the mono connection between the two body parts makes this separation quite pronounced.

  (If you do not want to buy ready-made McMurray ant bodies, you can make your own of foam, cork, or balsa. To do this, pick the foam, cork, or balsa cylinders of the correct diameter and cut them into the desired lengths. Generally, the forward head section will be about one-half to two-thirds of the length of the abdomen. Once they are all cut, you can pre-punch the hole for the mono, or use a mono-threaded needle to add the bodies to the mono core.

  To pre-punch the holes, rest the body or head end up on a solid surface and push straight down through the center with a bodkin. Remove the body from the bodkin, and alternately string the bodies and heads on mono of .010 to .015 inches in diameter.

  You can also thread the mono on a small needle, and thread the needle successively through the pre-cut heads and bodies. This can split balsa bodies, but this is less likely with cork and not a problem if using foam—although foam can create excess friction and thus be difficult. Both foam and balsa/cork bodies can be left squared off as cut, or rounded using the sandpaper for the cork and balsa and flame for the foam. Do this before threading onto the mono.

There are two ways to secure the bodies to the mono. One is to start by cutting the mono to length for the finished ant body, keeping the body and head in the center of the mono. Coat the ends of the mono with a thin layer of epoxy or CA glue, then carefully slide the body and head into position. (Use care that you do not pull the body parts off of the mono.) Another method is to position the bodies on the mono, then cut the mono about one-quarter inch longer than the body. Use a flame on the end of the mono to form a ball that will seal against the body to prevent it from coming off.

The foam bodies will be of the color desired, but cork and balsa must be painted. For this, dip each body—use two coats—into the appropriate color and hang to dry. A drying rack of a thin plastic

McMurray-style bodies can be made of foam, cork, or balsa by cutting the small cylinders and threading them onto a needle and then onto mono where they can be painted (if cork or balsa). These are glued in place with super glue or epoxy and then cut into sections to tie to the hook.

strip with "V"s cut into the edge by which to hang the bodies by the mono is easy to make. A variation of this is to thread a bunch of the bodies and heads onto the mono and dip the string of parts into paint, then hang up to dry by an end of the line. Repeat for a second coat and then cut, position, and glue the bodies.)

Once you have the McMurray ant body, tie thread onto the center of the hook shank and then hold the McMurray body in place. Tie down the mono mid-section so that the head and abdomen are arched and ride high on top of the hook shank. Finish with legs formed by wrapping a hackle, spinning a few strands of deer hair, or tying down and spinning a synthetic such as Ultra Hair. For best results, these are all tied to the middle of the fly between the head and abdomen.

Foam bodies of Live Body cylinders, Flycraft foam, or Rainy's Float Foam can be tied the same way, cutting the foam to the full length of the ant, then rounding the ends if desired and tying down, followed by adding legs. For best results, extend the wrap over the foam in the middle before adding the legs so as to make the typical and identifiable thin waist of the ant.

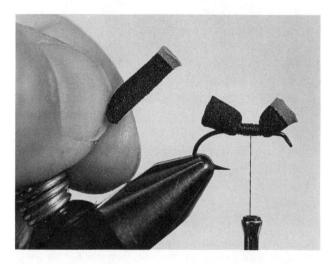

Example of Bill Skilton Flies-USA foam with spot on end for visibility. Here it is tied as for an ant pattern—hackle is yet to be tied down.

A variation of this is to tie a body of three segments—abdomen, thorax, and head. For this, the larger abdomen is tied down first, then the thread wrapped forward slightly (on the hook shank only), then the foam tied down again to separate the thorax and head.

Another variation with foam is to make separate bodies and then thread them onto the hook, securing with epoxy or a CA glue. Then tie down the thread between the sections and tie in the hackle.

A final variation (and the one suggested by Rainy Riding when using her foam) is to split the rod foam in half longitudinally, then

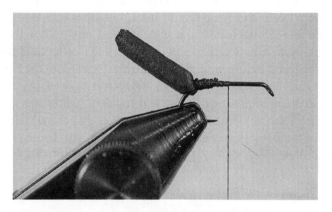

Foam from several sources (Live Body, Rainy Riding, Flycraft, Flies-USA) can be tied in and folded over to make a terrestrial body.

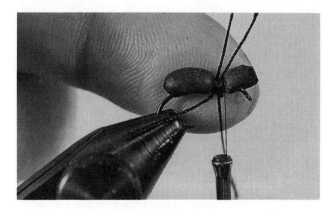

Tied-down body with thread added for legs.

cut out a small trough along the center of the flat side, and tie the foam down at the rear of the hook. Wrap the thread forward, then fold the foam forward, tie down and finish with legs and hackle as desired. If you wish, tie the legs in the middle of the hook and then wrap the thread forward, tying the foam down a second time behind the hook eye to make a head.

This fold-over method can also be used when working with any sheet foam, using FTM Wing Cutters to punch out shapes, or using the sheet foam or sliced strips cut and shaped, tied down, and then folded over to make an abdomen that is humped at the rear. Finish by wrapping a thorax constriction, cutting the end of the strip to make a head, and wrapping in hackle or fiber legs.

In two-segment ants, the legs are tied down after the body is secured. In three-segment ants, they are tied in after the foam is first secured, and before wrapping the thread forward on the hook shank to secure and separate the head and thorax.

Deer-hair ants are easily made using deer hair of the appropriate color for the ant (usually black, brown, or cinnamon) tied in at the tail of the hook. Choose a bunch of hair that will form an abdomen of suitable size. After tying in the deer hair just forward of the bend

A hair-bodied beetle is easily made by tying down deer hair and then folding it over to form the body.

Deer hair folded over to form the body of a hair-bodied beetle. A few strands of deer hair are splayed out at this point for legs.

Completed beetle—legs are then cut to size.

of the hook, wrap the thread to the center of the shank. Fold the deer hair forward and tie down with the thread. Pull out four to six strands of deer hair from the main bundle to form legs. Wrap the thread forward to just in back of the eye. Pull the bundle of deer hair forward (minus the strands removed for legs). Tie down the bundle of deer hair, clip the excess, and tie off the thread with a whip finish. Clip the strands of deer hair at the middle of the ant to a length that will resemble legs. Seal the thread with head cement and the deer-hair ant is finished. As with foam, three-segment deer-hair ants can be tied using the same basic technique.

- **Termites**. Termites are similar to ants, except that white deer hair, white painted balsa or cork, or white foam must be used. The main difference is that the thorax is thicker, so less attention need be paid to the thin waist. Otherwise, the instructions for any of the materials are the same as for ant patterns.

- **Bees and yellow jackets**. These are tied just as are ants, with due consideration for the larger size of the bees and yellow jackets and for the striped yellow/black bodies. Rod Yerger sells striped McMurray bodies for easy construction, and you can make your own, following the methods for making the McMurray ant bodies (see above); paint the rear of the body with three banded stripes to get yellow-black-yellow or black-yellow-black concentric rings of color.

    Other than the obvious size and color differences, bees and yellow jackets are the same tie as ants—using foam, deer hair, or similar materials. Wasp and hornet patterns can be made the same way, again in larger sizes appropriate for the natural insect, and in locally natural wasp or hornet colors (generally black or brown), and with a longer rear body form made in McMurray ant style or with longer sections of foam or other body materials as described for ants. For wings, consider some almost clear synthetics such as Krystal Flash or Ultra Hair, or make gossamer wings from the John Betts Z-lon or Zing.

- **Spiders**. Spiders are tied the same as above, except that they are often tied with a larger, wider abdomen (sheet foam is ideal for this), and in only one or two segments. The legs are of the same materials as those of ants, but are usually longer or, if clipped, left longer. Because of the body shape, these are often tied on short-shank hooks, although regular-shank hooks can be used. As with ants, the body can be threaded onto the hook, glued in place, and then the thread tied in to tie down the legs (hackle, deer hair, or synthetics) before tying off.

- **Crickets and hoppers**. Cricket and hopper patterns are legion. Most are surface patterns; they're tied with a floating body over which is tied a wing material—often mottled turkey wing or partridge (black wing material for crickets)—along with a Muddler-style, deer-hair head. The body can be of cork, balsa, foam rod, foam sheet cut to shape, or other foam materials. Often these are tied down with thread, but an alternative method frequently seen with foam is to impale the body on the hook, using a CA glue to secure the body in place. A wing of turkey (hopper) or black-dyed goose (cricket) is then tied in place, followed by a Muddler-style tie of deer hair that forms the legs and head, and also provides some additional flotation.

The main difference between cricket and hopper patterns is in the color, with crickets of dark brown, dark gray, or black materials; hoppers of green, yellow, or light brown, each depending upon the style of cricket or hopper and the season to be fished. There are many variations, including patterns with precise leg and antennae ties.

Crickets and hoppers can also be tied entirely of deer hair, using a folded (from the rear, as with ants) body, with the addition of wings and legs. Chauncey Liveley has a neat one-material pattern made by tying down deer hair along the shank of the hook, then folding the deer hair forward and tying down again, and finally folding the tips over to tie at the shoulder to resemble a wing.

Natural deer hair can be used for fall hoppers, black, dyed deer hair for crickets. For light green spring hoppers (and black crickets) brush over the deer body hair. Thick paint (such as fabric paint) is often the best, as it will not absorb or sink in between the deer-hair fibers.

Cork or balsa crickets and hoppers are also easy to make, shaping a crude hopper/cricket body from the material, first cutting a slot (as with a popping bug), and gluing it to the hook. Finish with quill rear legs and moose mane antennae inserted and glued into holes punched into the body. A variation of this is to glue a cork body to the hook, then wrap thread around the body for adding a turkey feather wing and deer hair for legs.

Examples of terrestrials from Rod Yerger include various types of McMurray ants, wasps, bees, beetles, grasshoppers, crickets, inch worms, and others.

Examples of ties by Rainy Riding. Top to bottom: ant, beetle, Chernoble ant, hopper, improved hopper, cricket, cicada, and salmon fly.

Rod Yerger makes a neat hopper and cricket pattern by shaping his balsa cylinders (one-eighth- and three-thirty-second-inch sizes available) into a bullet shape, cutting a slot to fit the hook, tying down a small bunch of deer hair, and gluing and wrapping the balsa in place. He then folds the deer hair over the balsa and criss-crosses with thread to tie down. A wing of turkey quill, and grizzly neck hackle stems for legs, are all wrapped in at the shoulder.

A large turkey quill can also be used for the body (see Chapter 6 for more details). Cut the quill to length, drill a hole in the end through which the hook can be inserted, and glue the hook in place with epoxy. At the same time seal the hole and the end of the quill by gluing in a rounded plug of foam, cork, or balsa. Wing material, smaller quill legs, and deer hair can be added with a body wrap.

- **Inchworms**. The best way to tie inchworms is with foam, using some of the light green color of thin sheet foam. or the foam cores by Flycraft, foam rod from Rainy's, or Live Body from Clemens. Since inchworms "inch" along by their front and rear legs, the best patterns are those that are tied at both ends on a hook or tied down in the middle so the ends will move in the current, simulating the live worm. Usually no hackle or other materials are used.

  Other variations are to tie a thin bundle of green-dyed deer hair to the hook shank, leaving the bundle extending past the bend of the hook, all held in place with a spiral, criss-cross wrap of thread. Cork or balsa cylinders or rod-type foam of the right diameter and length are also good, tied to the hook and then painted to resemble an inchworm. Rod Yerger makes some of clipped green deer hair— tedious to do, but a great pattern.

- **Beetles**. Beetles can be tied using deer hair, cork, balsa, rod foam, and foam sheeting. For the most part, they are tied using the same or similar techniques as those used for ants. Deer hair can be tied in at the rear and folded forward, then tied down, with a few fibers clipped to resemble legs and the rest clipped close and tied off and finished. Finished cork or balsa beetle bodies (such as those available from Rod Yerger, attached to a mono core as with McMurray ants, but with a single body) can be tied down at the head end and finished with a "bearded" hackle, spun deer hair, or similar bunch of synthetics for legs.

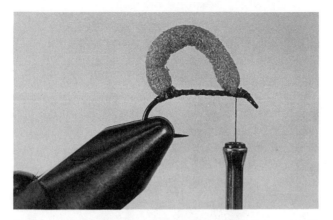

Inch worm from foam material (Flycraft), tied down first at the tail and then at the head after the thread is wrapped forward on the hook.

Examples of various inch-worm patterns of various types of foam, dyed deer hair, and the like. The clipped deer hair at bottom left was tied by Rod Yerger.

Examples of terrestrials from Bill Skilton of Flies-USA. These include beetles, ants, inch worms, and caterpillars.

Another popular leg is strands of thick thread, tied under the body and coated with paint or head cement to prevent unraveling. Foam beetle bodies are also usually tied in at the rear and folded over (as with deer hair), then deer hair or other leg material added to finish the fly.

Sheet foam can be used the same way. First cut or punch the foam to size and shape, tie in at the rear, fold over, and add legs. Fly tyer Floyd Franke of Roscoe, New York, hooks just the tail of the clipped and shaped foam after tying in the legs, then pulls the foam forward, tying it down at the head, and then gluing the legs to the underbody to maintain their natural position. This results in a very lifelike beetle.

A simple beetle can be made from wood beads, available from craft stores. To make these, use a sharp knife to split the bead in half along the grain. Paint the bottom, and when dry paint the top, adding any spots or stripes desired. Then wrap a hook with thread and use five-minute epoxy to cement the hook into the groove formed by splitting the bead in half along the hole. Lay the beetle on its back and lay several strands of coarse thread, deer hair, or other leg material into the blob of glue. Make sure that the hook stays at right angles to the body until the glue starts to set up.

- **Jassids**. Jassids are a form of beetle, but they are elongated in shape and thus best simulated with a cricket style of tying, first wrapping the foam in place and then finishing with jungle cock or similar materials, and hackle to simulate legs.

- **Ladybugs**. These are nothing more than small, colorful, rounded beetle-type patterns, and are tied the same way, with appropriate attention to painting to make these flies resemble the actual insect.

- **Leaf hoppers and tree hoppers**. Leaf hoppers have a sharply peaked body—like a pup tent—and so are best tied with foam that is covered with green-dyed feather webbing, raffia, or similar sheet materials folded to look like the leaf hopper body. Finish with hackle or deer hair, clipped short, for legs.

An alternative is to carve or shape a leaf hopper or tree hopper body from cork or balsa, then tie or glue (gluing is better) the body to the hook and paint to resemble the desired insect.

Most leaf hoppers are light green in color (camouflage for the leaves on which they live), while the similarly shaped tree hoppers are mottled brown in color to match tree bark.

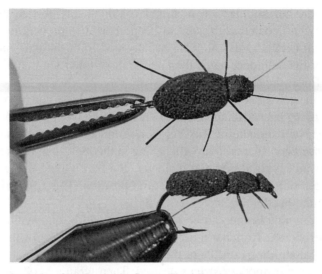

Examples of beetles tied by fly-tyer Floyd Franke. Note exact positioning of legs, glued into place on the underside of the foam.

Examples of beetles made by the author from wood beads, split in half and then glued to hooks to which thread or other leg materials have already been tied in place. Once completed, the beetles are painted as shown.

• **Caterpillars**. Caterpillars are tied like inchworms, but with larger-diameter foam rod, cork, balsa, dowel joints, or even wood dowels. Often hackle, peacock herl, or clipped deer hair is used at the head end to simulate the head, antennae, and legs.

Clipped deer hair, dyed the color of your local caterpillar population, can also be used, tying in a hackle at the rear, then tying and spinning the hollow hair on the hook shank (see Chapter 3 for details on spinning hair). Trim the deer hair, then palmer the hackle forward to resemble setae of caterpillars.

It is also easy to tie in palmered hackle when making foam caterpillars. Wrap the hackle around the hook, then glue the foam to the shank (the foam should be partially split with a razor blade so that it will surround the hook shank), the hackle sticking down and resembling the multiple legs of a caterpillar. Sometimes this resemblance to legs is closer when the hackle is clipped short.

Another method is to wrap the hook with thread, then first tie in, at the tail, a hackle to resemble the legs, then tie on caterpillar-colored (green, brown, or yellow are good) chenille or yarn. Wrap the thread forward, then wrap the yarn forward and tie off, finally palmering the hackle forward. Use a Dremel or other hobby tool with a small cylindrical grinder (I have also used three or four cut-off discs attached to the bit shaft) and grind out a slot in the foam. Do *not* make this slot any wider than necessary, or the resultant tie may not float well. Make the slot long enough to receive the wrapped hook shank, then fold the hackle over the body and glue the tied hook into the slot using a five-minute epoxy or gel-type CA glue. Clip the hackle to resemble legs. When cured, paint the foam with a caterpillar-colored fabric paint; allow to cure for twenty-four hours before using.

If desired, the foam can be extended to the rear of the hook shank, forward of the eye or both. Since some foam is cut away for the slot, the flotation of this bug will be different from those made with a slit, which does not remove any foam. Check for proper flotation before making many caterpillars this way.

Foam, cork, and balsa cylinders can also be used for this purpose; the foam, cork, or balsa is slit, then glued or tied to the hook shank, then painted, and finally wrapped with a palmered hackle. The same technique, without the palmered hackle, can be used to make imitations to resemble naked caterpillars (without setae or

Closed-cell foam strip wrapped around long-shank hook to make the body of a caterpillar. The hackle will be palmered forward to make the setae of the caterpillar.

Completed caterpillar with clipped palmered hackle, chenille head and wrapped green foam body.

Examples of caterpillars by the author of foam, wood dowels, chenille-covered foam, and other materials.

fine hairs). Another possibility for any of the above techniques is to use wood dowels cut to length, segmented, slotted, and glued to a hook, or the short dowel pins used for furniture making that often come segmented. They're available in several different diameters and short, caterpillar lengths.

If desired, cork, balsa, and foam bodies can be sanded to form the segmentation that some caterpillars have. Do this before any tying or other steps.

Thin strips of closed-cell foam can be wrapped on a long-shank hook, and either left bare or with a palmer wrap of hackle added to resemble the caterpillar setae.

- **Dragonflies and damselflies**. Both are similar, except for size and the fact that damselflies at rest keep their wings vertical and together; dragonflies hold theirs horizontal. The best method of tying is to impale or tie the forward end of a long section of foam (Flycraft cylinders or thin, colored Live Body) to the hook shank and then tie in spent or vertical wings of fur, synthetics (Z-lon and Zing are good), or feathers. These wings should use minimal materials and be light in color (or translucent) to closely resemble the gossamer wings of these insects.

Randy Swanberg of Flycraft suggests an alternative of stretching out the foam body and slipping blue or green Mylar tubing over the tail, tying down, then finishing as above.

Fly tyer Irv Swope makes dragonfly imitations using long, balsa pencil-popper forms, with a tail and wings added to the balsa body, and the body painted to resemble a dragonfly.

Examples of hair-bodied *(left)* and balsa *(right)* dragonflies.

See Appendix F for specific tying instructions and diagrams.

CHAPTER 3

Tying Hair-Bodied Bugs

H air-bodied bugs are a standard for bass surface bugs, and a comple-
ment to the cork bugs of the past. Just when hair-bodied bugs came
into being is anyone's guess, but records show that the basis for them
might go back to 1763, when William Bartram recorded that southern
Indians used a deer-hair "bob" on the end of a line to entice bass to hit.
The only problem is that, while it was used on the surface, it was described as being made or tied of white deer tail, which is not hollow and
does not float. James Henshall is credited with tying the first of the
modern trimmed deer-hair bugs, using alternate bands of black and yellow
deer hair, a splayed saddle hackle for a tail, and yellow bucktail wings.
Others soon followed and today the hair-bodied method of tying is used
not only on standard bass bugs, but also various forms of terrestrials (ants,

caterpillars, hoppers), panfish bugs, bodies of trout flies (the Irresistible), salmon flies (the Bomber), and others. The method is simple and, when well done, produuces a beautiful surface bug.

Tools, Materials, and Threads

The tools and materials are simple. You will want a clamp-style (for sturdiness when packing hair) fly-tying vise, good scissors for trimming (preferably with serrated edges to hold the hair without slipping), and a bobbin for thread spools. Materials will include a good supply of deer (or elk, antelope, moose, or other hollow-fiber) hair, along with any ancillary materials you might wish for tails, hackles, wings, eyes, or other applications. The best body hair will be taken from an animal in late winter (the hair will be longer and fuller), and from the back or belly of the deer.

White belly hair is the best for making the belly of two-tone bugs (in which the hair is not spun around the hook, but is stacked and positioned with white on the bottom and a dark color—usually natural brown—on top). White can also be dyed or colored with Pantone or felt-tip markers.

Different hair from different animals has different characteristics, as indicated by this chart from Rocky Mountain Dubbing, a wholesale supplier of materials available through local fly shops or mail-order houses. Used with permission of Rocky Mountain Dubbing, the chart on page 51 indicates preferred uses of each material.

Tail materials can be saddle hackles, bucktail, leather or chamois (for mouse tails), any of the synthetics, or combinations of natural fur, feathers, and synthetics. Some of the older styles of bass bugs had wings of bucktail tied in cross-wise to the hook shank (like wings on an airplane), and these can also be synthetics, bucktail, or other stiff furs.

Different tyers use a wide variety of threads, but any thread should be strong enough to pull down and spin the deer hair, not so thin that it will cut the hair, and easy to tie without slipping. Various choices include size A rod-wrapping threads, Kevlar thread from Gudebrod, cotton-covered polyester (preferred by Joe Messinger), or 3/0 Dynacord from Germany. Color is not critical unless the thread becomes a visible and important part of the head of the bug. For example, when tying a mouse pattern, you would want to end up with a black mouse nose, and thus use black thread for the final tie off.

TABLE 3.1

Type of Fur	Texture	Hair Length (inches)
Elk		
• Bull	Medium	1¼ to 2½
• Cow	Coarse	1½ to 2½
• Yearling	Medium	1½ to 2½
• Hock	Medium	¼ to 1¼
• Mane	Fine	3 to 6
• Rump	Coarse	2½ to 4
Deer		
• Coastal	Medium	½ to 1½
• Body hair	Coarse	1½ to 2½
• Texas Whitetail	Fine	¾ to 1¾
Antelope	Coarse	1 to 2½
Caribou	Medium	¾ to 1½
Moose		
• Body	Medium	½ to 3
• Mane	Coarse	3½ to 8

Hair Texture—Tying Characteristics

Fine	Will not flare. Excellent for wings and tails.
Medium	Will flare to a limited degree, maximum forty-five degrees. Excellent for caddis flies.
Coarse	Will flare to almost ninety degrees. Used for clipped hair-bodied flies like Muddlers and bass bugs.

Hooks for hair-bodied bass bugs are straight-shank, not the kink-shank style of cork or balsa bass bugs. Any favorite hook can be used, but it should be sturdy, with a longer-than-standard shank and straight eye. Mustad, Daiichi, Tiemco, Eagle Claw, Owner, and others make good hooks for this purpose.

Preparing the Hook

There are two schools of thought in preparing hooks for making deer-hair bugs. One is to work with a bare hook (my choice), since this makes it easier to slide the spun deer hair back along the hook and to pack it tightly.

The disadvantage is that there is more slip and a greater possibility that if you do not exert pressure against this packing, you can cause the fly body to slip down onto the bend of the hook. Other fly tyers like to prepare the hook by completely wrapping the shank with an even wrap of thread, arguing that this makes for a firmer base for the bug. It does require careful placement of the deer hair, since packing is more difficult.

Basic Bug Tying

Basic bug tying depends upon the bug being tied. Deer hair is used for basic Henshall bugs, moths, mice, frogs, Dahlberg divers, sunfish poppers, sliders, and more. The spinning and stacking technique is further used for the salmon flies such as the Bomber and Buck Butt; heads of Muddlers, crickets, and hoppers; the body on the Irresistible and Rat-Faced McDougall dry flies, etc. The basics for any of these are like those of most fly tying—begin at the rear and progress forward. Thus, the tail would be tied in first, making this as smooth and small a wrap as possible to allow spinning and stacking of the deer hair on top of this as the first part of forming the body. Legs of rubber or some other material are added as the fly progresses, and finally any wings (such as those on a Henshall bug), the ears, whiskers, or eyes on mice, or eyes on frogs. Finally the bug is tied off at the front, right in back of the hook eye, using several turns and half-hitches, finishing with a whip-finish, and finally cementing to secure the thread.

Tying down the tail for a deer-hair bug. (Heavier than normal thread is shown here for photo clarity.)

The details on patterns may be found in Chapter 4, but they all revolve around the basics of spinning and stacking deer hair on a hook.

Basic Spinning Steps

Spinning is the basic technique of making a deer-hair bug. It involves tying down hollow deer hair so that it will flare out and spin around the hook shank to make for a completely uniform and tightly packed body when trimmed to shape.

If you have not done this before, it is best to try it as a practice step before tying a completed fly. For this, first wrap and lock the thread on the hook shank right at the hook bend. (Ordinarily, you would tie the tail on at this point, but this is just practice.) With the thread secured, grasp a bundle of deer hair and clip at the skin. During practice sessions, you should try different sizes of bundles, but one the diameter of a pencil is about right to start. Use a comb to remove any underhair and clean the fur. Hold the bundle parallel to and over the hook shank with your left hand (all instructions assume a right-handed tyer—reverse if left handed) positioned so that the thread is positioned at the middle of the bundle. Bring the thread up and over the deer-hair bundle with two or three wraps, pull smoothly and tightly, and then, when pulling completely tight, make an additional wrap. As you do this step, release the deer hair so that it will

Making hair-bodied bugs begins with tying on any tail material, then clipping pencil-size bundles of hollow body hair as shown here.

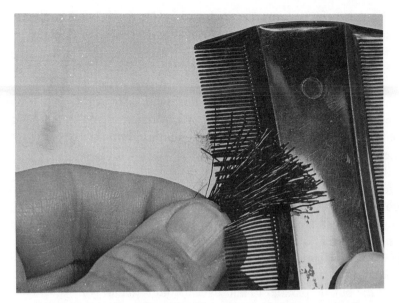

Use a small comb (a moustache comb as shown here is ideal) for removing the underhair from the hollow body hair.

Tying the first bundle of hair down by wrapping around the bundle and hook several times to allow the hair to flare and spin. (Heavier than normal thread used here.)

Flared and spun deer hair will spin completely around the hook shank as shown.

More bundles are added and the hair pushed back each time to compress it and make for a tight, compact body.

To add other colors, vary the colors of the hollow body hair so as to make alternating bands of color. By spinning, the band will completely encircle the hook shank.

This is close to completion, with several alternating bands of color of body hair. Head is tied off at this point; wings can now be tied on. (This streamlined bug will be made without wings.)

spin around the hook shank and flare out. If the deer hair does not spin completely, one trick is to use your left-hand fingers to physically spin and help rotate the bundle around the hook shank while pulling the thread tight.

Once the bundle is spun, flared, and tight, pull the spun fibers back with the left hand and with the right hand make two wraps of thread in front of (toward the hook eye) of the hair. At this time you can pack the hair, holding the bundle with the fingers of the left hand and using your hair packer in your right hand. This becomes more important with each successive bundle, since you will be packing all the bundles tightly to make for a tight body when trimmed. One word of caution: hold the fly securely with the left hand. Too much pressure with the right hand could cause the body to slip, or worse, impale a finger on a hook, should the point protrude from the vise jaws.

Once you have completely tied down this first bundle, half-hitch the thread to secure it. (This is not absolutely necessary, but does help to secure the bundle and prevent later loosening.) Repeat this step with a second bundle, cleaned and held parallel to the hook shank and tied down with several wraps of thread, then pulled back and the thread wrapped around the bare hook shank forward of the spun fur. Pack as above.

Any spun deer-hair body is built up by repeating these steps a number of times. Tails are obviously tied in advance of this step, and wings, feelers, ears (on mice), eyes (on frogs), and other additions are tied in as the bug progresses or when the body is complete. It often helps to tie up to the point where these additions will be tied down, half-hitch the thread to the hook several times, and then trim the bug roughly. This will prevent accidentally cutting these features off when trimming the bug later.

Note that in all of the above steps, the deer hair is tied to be trimmed to a smooth, compact body. You can also tie so that the loose tips of the deer hair form a ragged appearance, such as when tying some patterns of mice. For this, it is better to figure the total length of the hair you wish to form the untrimmed body, and position the bundle so that the thread will leave this length of fur exposed. To prevent the clipped ends from sticking through if the body is compact or the hair long, trim the clipped ends so that there is some hair extending (one-quarter to three-quarters of an inch) so that it will not slip out of the thread when pulling the thread tight and spinning the hair. The result is that the clipped ends do add bulk, but are hidden under the long, tapered tips. These tips ends are not trimmed, but form the ragged outer coat of some finished mouse patterns.

You can make a banded effect (like that of the original Henshall bug) by changing colors of dyed deer hair when desired (see below).

To get a denser body, you can tie a second bundle on top of each base bundle (in order, immediately after tying in the first bundle and before proceeding forward). To do this, place a second bundle right on top of the first, make several loose turns of thread, and then spin. To get it to spin completely, you will have to use your left hand to "coax" the hair around the body as you pull the thread tight. Then proceed forward as above. There is, however, a better way to make a dense body, using the stacking technique.

Basic Stacking Steps

Another basic method of tying in deer hair is stacking—adding bundles right on top of a previous bundle. This will add to the density of the packed hair and the tightness of the trimmed body. It is most often done on the rear or beginning part of hair bugs, since this area is often otherwise a little sparse.

It is also done with all bugs that are tied two-tone (light on the bottom and dark on top), such as mice and frogs. For this, each color of hair is stacked separately.

The technique here is to cut and clean a bundle, hold it parallel to the hook shank, and then make two or three loose wraps with the thread and pull tight. But here you want to hold the hair so that it will stay in one spot—almost like tying down a streamer wing that you do not want to spin to the side. In essence you want it to flare, but not to spin.

Start by first placing a bundle on one side (top or bottom) of the hook. Using the technique above, pull the thread tight while holding the hair so that it will not spin. Once the bundle is secured, add a bundle of contrasting color on the opposite side of the hook. This procedure is repeated all the way to the eye of the hook, or to the point where other features (legs, wings, ears, or eyes) are added. This procedure also requires moving the hook one-hundred eighty degrees each time, or using a rotary vise that can be locked in position each time.

In addition, stacking is used to make a denser body. For example, in many frog and mouse patterns, the technique is to add a bottom layer of white (white or yellow on a frog), then add up to four or five bundles of contrasting color stacked in one spot on the top of the hook shank to form the darker body. Then proceed forward, making the body as dense as desired, rotating the hook to stack the light bottom layers and darker top layers.

Stacking is a technique of adding body hair by which the thread is brought straight up in front and straight down in the back to hold the body material on one side of the hook. Here, black is added to one side—light-color body hair can be seen on the other. Usually it is best to remove and reverse the hook position (point up or point down) each time until you can practice to do this technique confidently.

Completed bug before trimming with the light color on the bottom (hook point is up here) and the dark color on top.

Trimming a hair-bodied bug that has stacked hair, light on the bottom and dark on the top.

Examples by fly-tyer Chris Helm of stacking and spinning. The frog on the left has stacked hair, with light on the bottom and dark on the top; the bug on the right has spun hair to create bands of color that completely encircle the bug body.

Working with Different Colors

Stacking is one way in which two colors are added to a bug. Spinning, as described above, can also add bands of contrasting colors.

It is easy to make deer-hair bugs with different colors of deer hair, using either natural colors (dark brown body hair in contrast with white belly hair) or bleached and dyed colors. You can spin fur in bands of color, like the original Henshall bug, so that the bug has the general appearance of a large bumble bee. To do this, use one or more bundles of one color to make the rear band, then switch to a second color to make another band, and then back to the first (or another) color for the final band. Most bugs are best with three bands like this, but smaller bundles can be used to make more, thinner bands of color.

Another method is to create spots of color throughout the bug using a different stacking technique. For this, use small bundles of colored deer hair, but instead of allowing it to spin, hold the bundle as you pull the thread tight so that the bundle of flared hair stays in one spot. Grasp the small bundle, clip the tip ends, fold it over the thread, and then pull the thread down to position the color spot where you want it. You can use this method to tie in concentric color spots—say for example, a green frog with a red spot within a yellow circle. For this, the yellow spot would be tied in as above into the green body, then the red spot tied down in the center of the yellow.

This method allows for random spots of color, as well as using different colors in different areas.

Adding Rubber Legs

Legs of rubber, Lumaflex, rubber bands, silicone skirt material, Rainy's Round Rubber Legs, Bug Legs (really Lumaflex) from Phil's Tackle, and other materials can be added as the hair-bodied bug is being tied. One easy way to do this is to stop adding hair at the position desired for legs, make an overhand knot of the material around the hook shank, and pull tight at the edge of the deer hair. Then wrap over and around this a few times to secure. Continue spinning and stacking the deer hair until the bug is finished. Legs can also be tied in place with the thread.

Using this method, legs can be added (at one or several spots) along the bug. The legs can be trimmed to length when the bug is complete. One fear is that the legs will be cut when trimming the deer hair. One way to

One method of adding a spot of color to a hair-bodied bug is to take a small bundle of a contrasting color, fold it over the thread and pull the thread down to place the stacked bundle in the right spot. This can be done while adding bundles (as shown here) or on top of existing spun or stacked hair.

Bundle of white hollow hair in a small spot on top of a bug. More dark hair will be added in front of the white bundle to complete the bug.

Completed bug with a spot of color, before trimming. In this case, the medium dark bug has a white spot with a center of dark in the middle. The dark hair is added the same way on top of and in the center of the white spot.

Example above, trimmed, showing the medium dark bug with a black spot of hair in the center of a white spot. Such spots can be made anywhere on any hair-bodied bug and of any size.

Completed bug of hollow body hair, here with strands of Lumaflex leg material added to the middle to be tied in place and glued to secure it. The excess material will be trimmed. The leg material can also be tied in while tying the body material. See text for details.

Example of a spun hair-bodied bug with full tail and rubberband legs.

avoid this is to roughly trim the deer hair before adding the legs. A better method is to pull the legs to the opposite side of the bug when trimming— pulling all the legs to the top of the bug when trimming the belly, for instance.

You can also add legs after the bug is finished, making a double overhand knot in the leg material and securing around the hook shank (worked through the deer hair), then pulled up tight. Spreading the deer hair apart and adding a drop of cement to this point helps hold the legs in place. Though not designed for it, one easy way is to use a Hackle Back as a funnel to direct a drop of cement right on the knot.

To make legs of rubber band appear jointed, tie an overhand knot in them at the desired spot. Rainy's E-Z Leg Tool (basically a latch-hook tool) in two sizes also works quickly for making the overhand knot in leg materials, as well as feather segments for terrestrials.

Folded-Hair Methods

In some deer-hair patterns you do not trim the spun deer hair, but instead fold it over and tie it down to produce a smooth, rounded body with no loose ends. If you are going to make a small bug, or ant and beetle terrestrials, deer hair works fine. For larger bugs that will require longer hair for folding and tying, consider moose or elk.

First decide if you are going to fold the deer hair toward the front or the back. If you are going to make a simple frog with two legs, then you want to tie in at the front, stack more deer hair to increase bulk, wind the thread back on the hook shank, fold over the body hair, and tie down with the tips extended.

As when making ragged patterns, it is best to tie the hair down close to the clipped end (don't clip farther, as you might do with the untrimmed bodies above), or use long hair to get the length needed to get the fold and make the legs. Once the folded hair completely hides the hook shank, tie down with thread and secure. Then split the resultant tail into right and left halves, figure-eighting the thread to separate the tail into two frog legs. If desired, make separate wraps around the leg "knee" joints with a piece of wire or pin to fold the legs forward or down.

Fold toward the front to make a hair-bodied popper. First tie in the tail of your choice (splayed or straight, fur, feathers, or synthetics) and then tie in deer hair, stacking again to get bulk. As above, tie close to one end of the deer-hair bundle (the tip ends are best here, but you must use a stacker to make sure they are all ending at the same place). Then wrap the thread forward to just in back of the hook eye. Fold the deer hair forward and tie down as above. Here you want the deer hair to flare, but hold most of it on top of the bug so that it does not completely spin around the body. This will also prevent a slight twist or angled positioning of the deer hair as the thread is pulled tight.

Once the deer hair is flared, make several more wraps to secure the hair and finish the bug. Trimming (to be covered later in more detail) involves clipping the hair ends (at the end of the popper face—not the body) so that you end up with a rounded body, constricted neck, and a flared popping face. Complete the flared popping face by coating it with several layers of head cement, paint, or five-minute epoxy to make the face sturdy enough to pop repeatedly.

Note that on all folded-hair designs, you will want to use some control over the spinning of the deer hair to minimize the hair on the bottom or belly part of the bug. This prevents creating a rounded belly that would partially block the hook and prevent hooking fish. In addition, make sure that you pull the deer hair so that it lies almost flat on the belly of the bug when folded over to maintain a wide hook gape.

Rough Cutting and Trimming

There are several schools of thought on the trimming of deer hair. One is to lightly trim the hair as each bundle is tied on, to reduce the amount of hair that must be trimmed off later. Most of us—myself included—prefer to wait until the bug is completed and then trim. There are exceptions to this, since when adding wings, mouse ears, mouse whiskers, and other accents to the front end of the bug, it's usually best to stop at the point where these are tied on, roughly trim the bug, then tie in the additional parts; finally, tie in any additional deer hair required to complete the bug.

I like to trim the belly of the bug first, trimming from one end to the other. I hold the bug by the hook and check frequently to assure that the belly is cut close to the hook shank (but not so close as to cut the thread), and that the flat or slightly curved belly surface is at right angles to the plane of the hook. Flat scissors are best for this; curved scissors best for trimming the convex body. Serrated blades are best to prevent slippage.

Once this is done, trim the rest of the bug in the general shape that you want, first blocking out the bug by trimming the sides and then the top. After this, it is easy to round off the corners and begin shaping the bug to final form.

Using an electric trimmer (battery operated, available from Fins 'N Needles) for the first trimming of the excess body hair.

Scissors can also be used for trimming hollow body-hair bugs.

Some bug makers trim with a razor blade, but this requires a lot of skill, a new blade, and a tightly packed bug that can be cut with the razor blade. Some are also starting to use electric moustache or hair clippers for rough trimming, usually holding the bug in a rotary vise and rotating while holding the clippers stationary.

Joe Messinger's Tying Methods

Joe Messinger, Jr., uses a completely different technique to tie his hair-bodied bugs, techniques and bugs developed by his father, who was famous for his Messinger Frog, Nitehummer, and Irresistible dry fly. The technique involves positioning the vise jaws in a vertical plane, which requires a vise with a pivot point or joint. The hook points straight up, and Joe rotates the jaws so that the hook can be positioned to view either the top or bottom of the shank. This allows Joe to stack deer hair to make the two-color bugs (light belly, dark top) for which he is famous. And instead of the standard fly-tying or rod-wrapping thread often used on such bugs, he uses a cotton-covered polyester thread similar to the button and carpet thread his father used.

The bucktail frog originated by his father also utilizes a central thread to spring load the legs, again a different technique from that used on most bugs. The tying methods are different, but make for a compact, fishable frog. I appreciate Joe's taking the time to instruct me on the basics of his tying methods, as follows. Serious students should also consider his video, "Tying the Bucktail Frog with Joe Messinger" (address in Appendix C).

Depending on the size and type of bucktail frog he is tying (generally #12 and larger), Joe favors a Mustad 3366 hook, Mustad 37189 or Tiemco 8089 in #6 and #10.

His technique for tying is to mount the hook in the vise in normal position (hook horizontal) and begin by tying the legs. The first step is to wrap thread on at the head of the hook, spiral down to the end of the shank and build up a bump of thread, then spiral back to the eye and tie off with a whip-finish. Head cement seals these threads and bump.

To maintain the two-toned look of the frog pattern, stack (do not mix) both light and dark deer tail (dark on the top, light on the bottom). A hair stacker used with each color helps to maintain even leg length and bundles. Tie these legs, in one bundle but maintaining color separation, to the hook shank, forward of the thread bump, with the tips pointing forward. To do this, reverse the vise direction so that the jaws point left, and hold

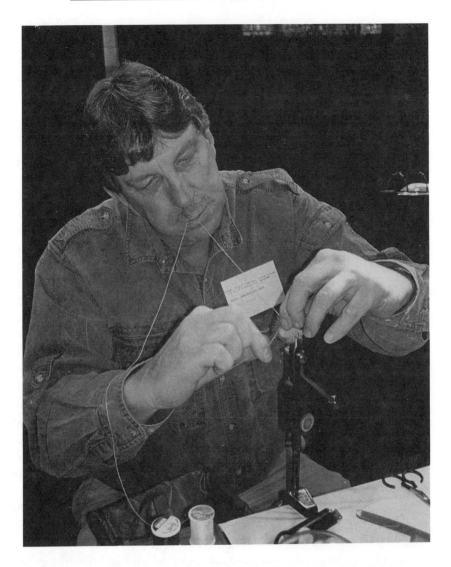

Joe Messinger, Jr., showing his unique method of tying his frog patterns in which he uses a vertical vise and holds the thread in his teeth to perfect the knots used to tie the legs and hair in place.

Examples of frogs from Joe Messinger *(left)* and his son Joe Messinger, Jr. The unique fly-tying method was developed by Joe Sr. and is still used by his son. The legs are tied forward and then pulled back, with a central thread to give the legs spring action in the water and a wire knee joint to form the bend in the leg. See text for details.

the leg bundle so that it is about two times the length of the hook shank forward of the thread bump. Holding the standing part of the polyester thread in your teeth, wrap around the leg bundle and hook shank, maintaining the dark deer hair on top of the hook, yellow underneath. Tie off with a square knot to secure and flare the deer hair. After tying the square knot, clip both ends, leaving approximately three inches of each end remaining. Pull the threads forward (toward the hook eye) for the next step. (This length of thread will be needed later.)

The next step is to remove the hook from the vise and trim the excess flared hair fibers in back of the legs. As you do this, push the bundle slightly forward, add a drop of medium viscosity (gel) CA glue to the bump, and push the legs back to the bump to seal them in place. (Liquid or thin CA glue would "wick" along the legs and ruin them.)

Then separate the leg bundle into two by feel and look. To keep the legs out of the way, tie separate strands of thread around each leg, including the strand of previously clipped polyester thread.

Remount the hook in the vise, this time with the vise positioned vertically. You can start with either the belly or back, but Joe starts with the back. Hold the thread in your teeth again, and position a bundle of deer hair parallel to the hook shank with your left hand. Wrap thread twice around the shank and the bundle with your right hand, and loop the thread around the standing portion of thread to pull down into the first part of a square knot. Pull tight to flare. Then turn the vise one-hundred eighty degrees, cross the threads behind the hook shank and in front of the hair, and pull to the side and down to pack. Add a second bundle of deer hair to the belly of the hook shank. This is done the same way, by holding the bundle in place and wrapping one end of the thread around the hook shank and deer hair. Tie a single overhand knot, then rotate the vise to proceed as before.

Repeated steps like this build up the body of the frog, while keeping it laterally separated by color—light on the belly, dark on top. Once at the eye of the hook, finish the body by tying securely with a final square knot and clipping both ends.

Trimming is next, holding the legs with the fingers of one hand to prevent cutting them (the legs) and using scissors to trim the body into a rough diamond shape, then rounded, and finally smoothed with a razor blade to remove any small stick-ups. One feature of the Messinger Bucktail Frog that is unlike many other deer-hair patterns is that the belly is bulkier than the back. Joe's rationale for this is that the belly will soak up a little water, make this part heavier, and thus contribute (together with the upturned dihedral legs) to the frog's always landing right side up.

Once trimmed, cut the temporary tie on one leg, insert a pin (stainless steel or nickel-plated brass to prevent rusting) into the center of the leg where the knee will be formed. Include the thread from the original tie, and then wrap with size A rod-wrapping thread. For a 1/0 hook, begin this wrap about three-eighths of an inch from the body, and wrap the same direction (toward or away from the body) on both legs to make them uniform. After a wrap of about three-eighths of an inch in length, tie the ends of the thread in a square knot, and clip the ends. Repeat with the other leg. Once both are complete, add head cement to protect the knee and then, with the pin in place, use pliers to bend each knee ninety degrees, with a slight upward angle to the leg. Hold the frog by the knee with one hand and, with the other, pull the thread to pull the leg back. Then use wire cutters to clip each end of each pin (without cutting any deer hair). Check the legs again, reposition if necessary, and cut the thread.

Examples of Messinger-style poppers in which the hair is pulled forward and then cemented in place (paint will also work) to form a stiff popping face or, as with these bugs, a cupped face.

For traditional eyes, use the plastic "jelly" that Joe makes from a plastic (polystyrene) hook box (he uses Mustad) placed in a jar of acetone to make it soft. Remove some of this jelly with a bodkin, roll it around with your fingers, and repeat, checking that each eye is the same size. Excess plastic can be clipped off if required. An option is to burn in eye sockets with a wood-burning tool before placing eyes.

Place a small drop of plastic cement (Ambroid or Duco) on the frog where the eye will be placed and work it in slightly. Stick the eye in place and shape with a small stick into a flat, raised frog eye. Repeat on the other side. Once dry, paint with acrylic or lacquer coating (gold and black, available from most craft stores) and allow to dry. Then add a final coat of Bug Glaze. At the same time add black lacquer and then a clear finish to the knee joints.

A variation of this basic tie is to trim the hair in front to a funnel shape to form a cupped popping face. The face is then coated with head cement or other clear finish to add strength. The Nitehummer—made to resemble a moth—is also tied the same way, except that it has a straight tail and forward wings in front of the clipped body.

Adding Henshall-Style Wings

Henshall-type wings are easy to add to any hair bug. The procedure for making the bug is the same as with basic bug making in that you tie in the tail, then spin or stack the body as desired until about two-thirds to three-

Example of Henshall-type wings added to a hair-bodied bass bug.
The hair wings are tied in line with the hook, with the wing material
aimed back (almost like a streamer wing) and then separated and
pulled forward to be half-hitched into place on the hook before
wrapping the head.

fourths forward on the hook shank. At this point, stop and half-hitch the
thread to the hook shank (tie off completely if desired) and remove the
hook from the vise for trimming. Trim the bug to rough shape to prevent
confusing the wings with the body later. Then replace the hook in the vise
and add wings. The wings are usually bucktail, since you do not want
them to flare. (If you do want a slight flare to make the wings more like a
moth, use the slightly hollow hair from the base of the tail.)

You can tie in first one wing and then the other, or both wings at once.
To tie in one wing at a time, form, trim, and comb the bundle for one wing
and tie in with criss-crossing threads that will hold the wing at right angles
to the hook. Then tie in a second identical bundle right on top of the first.
To make sure that both are lined up properly, push and work both together, then wrap tightly with criss-crossing threads to hold in place. If necessary, wrap several times around each wing, to isolate it.

To tie in both wings together, trim the bug and then make up a bundle
that can be split to form each wing. Comb and trim, then tie in with the
tips facing forward. To prevent gaps in the body, make the tie-down wrap
as short as possible and as close to the already-formed body as possible.
Then split into two wings, and separate with figure-eight criss-crossing
thread wraps. If necessary, add another bundle of body hair in front of the
wings and trim carefully to prevent harming the wings.

Example of a Chris Helm popper with a stiff (cemented) flat popping face.

Another method, if you don't care about the wings being trimmed (Henshall didn't), is to prepare a long bundle for both wings. Clean, trim, and comb, then reverse half of the bundle so that the tips and butts are mixed. Then tie this single bundle down, at its center, to the hook shank, figure-eighting around the bundle to maintain it in the right position.

A final alternative is to not tie in wings, but to completely spin and stack the body, then trim so that the body hair becomes the wings. Thus, the body is trimmed, but the hair that forms the wings is not.

Making Popper Faces

Making popper faces has been partially described under the method of folding deer hair to make a bug. In this, forward-folded hair was allowed to flare, then trimmed to make a rounded face that can be coated with paint or epoxy to make a hard popping surface.

However, this can be done on any bug simply by making the last bundle on the fly full, and controlling it so that it spins completely and evenly around the hook shank. If possible, minimize the amount of fur on the bottom of the bug to hold most of the deer hair on the top. Stacking helps to build up bulk in this area for a more dense face. Once finished, trim the bug as above, paying particular attention to the rounded face, and trimming away any stray fibers that stick out in front. Then coat with head cement, paint, or epoxy, and turn on a curing motor. (Clear coatings can be painted if desired.) The basic technique is to make a sturdy popping surface of deer hair that is stiffened with a coating for easier popping.

Making Legs

Legs can be made using the same methods as described in Chapter 10. Check this chapter for details on the methods, since they can be applied to making hair-bodied bugs just as easily as for cork.

Jointed Legs

Jointed legs, using the methods described in Chapter 10, or above using Joe Messinger's methods, are easily made. Check these sections for details on this.

Adding Weedguards

Weedguards can be added in many ways, all outlined in Chapter 9. Some types of weedguards are more suitable than others for hair bugs, but this also is outlined in this section. Typical weedguards include those of a full wrap of mono, wire weedguard, single short prongs, double short prongs, single long prongs, double long prongs, limb hopper style, jointed hooks, point-up-style body, and body-hair weedguards.

Finishing Touches

Once a hair bug is complete, finishing touches are possible. These include coloring white clipped bodies with permanent felt tip markers (Pantone is a popular brand with many fly tyers and bug makers), adding eyes, adding rubber legs (see above), and adding weedguards.

CHAPTER 4

Hair-Bodied Bug Designs

B ecause of the nature of the way in which hair-bodied bugs are made,
  they do not lend themselves to as many different patterns or styles as
do bugs or cork, balsa, or foam. They do, however, allow for some styles
(mice and frogs, for example) that are often far more attractive and
effective than the same patterns in hard materials.

Basic Hair-Bodied Bugs

The basics for tying hair-bodied bugs are covered in Chapter 3. All bugs
use the methods outlined in that chapter, with the variations in design and
style only in the type, position, and number of legs or tails; type of other
attachments such as ears and eyes; and how and to what extent the bugs
are clipped.

Poppers

Poppers are sometimes tied with bodies of hollow hair. The technique is tie the hollow hair right up to the hook eye, perhaps even stacking hair at the front to make for a denser hair body to hold the popping face. Then the bug is clipped into a popper shape, with a large, rounded front surface, flattened to pop or disturb water. Any hairs that are out of this popping plane are clipped away. To make the face rigid and the bug really pop, coat the face with light epoxy, paint, or several layers of head cement.

Another method involves the folded-hair technique (see Chapter 3), by which the hair is spun and stacked, then folded forward and the excess hair clipped to make a popping face.

Sliders

A hair-bodied slider is a bug that is designed to move water in a wake, rather than popping or diving. Thus, the tapered front body of the basic slider can be found in a number of more complex designs, or just as a slider design with a fur, synthetic, or feather tail (as found on a hard-

Examples of a mouse and frog from Chris Helm. Both have stacked hair to make them different color on top and bottom; also, the frog has doll eyes cemented to projecting fibers of the hair body to make the protruding and bulging.

Examples of minnow-like hair-bodied bugs from Florida fly tyer Alex Suescun. They include the Konehead (upper left, designed for Everglades fishing for snook, tarpon, and redfish), the X-Trail-Minator (*upper right*, designed for small tarpon, snook, and redfish and derived from a freshwater sculpin pattern) and the Mirrolure (*bottom*, with red head and white body for snook, sea trout, redfish, and tarpon). All are tied with hair bodies or heads.

bodied slider). As a result, these are among the easiest of hair-bodied bugs to tie, since they do not require the attachment of wings, eyes, ears, rubber-band legs, or other additions.

Frogs

Frogs are designed to look and, more important, act like frogs. Thus, most have the tail split into two legs, (some with jointed legs or bent knees), most have large eyes to emulate frogs, and some even have front legs or rubber-band segments to suggest forelegs.

The legs are tied in at the tail area first, then often finished only after the bug body is complete and trimmed. There are a number of patterns, but most have the legs cocked up slightly so that the frog floats with the body at an angle and the legs in the water, with the hook down for better hooking.

Folded-Hair Frogs

The technique for tying folded hair-bodied frogs is covered in Chapter 3. It is really no different from tying any folded-hair bug, except that the fold is made to the rear and the excess hair is then split into two legs and separated by figure-eighting the thread.

Mice

Mice are tied almost like a simple slider pattern, except that they have a tail of a strand of UltraSuede, chamois, or Bugskin tied in first as a tail. The rest of the bug is tied as is any hair-bodied bug until close to the front, at which point ears, eyes, and whiskers are tied in, then a final stack of body hair added, and the bug finished. Most tyers will add hair until at the point for the additions, then tie off the bug and clip the body at least roughly to avoid mistakenly clipping an ear or whisker later. Ears of UltraSuede or Bugskin are folded and cut into a dumbbell shape, then tied to the hook shank with figure-eight crossing threads.

Eyes of singed mono or other materials can be tied in at the same time, then the final stack of hair added and clipped, taking care not to hit the ears and eyes. Whiskers of synthetics or moose mane can be added at the front and then the thread tied off to resemble a black nose.

Snakes

Snake patterns are nothing more than slider-type mice bodies with long tails. The tail can be made of thick chenille, UltraSuede, Bugskin, chamois, long lengths of bucktail or synthetic materials tied together at the end to make them rope-like, a thick strand of the Kreinik braided body material, or thin strands of Kreinik braided material tied together at the end. Often it helps to mix materials for greater bulk, flash and color, as mixing Flashabou in with Kreinik braided strands, or Ultra Hair with bucktail. With stranded materials such as the Kreinik braid (and all the chenilles), a few coats of epoxy or head cement on the tip end will prevent unraveling.

One style of a rat or mouse style of bug with a chamois tail. Note that the upper part of this body is left untrimmed, but that it is trimmed on the belly for proper hook clearance.

The body should be the slider type, tapered narrow at the back and thicker and flatter at the front to simulate a snake's head. Eyes can be added if desired. While snakes can be made of cork, balsa, or foam as well, they are often better when made of hair, since they will sit more naturally (low) in the water and more nearly simulate the typical swimming wake of a snake than will hard materials.

Moth Patterns

Moth patterns are tied like a basic slider, with the addition of wings that extend out from the sides of the body (almost like a Henshall pattern), or flared and fanned over the top of the bug. The extended wing style is made like that of a Henshall bug (see Chapter 3), except that the wings are a little fuller and fanned out more. The same techniques can be used.

Gerbubble Bug

A variation of the hard-bodied Gerbubble Bug is to tie it in a hair-bodied style, with the side feathers (or saddle hackle or marabou) tied in at the

Examples of various types of Gerbubble bugs, including modern hair-bodied variations. They include *(clockwise from upper left)* an original Tom Loving type Gerbubble bug, one tied by Norm Bartlett using marabou for the tail and wings, a hair-bodied style with standard hackle and wings, and a hair-bodied style with rabbit (like Zonker strips) for the wings.

rear along with the tail. Then tie the rest of the bug and clip it, finally pulling the side feathers forward and working them into the body, then tying them off at the head of the bug.

Basic Henshall Bug

The basic method of tying the wings of the Henshall bug is described in Chapter 3. While this technique can be used with any hair-bodied bug, the original Henshall bug had a splayed, flared tail of four saddle hackles. Often they were arranged with the feathers horizontal, but still curved so that they flared apart.

Dahlberg Divers

Dahlberg Divers are tied a little differently, and act a little differently as a result. Unlike most bugs with deer-hair bodies, these are begun in about the middle of the hook, where the tail materials of feathers, fur, Krystal

Example of a Dahlberg Diver type of surface bug with a stacked "shelf" in back of the trimmed head to make it dive on retrieve, float at rest.

Flash, or Flashabou are added. Then the body is begun, first spinning a bundle of body hair onto the hook immediately in front of the tail. To make the "mane" or "collar" (upward angled fibers that cause the bug to dive), additional body hair is stacked on top of the bug to add bulk and density. Then the rest of the bug is finished, using spinning or stacking techniques as preferred. (The only reason for stacking forward of this point is if you want the bottom and top of different colors and laterally separated.) Once all the body hair is added and the bug tied off, it is clipped so that there is a pronounced upward "lip" of hair immediately in front of the tail area, with a smaller slider-shaped body in front of this.

Muddlers

Muddler Minnows are classic fly-rod patterns (the basic Muddler has spawned many variations), and all involve a streamer fly with a finish of deer hair that makes for a wing topping and also a clipped head. The basic Muddler pattern as designed by Dan Gapen in 1937 is tied as follows: tail of brown turkey quill; body of gold tinsel; underwing of gray squirrel tail; wing of matched sections of mottled turkey quill; collar or overwing of brown deer hair; and head of clipped brown deer hair.

Combination Poppers

I've never seen it described elsewhere, but it is also possible to make poppers that are combinations of deer hair and foam. For this, make a standard deer-hair body, but tie off about one-quarter inch in back of the hook eye. Then add a quarter-inch-thick section of round foam cylinder for the popping face. For this, make a hole with an awl or drill bit through one edge of a foam disc, and use epoxy to glue onto the hook shank and to the face of the spun hair body. Trim the hair body to correspond to the diameter of the foam face. A brightly colored foam makes the fly more visible.

Cork Bug Construction

I n this chapter, we will cover the basics of cork bug construction. (Tying methods and painting methods will be discussed in subsequent chapters.) Note that, depending upon how you wish to make cork bugs, you can tie the tails on first and then glue the corks in place, finishing by painting them, or you can glue and paint the cork bodies and then finish by tying. Thus, this chapter may or may not be in order of your cork bug construction. The traditional method is to glue the cork body in place on the hook, paint it, and then tie in the tail material.

Materials and Tools

Materials for making cork bugs include the cork, glues, hooks, thread, and any wire forms necessary for the addition of legs or separate tails.

Corks will be easiest to work if you buy them in the shape and size you want for a particular pattern or design. Typically these will be tapered and rounded—both standard and longer, slim designs are available, some with cupped or shaped faces. One design is not necessarily better than the other—they are just different. Build the type that experience has proven best for your fishing.

Cork is cellular, and can have holes and pits. These must be filled before painting for best results and appearance. (The fish won't care about any holes or pits, but your friends might kid you a little.) I do believe that good-quality, accurately tied bugs with smooth finishes inspire confidence on the water, which does affect results at the end of the day. It is just as easy to make a good bug as to make a sloppy one.

You will also need a proper hook and usually this means a hump-shanked (sometimes called a kink-shanked) hook. Many styles are available from the major manufacturers such as Mustad, Eagle Claw, Tiemco, and others. Mustad makes the 33900, a ringed, bronzed hook with a single kink in #12 through #2/0; the 33903 double kink (one up and one down) hook in long-shanked sizes #14 through #1/0; the #2/0 9082S stainless hook with double kink in extra long shank; and the #1/0, 3X strong single kink 32669CT tinned hook. Tiemco has a similar 511S stainless steel extra long #2/0 hump-shanked hook. For special purposes you can consider other straight-shanked and special hooks, some of which are described later.

Thread must be wrapped onto any straight-shanked hook before gluing it into the cork body. Kink-shanked hooks can be wrapped too, but it is not as necessary. This helps to give the smooth hook shank some "tooth" for better hold when glued in place. Coarse thread is better than fine thread for this, for obvious reasons. For some purposes, you might even consider thin yarn or chenille on big bug bodies.

As part of the research for this book I did a few tests, wrapping both straight-shanked and kink-shanked hooks with thin thread, very coarse thread, medium chenille, and spiralled chenille. The material was spiral-wrapped up and down the shank of the hook: once in each direction for the coarse thread; twice in each direction with the fine 3/0 thread. The chenille was wrapped tightly. The slots cut into identical corks were made just wide enough for the individual plain or wrapped hook. I used five-minute epoxy, with one batch mixed for all tests for consistency. Once cured, the point of the hook was attached to a precision Amtek industrial tension gauge and pulled sideways (to twist or rotate the hook in the cork) until the hook broke free of the bond and rotated freely. The results are as follows, with the figures averages of several tests of each material.

TABLE 5.1

Hook	Strength (pounds)
Kink- or Hump-Shanked Hooks	
Bare hook	3.5
Wrapped with fine thread	3.5
Wrapped with chenille	11*
Straight-Shanked Hooks	
Bare hook	2.7
Wrapped with fine thread	2.7
Wrapped, coarse thread	5.0
Wrapped, chenille, tight	8.2
Wrapped, chenille, spiral	10.2

*Actually bent and rotated the hook at this point; did not break free.

The point is that if you want the strongest bond, even with a kink-shanked hook, cut a wide slot and wrap the hook shank with chenille or yarn (wrapped down with thread as in standard fly-tying procedure). And coarse thread at least is a must for any hook lacking a humped or kinked shank.

Everybody has their own ideas about glues. I like epoxies for cork. Consider the gels for filling wide slots. The gels do not have the strength of the liquid form, but they will not run, and thus make it easier to fill up a wide slot in the cork and surround the hook with a solid bond.

The only tools needed for this step are a jig and saw for sawing the slot in the cork (previously described in Chapter 1), and any sanding and shaping tools that you prefer. Simple shaping requires nothing more than sandpaper or an emery board, while for more complex shapes (and to cup the face) you might want a rotary hobby tool and the appropriate cutters and sanders. For mixing glue I like a tip I learned from expert tyer Bob Popovics: use a stack of Post-It notes to mix and prepare glues. It is easy to pull off a sheet when mixing a new batch. For mixing, I like the coffee stirrers available at fast-food places—they are effective, free, and disposable.

Shaping the Cork

Assuming that the cork is not shaped when you buy it (many are) you will have to shape it. If working from a large block of cork or larger-than-needed wine cork, first use a fine-toothed hack saw or X-Acto saw to cut the cork into small, rectangular blocks of appropriate size. Then plan the design of the bug and draw it on all sides of the cork block. Cut or sand away cork on the sides, top, and bottom of the bug shape, making a silhouette to make it easier to remove the rest of the material. (I like to shape the top and bottom first, since this makes it easier to shape both sides to make a symmetrical bug.) After this, it is easy to round off the corners to finish the bug, sanding it with successively finer grades of sandpaper to finish it. Generally, bugs are shaped into a rounded, tapered body that can then be used for either popping or slider styles. However, this is also the time to cut and sand body segments to make bumblebee shapes, slim pencil-popper shapes (although these are better made of balsa), flattened Gerbubble Bug shapes, or other specialized designs.

In some cases, you do not need to shape freehand. The use of cutting jigs, such as the jig previously described for Lefty Kreh's Potomac River

Cork bodies can be cut with a knife or razor blade, but should also be sanded. Emery boards are ideal for this, since they are stiff and provide two different sanding grits.

Popper, allows simple cutting of a tapered bottle cork to come up with a completely finished, though simple, cork bug body. Sand the cut surfaces to smooth them.

Carving Heads

This is really just an extension of the above, but this is one area where small power tools such as the Dremel Moto Tool or similar high-speed hand drills are useful. Various round and tapered cutting bits, sanding drums, and routers make it easy to shape concave bug faces, small sockets for eyes, curved faces for saltwater poppers, cut slots and grooves for "spouting" faces, and holes for insertion of legs and wings.

These tools are small enough and light enough to make it possible to hand-hold and shape the cork, or you can buy small holders that support the tool, or drill press attachments in which the tool can be mounted. The faces and shapes that you can make are only limited by your imagination and the cutting bit available. Dremel has a wide variety of tool bits available; some that I like for shaping include:

- **Small sanding wheels.** These accept replaceable sanding drums that are ideal for making curved faces (like a chugger plug), and cow-catcher faces that spout water.

- **Small grinders**. These are not thick, and thus are ideal for cutting horizontal slots in the face to make darter heads, cutting vertical slots for spouters, and more.

- **Cut-off tools**. These are ideal for cutting slots for hooks (though the slots must be straight, which is more difficult with a rotary tool like this than with a straight saw blade).

- **Ball and acorn bits**. These are ideal for making cupped faces in poppers. The size of the ball in relation to the diameter of the popper will determine the shallowness or depth of the cut.

- **Small grinding bits**. These are perfect for boring straight, smooth holes for inserting tied bundles of fur or synthetics for legs, wings, and tails. These are much better than drill bits which, because of their construction and lower speeds, tend to chew up cork.

Small ball or tapered grinders that fit into drills or rotary hobby tools are ideal for making cupped faces in cork and balsa popping bugs.

These bugs are painted, but show the cupped faces that can be easily formed by a small sanding drum such as the one shown.

Slotting the Cork for the Hook

Slotting the cork for the hook is simple. You can use a cut-off bit in a Dremel Moto Tool as outlined above, or use a straight saw blade in a jig as described in Chapter 1, or cut the slot freehand by holding the bug and working the saw blade back and forth. All three methods work well. The quickest way is with the cut-off bit, although this must be done freehand and as a result the slot will only be as straight and accurate as your skill in holding the bug and working the tool. Drawn guidelines sometimes help. The best way is with a jig and saw blade, since the jig automatically holds the cork in proper alignment. Another way is to use a large but fine-toothed saw—like a back saw—with the saw held in a vise and the bug body held in the hands and worked with the slope of the teeth to gradually cut a slot. Naturally, the same can be done with any saw blade.

For wide slots use two or three blades together, the tooth direction alternately reversed for easier sawing. If making a sawing jig for this, plan on this for the vertical saw cut through which the saw blades will ride.

In all cases, cut the slot deep enough, but not any deeper than necessary. One problem is that the kink or hump in the hook shank seems to require a deeper slot than would be necessary for a straight hook shank. One tip to prevent cutting deeper than necessary is to use a bodkin or a cut, tooth end of a hacksaw blade to dig out the cork in the area of the shank hump. This then allows room for the hump without making an abnormally deep cut.

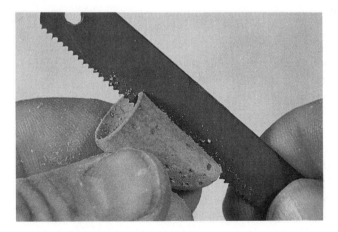

Hacksaws or similar saws are ideal for making the slots in the base of cork bugs for gluing the hook in place.

Several saw blades, bolted together as shown here with the teeth alternating in direction, are ideal for making a wide slot in cork or balsa for gluing wrapped hooks or hooks with added extensions.

Another way to cut slots is with a razor blade (cutting freehand), using this cut to force glue and the hook into the slot. I don't like this, since it tends to deform the cork and make gluing difficult. Another method is to use a razor blade to cut a moderate wedge out of the bottom of the cork bug, leaving a small straight "V." Then glue the hook into this "V" and at the same time glue the removed wedge of cork back into this groove. I don't like this either, since it difficult to get a cut "V," about impossible to get the wedge glued back smooth with the surface, and it seems an unnecessary waste of time and effort when there are simpler methods.

One additional consideration involves the order of bug construction. You can tie first and then add the body and paint it, or glue the bug on the hook, paint it, and then tie. For the former, you can use more of a finishing wrap on the hook shank to hold materials in place, almost building it up like a head on a fly or streamer. This will make more bulk in this area— bulk that will not fit into the slot in the bug. To adjust for this, increase the slot width at the rear of the bug by using a small grinding bit to cut out this area to fit the thread.

If you plan to add other features that require slotting, do this now. Possibilities include slots cut in from the top or bottom crosswise to the bug and at several angles to hold rubber hackle, horizontal slots along the

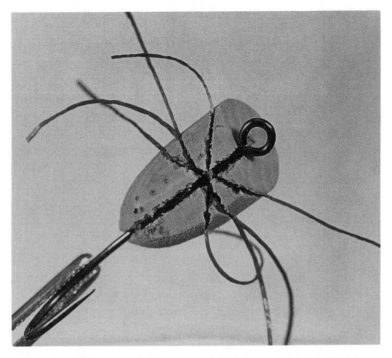

One way to add rubber or other legs to a cork body is to cut slots into the belly and glue in the legs as shown.

sides to hold hackle as per the design of Tom Loving's Gerbubble Bug, slots cut longitudinally in the top for a wing or fin of hackle, or horizontal slots cut into the tail of the bug for inserting a fan-shaped tail. If you plan to add wires to hold jointed legs, you may also need slots for placing the leg wires in the cork body.

You can also place the hook into the cork bug through a hole punched or drilled lengthwise through the cork, as will be described shortly.

Drilling and Other Shaping

At the same time that you slot the cork, drill any holes for legs or a tail. This is best done with a small grinder bit, since drill bits tend to chew up cork. Typically, the only drilling is for legs (placed at an angle on each side of the tail, straight into the tail for a skirt or tail of fur or synthetics, or straight through the forward part of the body for wings), or gluing rubber hackle or yarn for front "legs."

If you plan to later add a worm rattle, this is the time to drill the hole for it. You can place the rattle (and thus drill the hole) straight into the bug body in line with the hook shank, in line with the hook shank but at an angle so that the forward part is down, crosswise through the body, or into the tail area. Of these, I like placing the rattle crosswise through the body or at an angle, with the latter the best method. My argument for this is that the ball in an in-line rattle pointing down will be thrown back (and make a noise) with each twitch or pop of the bug. A straight-aligned rattle may not do this, and a crosswise rattle will react best only with bugs that wobble from side to side on retrieve. (For more on rattles, see Chapter 10.)

One variation in gluing the hook into the cork body is to use a small drill bit to drill a hole lengthwise through the cork, or to use a large bodkin to punch a hole through. Work the drill bit or bodkin back and forth to slightly enlarge the hole for easy insertion of the hook. Naturally, this hole should be placed as close as possible to the belly surface of the cork bug.

Hook Preparation

Hooks should be prepared for gluing by first wrapping them with thread or other materials to create a larger surface for the gluing bond. Coarse thread is best for this, although any fly-tying thread can be used. For best results wind the thread back and forth in a spiral fashion. This provides a greater surface area to allow for penetration and contact of the glue with the thread, hook shank, and cork. Fine chenille or yarn are also possible choices for a wrap, since they too will absorb glue and will make for a greater hook-to-cork bond. With any of these, you can just tie off with half hitches, since the knot and the material will be hidden when the hook is glued in place.

In some cases, you may wish to use a hook that is not a standard hump-shaped cork-bug hook. For straight-shanked hooks, heavier wrappings are a must. (Another possibility, although it is a nuisance, is the method that was used years ago by Tom Loving on his bugs on long-shanked hooks. He would remove the finish from the hook shank and, in the center, solder a small clip of metal from an Acco paper clip, keeping this clip in line with the hook plane.)

Another possibility is to add lead wire to the hook shank to add a little weight to bugs that are to be tied with very air-resistant materials, or to make bugs float lower in the water, or low at the back for better hooking.

Once glue is added, set the hook (wrapped with thread here for more strength—see text), then more glue is added to seal the belly.

The addition of weight to make a bug float lower is seldom done, and then primarily added to larger saltwater bugs. The rationale is that lower-floating bugs will bubble, splash, pop, and disturb more water on retrieve to make them more attractive to saltwater fish. They also help when retrieving through a chop—common in saltwater fly-fishing—to keep the bug "plowing" through the water rather than dancing and bouncing around where it might catch the leader. Standard fly-tying lead wire in different sizes is available for this and experimentation is a must to determine the correct size, amount, and position of the lead for each size and type of bug. Two general rules are that too little wire is better than too much, and that the wire should be evenly distributed or placed to the rear of the bug to keep the hook point down on retrieve.

Naturally, with the chenille, yarn, or lead wire you will need a wider-than-normal slot, while with the paper clip addition, you will have to dig out more of the cork for this large additional strip of metal to fit into the cork body.

Gluing the Hook in Place

I like to use epoxy cement for gluing the hook in place. First, make sure that all cork dust is out of the hook slot. Check the hook for size and position and make any required adjustments.

Mix the epoxy thoroughly and then use a small needle (I make small needle bodkins for this) to place glue in all parts of the slot. Use the same

Either five-minute epoxy or regular household cement works well for gluing hooks into the slot in the cork as shown here. It is usually best to add glue to the slot, then add the hook, then add more glue to seal the hook in place.

bodkin to add glue to the hook shank, thoroughly soaking any wrappings. Place the hook in the bug by pushing it straight down into the slot. (Doing this will most likely push small blobs of glue out of the slot at both ends. Remove these with a bodkin before they clog the hook eye or cover the hook shank where the tail will be tied.) Pushing the hook into the slot will also leave a void in glue at this point, so add some more epoxy to the slot, slightly overfilling it for any shrinkage that might occur during curing. Hang the bug up for curing. If the glue is very runny and tends to flow out of the slot and onto the hook, place the bug on its back so that any glue pools at the slot, or place it on a curing motor. Check at this time to be sure that the hook is positioned properly in the bug and not canted to one side.

It is also possible to glue a hook in place without a slot, by using the hole punched or drilled through the cork as previously mentioned. For this, soak a bodkin with glue and run it back and forth through the hole to get as much glue as possible in the hole. Then coat the thread-wrapped hook shank with glue and run the hook from the tail to the head through the cork bug. Work it back and forth slightly, twisting at the same time, to assure as much glue contact as possible. Glue will have coated the hook eye; remove it now, check the hook for proper alignment, and then hang up to cure.

At the same time, glue in any rattles or other additions that you might want. Generally, you do not want to glue in any legs, tails, or similar additions that are to be added to the drilled holes, since this makes it very difficult to paint the bug later. By painting the bug before this step, it is then easy to glue in tied bundles for tails, legs, and other additions.

Also, if there are any pits in the cork, now is a good time to fill them. Fill any pits with glue or with a glue/cork dust mixture. I like glue with cork dust best, since it is a little easier to work and sand when cured.

As a final thought, if you are cutting slots in the belly or back to hold rubber-band legs, add these now, filling the slot so that the surface will be smooth.

Sanding and Sealing

Once the glue is cured (usually twenty-four hours) check the results for proper hook placement, hook alignment, and excess glue on the hook eye or shank. Then sand off any excess glue that is on the belly of the bug.

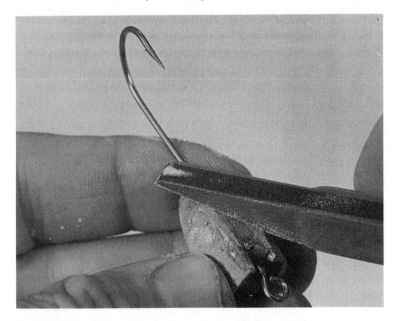

Sanding sticks, which consist of a thin belt on a spring-loaded bar, have tapered ends that make them ideal for sanding smooth the belly of bugs and for working in small areas under the hook point.

Depending on the size of the bug and the amount of excess glue, you can use a fine file or coarse emery board. Often it helps to file the base flat a little for greater hook clearance and a better bite. Once the bug is completed to your satisfaction, seal with a paint sealer compatible with the paints that you will ultimately use.

Special Construction Methods

Some designs require special methods of construction such as extending hook shank lengths with wire extensions, joining hooks to the bug body, jointing bug bodies, and double hook designs. These are covered in detail in Chapter 10.

A completed bug by fly-angler and fly-tyer Norm Bartlett, made by sealing a tail with a glue gun, then adding the hook to the body with a glue gun. Though Norm does not paint his bugs, he catches as many fish as the rest of us.

CHAPTER 6

Balsa, Wood, Quill, and Silicone Bug Construction

W hile cork is a traditional material for making surface bugs and foam is a new innovation that has proven its worth in fresh and salt water, materials such as balsa and other woods are also used for specific purposes. In addition, quill is occasionally used. Silicone used as a coating over fluffy body materials also adds an entirely new dimension to making surface bugs.

In most cases, the techniques used for working with balsa and other woods are not unlike those used for working with cork. Thus, Chapter 5 should be read for basic information.

The use of quills is not unlike that of the old technique of making quill shad darts (except that for these surface bugs, the quill is not filled with lead). And the construction of bugs with a silicone coating over other materials, a technique developed and popularized by fly-tying innovator Bob Popovics, utilizes basic fly-tying methods until the silicone is added.

Miscellaneous Materials Available for Making Bugs

The materials for making bugs covered in this chapter are not hard to find. Some balsa bodies and cylinders are available from fly-tying and lure- and bug-making suppliers, and balsa is available in many stock forms from most hobby shops and some craft shops. The advantage of balsa is that it is lighter than cork, but it's sometimes not as durable. Unlike cork, which has a cellular structure, balsa has the typical grain associated with all common woods. As a result, it lends itself to making long, streamlined bugs, minnows, pencil-poppers, and other shapes for which cork is less suited or not available in the right body form or length.

Other woods can be used, but be aware of the weight and specific gravity or flotability. For example, I have bought wood eggs that are designed to

A mouse made by the author using a craft-store wood egg (used to make Easter crafts) with dress pin eyes, deer-hair whiskers, and a braided Kreinik tail. Ultrasuede or chamois can also be used for mouse tails.

make painted eggs for Easter and decorations. By using the narrow end as a nose, these also make fine small mouse patterns. They are heavier than balsa or cork, so they cast more like a weighted fly than a bug.

I have also used the short fluted or spiral-grooved dowels used for furniture construction and repair as raw shapes for making hoppers, crickets, caterpillars, and poppers. The spiral grooves make them particularly good for simulating the segmented bodies of caterpillars, while those with fluted surfaces can be filled or sanded, then shaped, to make other bugs. Dowels of any diameter can also be cut to the length desired for the same purposes. They are generally of hardwoods, so shaping and sanding will be more difficult than with cork or balsa.

Other wood scraps and blanks available from wood and hobby shops are available—try small samples of cedar, basswood, poplar, fine-grained pine, and similar woods.

Any wing quill material can be used to make hollow-bodied bugs that will closely resemble the body shapes of grasshoppers, crickets, and caterpillars. Most commonly used are those from turkey primary wing feathers, but other feathers can be used or gathered provided that they are legal to obtain and collect. (For some animals and birds, it is illegal to even gather or retain possession of roadkill furs and feathers.) The butt end of the quill is used, cut to the right length, drilled or ground at the end for inserting a hook, and sealed at the open end with cork, wood, or a foam plug.

Silicone bugs are an unusual and recent addition to bug-making. The frogs, lipped divers, and various other patterns developed by Bob Popovics are made with a body of fleece, brushed to make bulky, trimmed to shape, and then coated with a silicone that in essence makes them almost airtight and watertight, and thus floating—at least for a long time.

The silicone used for this is standard caulking or glue-type clear silicone sealer, available in small tubes or larger caulking cylinders. The small tubes are best, since they have a screw top for sealing after each use.

Photo Flo, a Kodak liquid for reducing water spots on film, is the best solution for wetting the fingers for shaping the silicone without it sticking. It is available from photo and darkroom supply shops.

Balsa and Wood Bug Construction

The basic construction methods of shaping, slotting, sanding, making cupped faces with electric ball grinders and routers, and similar construction and preparation involved with cork works with balsa also. The only differences are those between the cellular body of cork and the grain of balsa or other woods. Be sure to check Chapter 5 for details on shaping methods that will apply to balsa and other woods.

I like balsa and straight-grained woods best for making long pencil poppers, cigar-tapered pencil minnows, or flat-sided minnow imitations. Some of these are finished with a tied-down tail or left plain, almost like a lightweight, miniature version of some topwater plugs.

When making bugs of balsa, make sure that the grain runs in the long direction of the bug. Also, there is a difference in balsa. Most of the light-colored balsa is softer (and thus more fragile) and also lighter (floats higher) than the darker and more heavily grained balsas. For toughness, pick the darker balsas.

I usually roughly shape the bug, then slot the bottom using a hacksaw or similar blade as with cork, then glue the hook in place, and finally shape around the hook shank. As with cork, it helps to wrap the hook with cord for better adhesion. This is particularly important if using a straight-shanked hook in place of a hump-shanked hook.

Sometimes an extra-long, straight-shanked hook must be used in place of a kink-shanked hook for the added length required of pencil poppers

Plugs cut from a block of balsa using a core cutter shaped from a sharpened length of tubing.

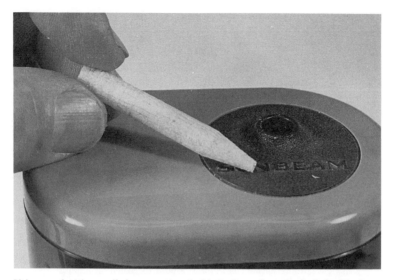

Using an electric pencil sharpener to grind into shape the end of a balsa blank to form a pencil popper. These electric grinders work better than small pencil sharpeners, which tear up the balsa.

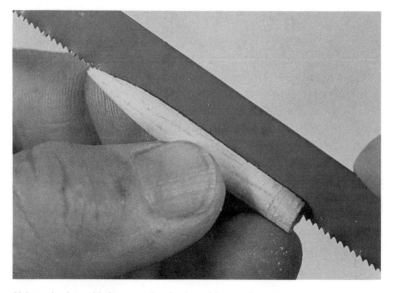

Using a hacksaw blade to cut the slot in a thin pencil popper.

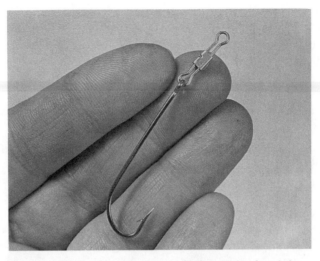

Using a terminal-tackle connector as a hook extension for a balsa bug. While this can be used for any bug, they are mostly used for the longer bodies on balsa pencil poppers.

Here a simple minnow pattern is being made by tying in a simple hackle tail and adding a balsa body to make a slim popper.

and minnow styles. It is also possible to use a connector link or double-eye wire form to extend the length of the hook, or to use two hooks joined together to produce a bug with two single hooks glued into the body.

One of the advantages of balsa and other woods is that it comes in relatively large blocks from hobby shops, and thus can be cut to size, with templates used to lay out certain shapes of bug bodies. By cutting one large block into the right lengths and then using templates to draw outlines of the bug shapes (primarily for the longer pencil poppers, pencil minnows, and slab-side minnows), it is easy to saw them on a jigsaw for final shaping with a knife and sandpaper.

Once you are finished and the bug body is properly shaped and glued on the hook, it must be sealed for painting and to prevent water absorption. Special balsa sealers are available from hobby shops, or you can use a tip from my fly-rodder friend Norm Bartlett. He uses thin Duco cement mixed with acetone to a watery brush-on consistency for an impervious sealer.

Balsa Bug Designs

While balsa and other woods can be used for any design of popper, slider, skipper, or basic bug, they are probably best for those bug shapes that do not work well in cork. As a result, I like balsa best for the following:

- **Pencil poppers**. These are long-bodied poppers, most often used in salt water, and usually lack the splayed hackle that characterizes most freshwater bugs. They must have a long-shanked hook, or be made on a hook to which extenders have been added. (See Chapter 10 for details on these.) They can be made in a range of sizes. All have a popping face, which can be cupped or left flat.

- **Pencil minnows**. Just like pencil poppers, but they have a rounded or sharply tapered end that will not pop, but will make a wake, and are thus most similar to sliders in action (although more lifelike looking and natural in the water). They are usually tied with tails, just like poppers. Hooks with extra-long or extended shanks are usually a must.

- **Slab-side minnows**. These are also long-bodied bugs, usually made on extended or long-shanked hooks. They are like the pencil minnows, but with a narrow body that more closely resembles a live minnow in shape. This makes them slightly harder to slot, since

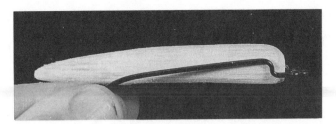

Here a worm hook with a double offset bend is shown beside a completed bug body, showing that hooks other than kink-shank worm hooks can be used for making bugs.

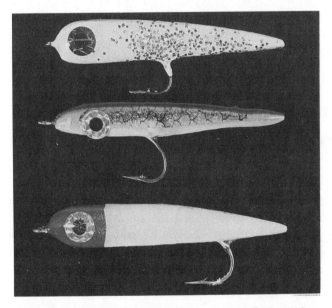

Examples of tapered minnows, in these cases with no feather or fur tails added. While these minnow fly rod bugs resemble larger lures and are very effective surface patterns, the extended body makes them fragile.

you are slotting on the thin edge of the shaped body. They can have a tapered or flat front (although it will not have the surface area to pop properly). Slab-side minnows can be made so that the body is wholly contained on the hook shank, with or without a tail tied at the end, or with the rear of the body extending behind the hook (also plain, or with a tail inserted into a hole drilled into the end of the balsa). Note that these designs, particularly those with extended bodies, are not as sturdy as some others and are often broken by fish.

• **Injured slab-side minnows.** These are like the above, but built so that the flat side floats down, almost like an injured minnow would float and flap on the surface. As a result, they are easier to slot and glue. The variations of body length, hook placement, and presence or absence of a tail apply as above. These shapes, too, are more fragile than traditional bug shapes.

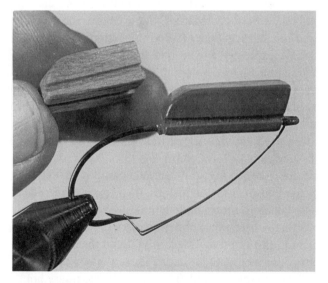

This Gerbubble bug made by Norm Bartlett shows the bug before adding to the hook, and the completed balsa bug body glued and painted on the hook. The grooves on the sides for adding the wings are visible. Norm likes the nylon-bonded wire weedguard Eagle Claw hooks for his Gerbubble bugs.

- **Long Sliders**. These are like sliders, but of an exaggerated, long body, often slimmer in proportion and often built on extra-long-shanked hooks. The body length is usually the same as that of the hook shank. The tail is usually fuller than on traditional surface bugs, and wrapped separately and inserted and glued into a hole drilled into the back of the body. As a result, these more closely resemble a minnow in shape and action.

Bugs from Wing Quills

Wing feathers from turkeys, swans, and other large birds (buy from reliable fly-tying sources or check state and federal laws as to legal use of other feathers or roadkills) can be used for making hollow quill-bodied surface bugs. The butt end is used, so that the rest of the feather is not harmed for other fly-tying purposes.

Mostly, quills are used for making the bodies of hoppers, crickets, and caterpillars, but in larger sizes they can be used for sliders and small poppers. These, and the similarly shaped balsa bodies and those from straws and tubing, are called "Marms" in the South, according to Charles Waterman in *Black Bass and the Fly Rod* (Stackpole, Harrisburg, Pennsylvania, 1993). He explained to me that the term originated in the early 1950's, when casting anglers (spinning was in its infancy then) fishing for schooling bass on the St. Johns River used such lures as trailers (with thirty inches of mono) behind their standard surface lures. Waterman then decided that the small feather- or fur-tailed trailer could be cast with a fly rod. It has been used and developed independently in many other areas, with "Marm" a regional Florida term.

The technique for making quill surface bugs is to cut the last two inches from the end of a larger feather, then use a razor blade or fine-toothed saw to cut the quill to the length desired for the bug being made. In most cases this will be about three-quarters to about one-and-one-half inches long, and must fit on the hook used. Sand the cut edges to remove any roughness. Use a crochet hook or thin saw blade to snake the fibers out of the hollow core of the quill. Then use a file or rotary hobby grinder to make a small hole at the very end of the quill for insertion of the hook. Check for size (the hook eye will have to fit through the hole) and length.

Make a small cork or foam "stopper" that will fit into the open end of the cut quill. This can be left flat (as for a popper) or rounded off into a

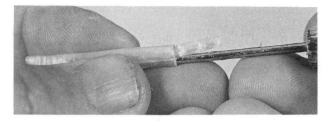

A bodkin is used to remove the fibers from the center of a turkey quill to make a slim quill bug. The quill has been cut and a hole drilled into the tapered end.

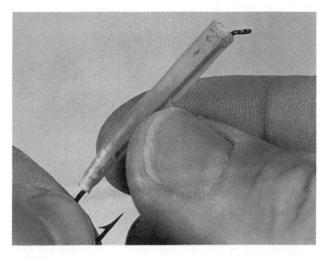

Here the hook is checked inside of the quill body before gluing. The hook will be glued to the belly of the quill and a small cork used to glue shut the open end.

A tail has been tied to the hook and the hook inserted and glued into the quill with a cork cap added. The quill bug can be left as is or painted as desired.

bullet shape (as for crickets and hoppers). For sliders, in which the quill is added in reverse, either type of button can be used.

To fit the hook shank to the quill, first wrap with thread for additional bonding to the glue. Then mix some five-minute epoxy and smear some with a bodkin on the inside of what will be the bottom or belly of the finished bug. Insert the hook into the quill. If making a popper, cricket, or hopper, insert the hook through the tail hole and "aim" it so that it does not come in contact with the glue until in proper position. Then lower the hook into the glue, twist slightly for a good glue bond, and allow to cure. Fill the hole in the end with epoxy and glue the button into the open end to seal the hollow body. Remove any glue that might have clogged the hook eye.

If making a slider or minnow, insert the hook through the open end, and then poke the hook eye out through the hole in the end of the quill. Rotate slightly for good glue adhesion, glue the button closure into place, clear any glue from the hook eye, and allow to cure.

Once the bug bodies are completed, they can be painted, left plain (the translucent look is very natural), and tails added to poppers and sliders, legs and wings to hoppers and crickets. In any case, the "stopper" in the open end should be sealed and then painted to protect it.

Another alternative is to cover the body with Mylar tubing tied at both ends. Other possibilities include tying the tail onto the hook shank first and then inserting the hook into the hollow quill, where the thread ties will be sealed in the glue.

If making hoppers and crickets, the above will make the body; adding legs involves gluing and tying on small ends of standard wing quills. For this, fasten the completed quill body in a vise, wrap the forward part of the body with tying thread, and then, using glue (epoxy or CA), glue and tie the wing quills on each side, cocking them at an angle so that they resemble legs. Finish with a wing of turkey feather (hopper) or black-dyed duck or goose (cricket) and with deer hair as with a Letort Hopper.

Straw and Tubing Bugs

Using the above techniques for quills, I have made surface bugs from large-diameter plastic drinking straws and from thin-walled plastic tubing available from hobby shops. Since the tubing is parallel (not tapered), both ends must be plugged as outlined above.

First tie in thread and wrap the shank, then tie in the tail of materials of your choice. Cut the tubing or straw to length to fit the long-shanked hook, add some quick-drying glue (CA or five-minute epoxy) to the hook shank,

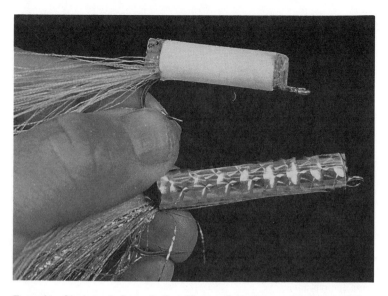

Examples of bugs made from plastic tubing, available from craft stores: *(top)* the plastic tubing has been cut to length, slipped over the hook shank to which a tail has been tied and plugged with corks; *(bottom)* the corks have been trimmed and foil from Phantom added to the body to finish it. The bodies can also be painted to finish.

and slide the straw or tubing in place so that the tail wrap is covered and the hook eye exposed. Place the body on a shelf with the hook point hanging down so that the glue dries in place and maintains maximum gape. Then plug the ends as outlined above and allow the glue to cure. The resultant bug can be finished as above—painted, trimmed with foil, covered with Mylar tubing, sprinkled with glitter. For a neat effect, tie the Mylar at the head end and reverse it over the straw or plastic (folding it inside out) and then tie off at the bend of the hook to make a prismatic minnow. Because of the weight of the bend of the hook, most of these minnow imitations will float head up/tail down, allowing for a realistic skimming motion on the surface when retrieved with short strips and twitches.

Construction of Silicone Bugs

Bob Popovics, one of today's most innovative tyers, developed this method of tying bugs. While they do float (the silicone forms an almost airtight sphere), they will waterlog in time. They will vary a little with how

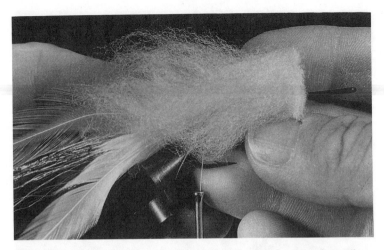

Making silicone bugs as designed by Bob Popovics involves first tying in a tail, then adding sheep fleece over the hook shank (not on top of it) then tying down to secure and repeating.

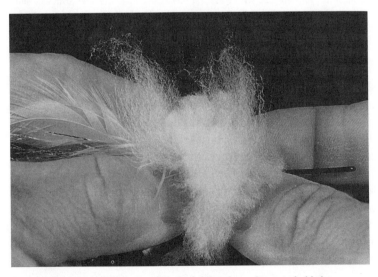

Here the fleece is pushed back, using the left hand as a brace to hold the developing fly. More fleece is added the same way until the hook shank is full.

Here the hook shank is tied with fleece and ready to be tied off.

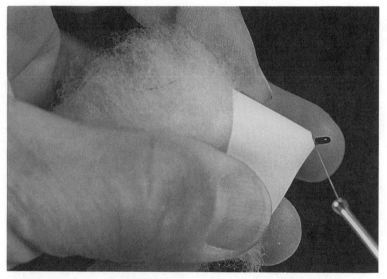

Since fleece is bulky, a Hackle Back is handy for tying off the end of the silicone bug.

Once the bug is tied off, trim with scissors or with the electric trimmer as done with hair-bodied bugs.

Clear silicone glue and sealer and Kodak Photo-Flo are required to complete the bug—the silicone to make the bug body waterproof and the Photo-Flo for ease in handling the silicone.

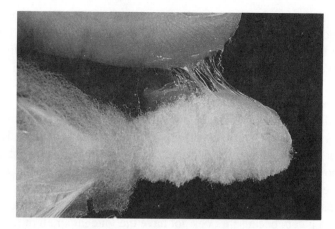

Add the silicone to the bug body to coat completely the body with the sealer. Note that without the Photo-Flo, the sealer is very sticky and messy to deal with.

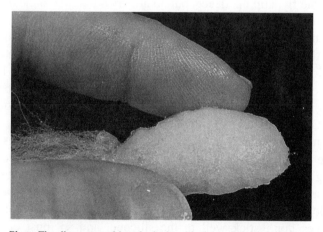

Photo-Flo allows smoothing the body with the sealers as shown. Several coats are added for durability.

they are made, but Bob has found most of them to float for at least twelve hours under fishing conditions. They can be soaked and squeezed in water to make them sink, if desired. Thus, while they do belong in this book, they will sink or can be made to sink, and their construction and methods of fishing almost make them a hybrid.

Bob came upon the design of coating sheep fleece with silicone to make a floating bug or fly when considering the various complex ties for crab flies—primarily those used for permit—used in salt water. He made some out of wool, then decided to add silicone to make them smooth and the Popovics Siliclones (minnow patterns) and Pop Lips (a wobbling diver) were born.

For making any of these, Bob likes GE II Silicone, available in small tubes with a cap, because it does not have the vinegar smell of many such sealers. To tie the flies, Bob inserts the hook in the vise, ties in whatever tail he wishes, and then proceeds to add the sheep fleece. For this, he likes Rocky Mountain Dubbing Sheep Fleece, claiming that it is fluffier and coarser than others—properties that he wants in these bugs.

To tie the fly, clip the fleece, but do not lay it parallel to the hook shank or try to tie it on like deer hair. Instead, poke the fleece over the eye of the hook so that the hook goes through the center of the fleece bundle. (For the first tie at the tail, make sure that the tips are facing to the rear.) Tie down with several turns of thread and move forward, almost like tying down deer hair. Repeat with another bundle, tying repeated bundles to build up a tight, compact bug body. With each bundle, fray out with a bodkin. Once at the eye of the hook tie off with a whip finish. Then use scissors to trim the body, making sure that most of the fleece is trimmed from the belly of the bug to assure a wide hook gape. Once finished trimming to size and shape, add the first of three coats of silicone, rubbing it into the body, as of you were wiping your fingers on the bug fleece. Then add an eye of self-adhesive prism tape on each side of the bug. These eyes don't stick well to the silicone, and so must be carefully positioned and then covered with a blob of silicone.

Then add second and third coats, using Photo Flo (a solution used to dry photographic negatives without water spots) to keep your fingers clean and clear of the silicone and to smooth the body. If desired, the silicone can be coated lightly over the base of the tail to reduce the tendency of the tail to wrap around the hook on a cast, and to keep it straight, yet flexible.

Using this system, mice, frogs (with two legs in place of one tail—Bob Clouser makes a neat one), Muddlers, and minnows are all possible and easy with the same basic procedure, and vary in the legs, colors, hook length, and body shape.

A variation of the above produces the lipped Pop Lips bug, which floats at rest, but will dive on retrieve—almost like a hair-bodied Dahlberg Diver in performance, if not in design. The technique here is just like that above, except that the body is stopped one step short of the above, so that there is a short length of hook shank exposed with the material tied off. Trim the bug to the finished shape and size with scissors. Then re-tie the thread, and tie in one last bundle of fleece, and then trim it so it forms a small "beard" of fleece pointing down. Tie off, then trim this beard to shape and coat the entire bug with three coats of silicone. The small beard forms a lip that pulls the bug down on retrieve, while it floats at rest. After the silicone is added, and the beard shaped at a downward angle, the beard is trimmed with scissors, first by cutting it square along the sides and bottom, then cutting the corners formed and finally rounding them.

CHAPTER 7

Molded Bug Construction

U ntil recently, there were only a few ways to make your own poppers, as outlined in other chapters. Corks for carving to shape, pre-
shaped cork bodies, and corks cemented on hooks are all available, as are
balsa and wood poppers, hard-foam popper bodies, and foam bodies with
molded-in hooks, along with closed-cell soft foam poppers.

Types of Molds

Enter Hilts Molds, by which you can pour your own poppers using readily
available polyethylene molds, a simple two-part polyurethane plastic
foam, and some simple mixing cups and measurers. The foam is non-
toxic, the steps simple, the cost low, and the results good.

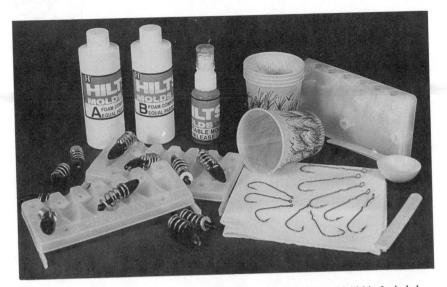

The tools and materials for making hard foam poppers using the Hilts Mold kit. Included are the two parts of the foaming compound, and the two-part mold with fasteners, hooks, and mixing cups.

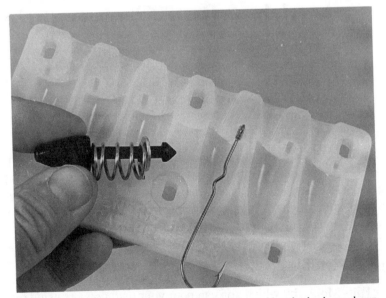

Here the spring-loaded fasteners and one part of the mold and a hook are shown. Certain size and style hooks are designed for each mold and each mold makes six to eight bugs at a time.

Except that they are of lightweight plastic, the molds are like the aluminum molds used for molding lead sinkers and jig heads. Different popper molds are available from Hilts Molds, (along with other molds for making foam plastic plugs and crankbaits). Molds for making the larger-sized poppers are six-cavity; molds for the smaller panfish bugs are eight-cavity. Each mold has cavities for the poppers, a recess for the proper hook, and a small funnel area (called a gate or sprue hole), for pouring in the plastic foam. Where required, legs on each mold make it easy to set it vertically for pouring and resting during the curing process.

Since the molds are lightweight and since proper alignment and close fitting of the two parts is a must, Hilts Molds has devised a clever way to secure the two mold halves. Key spring-loaded pins fit through the mold in several areas to quickly and easily secure the two parts. Thus, they can be inserted and removed quickly for rapid molding.

Hooks for Molds

The different molds make different sizes of poppers. The ⅝" X ⅞" and ½" X ⅞" poppers both use Mustad 37190 hooks, size #2 and #6, respectively. The ⅝" X 1½" and the ½" X 1½" poppers use a Mustad 9082N, #2/0 for both molds. The smaller panfish poppers are ⁵⁄₁₆" X ¾" and ⁵⁄₁₆" X ⅝" long, taking a Mustad 33903 hook in #6 and #8, respectively. All the hooks are hump-shanked to keep the body from turning on the hook, although adhesion of the material to the hook is excellent. The large bugs come six cavities to the mold, the smaller eight cavities per mold.

Foam for Molding

The foam plastic—which is non-toxic—comes in two parts, and is a 50/50 mix for simplicity. While the two parts are liquids, when mixed they react and foam, expanding up to twenty times the original volume, with the foam forming the bubbles (closed-cell) that float the popper.

Ideally, you should mix the foam with good ventilation (although I notice no appreciable smell when working with it), and at a temperature of seventy-five to eighty-five degrees. Foaming action is slower at cooler temperatures, faster at warmer temperatures. Do not overheat (the foaming action is fast enough as it is), since hotter temperatures not only make the foam set up more quickly, but also tend to make the resultant bug brittle and crumbly.

The two parts used for mixing are two different colors, so that even, smooth mixing is easy to check. The foam is available in half-pound, four-pound, twenty-pound, and, for the really heavy user, 100-pound sets. A stirring stick and measuring spoon of polyethylene (so that the plastic does not stick) are included in the half-pound and four-pound sets.

The one disadvantage to the foam—although it is more perceived than real—is that, once mixed, the plastic foams *fast* and must be used *immediately*. You have only thirty-five seconds from the time that you pour the two liquids together until the foaming and expanding action begins.

You will also need a measuring spoon or cup, stirring stick (included with the foaming plastic), some waxed-paper cups to mix the foam, and molding spray. In addition to the polyethylene stirring sticks and mixing spoon, you can use wood craft sticks, and the small polyethylene disposable pharmaceutical measurers often used for mixing epoxy finish for rod building. Waxed cups for mixing are readily available at food stores. The mold-release spray is used to aid in freeing the completed poppers from the mold. I've used the foam both with and without the spray, and the spray definitely helps. It's available from Hilts Molds, although a common and effective substitute is Pam cooking spray.

Molding Steps

Steps for pouring your own poppers include:

1. Begin by making sure that you have a good work space, adequate ventilation, and everything properly arranged for the rapid mixing and pouring that is a must with these molds.

2. Spray the two halves of the mold with Pam or mold-release spray. Then place one mold half on its side and add the proper hooks. Place the second mold-half on top of the first, lining up the registration pins and making sure that the hooks stay in their molding cavities. Use the spring locks to secure the two halves.

3. Use the spoon or polyethylene mixing cup to measure parts A and B. For best results, mix a minimum of one tablespoon of each part (the size of the yellow mixing spoon provided with the foam), and never mix less than a teaspoon of each. Mix in a waxed-paper cup, first forming a folded spout in the cup for rapid pouring.

4. Whip the mixture vigorously for about fifteen seconds (bubbles don't matter, since you want the mix to foam anyway). Note that parts A and B are different colors, so that a uniform color assures complete mixing.

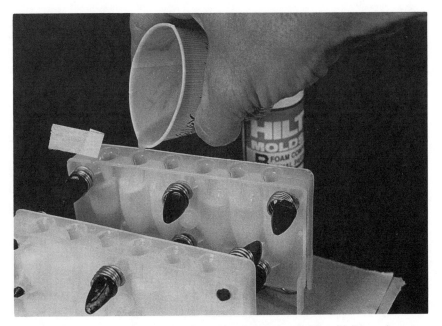

Here the two parts of the foam have been mixed and are being rapidly added to each sprue hole of the mold. Speed is important here, as explained in the text.

5. Once the two parts are completely mixed, pour it rapidly into each funnel-like sprue hole in the mold. Since you have limited time, one tip here is to completely fill the funnel-like gate opening, then move on to the next cavity. The plastic will drip down into the mold rapidly and will be enough (according to Hilts Molds) to completely fill each cavity. (Realize that with the expansion of the foaming plastic, you do not need to and should not fill each mold cavity, since this will only cause waste.) For complete filling after expansion, fill no more than one-third to one-half full—less with practice.

6. Once all the cavities have sufficient plastic, allow the mold to stand upright for at least thirty minutes.

7. Thirty minutes after filling, remove the locking pins and open the mold slowly and carefully, opening like a book with the bottom the open side, and the top or sprue-hole side the "hinged" side. This will aid in protecting the undercut areas of the popper faces. Lift the rear of the hook and pull the molded popper out of the cavity. At this point, you will still have the sprue plastic attached, and may have some flash or plastic along

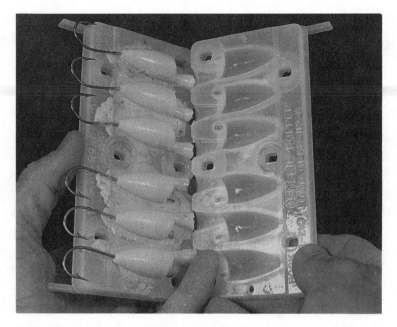

Mold with completed bug bodies being opened to show the result. Any flash (excess molding compound) is easily removed.

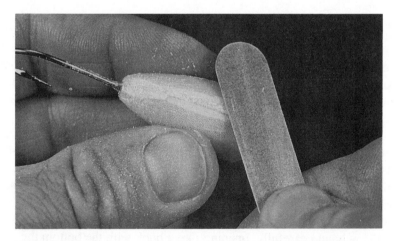

The finished bug can be trimmed of any flash and then sanded as shown to smooth before painting and finishing.

the mold seam line. You can trim this at this point, but I prefer to allow the poppers to cure overnight and become harder before trimming with a razor blade, scalpel, or X-Acto knife. Sometimes I use a Dremel Moto Tool or similar electric hobby tool with a small router or drum sander to smooth the sprue surface. I also like stiff emery boards to clean up any seam lines or similar rough areas.

8. Clean up by washing with soap and water; when the plastic is hard, peel the foam off of the mixing spoon and stirring stick.

9. After curing overnight, you can paint the poppers using any paint that will not react with polyurethane. Hilts Molds recommends their Roy's Benchmark Paint, but any good waterproof lure or bug paint can be used. However, test first with one popper to check for any reaction.

Finishing Molded Bugs

Once the poppers are complete, tie up as you would any cork or foam popper, using legs, tails, and hackle or skirts. (See Chapter 9 for details on tying methods for all hard-bodied bugs.)

There are variations on the above. For example, the flexible plastic molds do allow some modifying with a knife or scalpel (using care of

Completing a Hilts-molded bass bug after it has been painted.

course) to enlarge or extend the slot for the hook shank for larger hooks. The molds are thin, however, so that you must not carve deeply or radically change the shape of a cavity or resulting bug.

Coloring Molding Foam

You can mix color into the plastic, although this requires some experimentation. Hilts recommends powdered color, mixing it into part A *before* mixing it with part B. This allows for plenty of mixing time, since the two foaming components are not yet in contact. You need to add a lot of color, since the foam expands twenty times. Too much, however, will slightly inhibit the foaming action. As with any construction method like this, it is best to measure the amount and shade of color added to the amount of foaming components and to keep records of the results so that you can repeat results when desired.

Examples of completed bug bodies from Hilts Molds. Included are panfish, bass, and salt-water poppers. Colors can be added to the foaming compound to eliminate painting later.

Variations in Molding—Rattles and Weights

Other variations can include molding in rattles. Small rattles are best (usually these are glass, plastic, or aluminum), tied or glued to the hook shank to keep them from "floating" to the surface of the mold cavity and showing through the completed body. This is easiest in the larger, bass sizes that will completely encapsulate the rattle, but is also possible with all sizes, if you're careful when placing the rattle on the hook shank.

Roy Hilts, of Hilts Molds, also suggests that rattles can just be "dumped" into the mold cavity when the halves are open and when the hooks are added, the rattles encapsulating in the foam, but leaving a thin skin of foam over the surface. With painting, the rattles—even when just under the surface of the popper—are not visible. Roy Hilts has used up to four small glass rattles in one bug this way.

Other possibilities include adding weight to the popper so it will float lower, or float at more of a "hook down" angle in the water. For this Roy Hilts just dumps lead shot (he likes shotgun shot in sizes 8 through 00) into the mold cavity, turning the mold after pouring the foam so the belly is in a down position when the foam cures. This places the foam in the belly and roughly centered in the bug for even flotation. However, since the Hilts popper molds are made with cavities facing each other (three or four on each side of the mold), it is necessary to work with only one side of the mold at once, turning the mold so that the bellies of the poppers are down for the lead shot to settle before the foam cures. Try to do this in the first minute or so after the foam is poured. If necessary, slap a quick layer of tape over the sprue holes or gates to prevent foam from leaking out and leaving voids in the cavities. To make the most of the molds, fill all cavities with hooks and shot, mix only enough foam to fill half of the molds, fill these and, after fifteen to twenty minutes (enough time for the foam to partially cure and prevent shot movement), mix more foam and fill and position the other three mold cavities.

Lead shot can also be positioned on the hook shank with glue, and small split shot can be crimped onto the shank to hold it in place near the belly of the bug. A third possibility is to use fuse wire or lead wire such as that used to tie weighted flies. Using these methods, it is possible to fill all mold cavities at once.

The addition of a rattle, lead shot, or lead wire will require slightly less foam with each bug; with care you may be able to adjust quantities of foam or number of molds filled. Be sure to keep records of the amount of shot or turns and size of wire for each bug size, so you can repeat good results and adjust those that are too light, too heavy, or misplaced.

Other Variations in Molding

It is also possible to mold in wire or mono with the hook to make other bug variations. One possibility is to mold in mono or wire that extends in back of the bug body for the addition of a long tail tied to the wire or a propeller blade on the mono or wire. (A tail can't be used with such bugs, since it will interfere with the blade.) For this, tie the mono or wire securely to the hook shank, with the wire or mono positioned so that it will extend in front of or behind the bug. For proper closing of the mold, use a razor blade or hobby knife to slightly enlarge the slot for the hook shank. A good way to do this is to first cut a straight line at a slight side angle, then cut again parallel to this cut (at the opposite angle) to form a small gutter or channel. Do not make this any larger than necessary, and make it only on one side of the mold. (It would be nearly impossible to try to match grooves on the two halves.)

Once the mono or wire is molded into the bug, it is easy to finish by adding small propellers, spinner blades on clevises, lightweight plastic buzz blades, or similar attractors to the front or back of each bug. Make sure that the blades are small to prevent unbalancing the bug. (See Chapter 9 for more.)

Final Molding Considerations

Some final considerations: Either before or after painting, but before tying in tails, grind or drill any sockets for legs, tails, eyes, or wings. A small drill bit (about ⅛" is right) or tiny rotary grinding bit will serve to cut one socket into the tail of the bug for adding a wrapped, glued-in tail, or to cut two such sockets for frog legs. Similar recesses can be used for plastic bead eyes, or drilled holes of the appropriate size for stem eyes.

Costs of Molding Bugs

Cost of making these hard-foam poppers is low, provided you make a lot of them. Prices of the molds and foam will vary with time and inflation, but after amortizing the cost of the mold, and with experience that will

Examples of various bugs made from Hilts Molds.

help to eliminate waste, such poppers should cost about one-third or less the cost of a finished molded popper body (unfinished) available from a store or mail-order catalog. That would be for a bass-sized popper—panfish-sized bugs would cost even less.

Because of the curing time and the minimum quantities of plastic required, it does help to use more than one mold. That way, sufficient plastic can be mixed to fill all the mold cavities, with reduced waste. The first time that I used the system using two molds, I used too much plastic and ended up with a waxed cup full of excess foam, in addition to completely filled mold cavities and sprue holes. Conservatism is the key to eliminating waste, while speed in mixing is the key to properly formed poppers.

Other Molded Bugs

In addition to molding your own with the Hilts Molds as outlined above, you can also buy bug bodies with and without the hook already molded in place. Mystic Bay sells a popper bug with a long-shanked 2/0 hook in place and sockets molded for adding eyes. The bugs are available in color for simple finishing by tying on a tail, but they can be painted if desired.

Lefty's Popper is available in molded plastic, and other bug shapes and sizes (manufactured by Wapsi and others) are available through standard fly-tying suppliers. Sliders, poppers, and pencil poppers are typically available, both with and without hooks.

In addition, you can use other molded products. I've used the rigging floats that are designed for walleye bait rigs. These small, hard, symmetrical bean-shaped closed-cell floats in fluorescent colors are available in sizes from $\frac{1}{4}''$ X $\frac{5}{8}''$ to $\frac{3}{8}''$ X $\frac{3}{4}''$. Some now have slots cut in them for quick rig changes, which makes it easier to add a hook. Before finding these, I cut a slot with a hacksaw blade to glue in a kink-shanked hook to make a small slider bug. I've used these with regular slider ties, along with other ties in which I added a tail and then large soft hackle fore and aft of the body for a different look, to make what I call a splider—a combination slider and spider.

CHAPTER 8

Soft-Foam Bug Construction

C losed-cell plastic foam is one of the more interesting materials to come along for making bugs. As it's closed-cell material, it will not sink, and in its various forms it is appropriate for everything from tiny terrestrials to big bugs for big-game fishing. It is easy to work, easy to shape, and easy to glue in place. Best of all, it comes in colors or can be painted to make any color bug desired.

Foams for Making Bugs

Foams for making bugs of all types include a wide range of foams sold for the fly-tying trade, as well as foams designed for other purposes. Most are "soft" foams, which made be firm or soft, but which do recover when

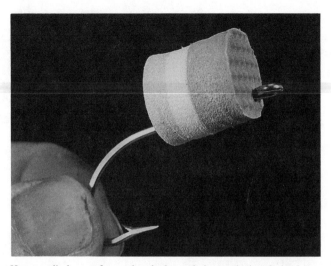

Here a cylinder cut from a beach shoe sole is punched and glued to
a hook to make a simple soft-foam popper body. Note the three
colors in this bug body, a result of the three layers of the shoe sole.

compressed. For example, Jason Shiba of EdgeWater makes a wide range
of bug bodies for the component builder, including poppers, sliders, slim
pencil poppers, and cylindrical big-game popping bodies. Dick French of
Dale Clemens Custom Tackle sells their Live Body foam (also available
elsewhere) in sizes from one-thirty-second- to three-quarter-inch diameters and in eight colors. Greg Snyder of King Neptune's Flies sells round,
rod-formed Ethafoam in one-half-, five-eighths-, three-quarter-, and one-
inch diameters in popper bodies, and by the foot for cutting to size. Rainy
Riding of Rainy's Flies and Supplies offers a series of molded foam
"rods" (in various sizes and colors) that are ideal for cutting to length,
trimming, and making into small foam poppers and sliders, as well as
terrestrials. Randy Swanberg of Flycraft supplies cylindrical bodies that
are easy to shape into poppers and sliders. In the hard (non-compressible)
foams, Jeff Hahner of Mystic Bay molds a hard-foam body on a hook, and
Tom Schmuecker of Wapsi has developed and sells hard-foam popper
bodies in several designs and sizes for gluing onto the hook of your
choice. He used to sell the bodies (such as Lefty's Bug) on hooks, but
found that too many anglers wanted a different hook for their own reasons. "No matter what I made, everyone said they wanted it on another
style hook," Tom explained.

In addition, foams meant for other purposes can also be used. If you have a discarded fishing rod with a foam grip, you have a source of foam, since many of these grips were of closed-cell EVA foam—the same material used by some companies marketing foam bodies. Discarded rubber-sole thong-type beach shoes are also a good source of material, as are broken foam surfboards, lobster and crab pot floats, etc. Some of these are EVA, some are PVC, and some are other materials, but the key to any of this found bug-body stuff is that it be a closed-cell foam. Ethafoam used for packing material for delicate electronic parts is also good, particularly for large bug bodies. (This not the brittle, breakable foam sometimes erroneously called Styrofoam, but a closed-cell, squeezable foam easily cut into bug shapes with a sharp knife, razor blade, or cylinder cutter.)

The foams will vary in density and usefulness. For example, Mystic Bay was making PVC foam bodies by coring out cylinders from lobster-pot float material. They no longer supply these, but do supply bodies of hard PVC foam. These bodies are dense, with tight cells. I have made some by coring out sections of similar crab pot floats that, while still useable, are lighter, less dense, more fragile, and larger-celled. Ethafoam is also a large-cell material that, while fine for big-game bugs, is less useful for smaller bugs of any type.

Naturally, with many materials available, not all glues will work uniformly. When trying a new foam or source of found foam, follow the manufacturer's or supplier's recommendations, or try various glues to test compatibility and strength. One common problem is the use of airplane-type glues (like Testor's model cement) on the non-compressible foam bodies (such as Wapsi). This glue will dissolve the plastic foam. The best glue for these bodies is epoxy. Similarly, CA glues are good for most foams, but will not work at all on Ethafoam, which requires epoxy or AquaSeal.

Cutting Methods for Foam Blocks

Cutting methods for foam vary widely, depending upon the foam and equipment available. One of the best methods for cutting out cylinders from materials such as Ethafoam, beach shoes, foam blocks (some companies sell it this way for your own cutting and shaping), or lobster and crab pot floats is to use a cutting tube that will cut out a cylinder. In theory, it is just like coring an apple with a round-tube apple corer. You can make your own foam cutters as outlined in Chapter 1.

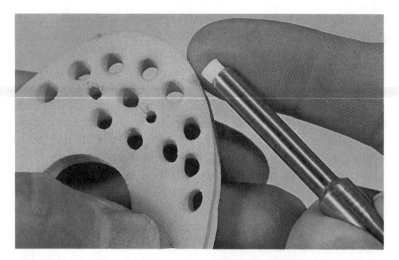

Small bug bodies are cut with a coring tube cutter from a closed-cell beach-shoe foam.

Perform all cutting against a firm support or bench, either by hand or drill. I've found that careful hand cutting works fine, but Jason Shiba of EdgeWater recommends using a power tool at about 800 to 1,000 rpm for best results.

Foam can also be cut into rectangular blocks with a fillet knife, the blocks squared on the end for subsequent shaping with the knife, a razor blade, or sandpaper.

Shaping Methods for Foam Bodies

While foam bodies can be shaped with a sharp knife as outlined above, the best method is sanding. One way to do this is to cut a cylinder with a cutting tube, pull enough of the foam out to shape the taper you want, and then chuck the tubing into a drill (following above instructions) and turn it at an angle against a stationary or moving sanding surface. (The moving sanding surface is best to avoid clogging the sandpaper.) I like to use a separate tube of the same interior diameter to keep the sharp edge of the tube from making contact with the sander.

This method is best only for short bug bodies, since long bodies have no internal support to keep them from chattering when rotating—you won't get a true round shape.

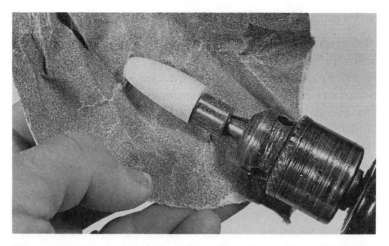

Here an EdgeWater shaping tool is used to hold a cylinder of foam (EdgeWater supplies blocks for coring and cylinders as well as pre-shaped bodies) for shaping against sandpaper.

A different system is used by EdgeWater, which sells a shaping tool that consists of a central point and two side prongs (like a pitchfork) with a shaft to fit into an electric drill. They recommend about 2,000 to 3,000 rpm for the motor turning the foam cylinder, again shaping against a moving sanding surface if possible. An alternative is to use sandpaper glued to a board. Medium sandpaper is best, since it gives some texture. Too coarse a sandpaper leaves a coarse, open look to the foam, while too fine a paper makes for a frosted or glazed appearance.

A third method is suggested by Frank Wentink in his book *Saltwater Fly Tying* (Lyons & Burford, New York, 1991), who describes using a sheet metal screw through the foam, the parallel sides of the screw held in a drill chuck and the turning body tapered and shaped by holding it against sandpaper or sand screen. (Sand screen shapes rapidly and is an abrasive material used for sanding drywall joints; it's available from most paint and hardware stores.) Speed is critical for this operation—too fast will melt the foam; too slow will tear the foam and produce a rough surface. The best angle is about thirty-five to forty-five degrees, to form a tapered or bullet head.

If you want spouter heads with bow-shaped sides, or slots cut into the front of the head, use small stone grinders, sanding drums, or metal router bits in a rotary hobby tool.

Hook-Gluing Methods with Foam Bodies

There are several gluing methods for foam. Most of the CA glues work very well with foams. They glue easily and quickly; just be sure you don't get a finger glued semi-permanently to a foam body in the process.

There are two basic methods of gluing hooks into foam. One—recommended by Jason Shiba of EdgeWater for their products—is to use a small-diameter drill or awl to punch or drill a hole through the foam bug at the desired location. Then wrap the shank with thread so that there is more surface area and "tooth" to the hook. Use Aron Alpha Ethyl Blue Cap Type 232 to bond the thread to the hook. According to Shiba, this adhesive has good bonding to metal, but it's not the best for bonding the hook to the foam, since it is fast acting (you might not get the hook in proper position before the glue cures), and it also leaves a white residue that could discolor the exterior of the foam. (However, if a glue is not used to bond the thread to the hook, the thread might be pushed out of place—pushed back—when you insert the hook into the hole in the foam.) The Type 232 sets up almost immediately, so it is possible to add this adhesive, wait a few seconds, and proceed to the next step, which is to coat the thread-wrapped hook with Aron Alpha Ethyl Blue Cap Type 202 (a moderately fast curing adhesive), and then insert the hook into the foam. Work it back and forth slightly while rotating it to assure good adhesive distribution, and then set it in position to cure.

Jeff Hahner likes Satellite City Hot Stuff, a thin, watery CA glue. His method is to slit the foam for the hook (his foam bug bodies, the soft version of which he no longer supplies, were a PVC plastic), insert the hook, and then hold the body together while adding a drop of the glue to the tail of the bug. The thin glue will "wick" to the other end and completely glue the hook in place, and seal the slit at the same time. This works for straight-shanked hooks as well as kink-shanked hooks.

Some foams will vary in their ability to take glues. Rainy Riding, who sells the foam rod used primarily for making terrestrials, notes that there is a different chemical formula for her black foam than for the yellows, oranges, and whites. I have found that Hot Stuff works fine for the black, but not so well for the other colors. Rainy recommends the thicker, gel CA glues, and has had good success with all her foams using Quicktite Super Glue Gel made by Loctite.

While a number of different brands and types of CA glues are available for foam, it is possible to use other glues, such as the gel and low-viscosity epoxies, PVC pipe glues for PVC foam, and other types of firm,

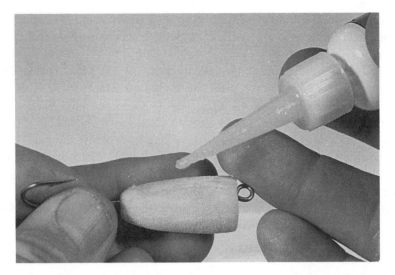

Fast-acting CA glue is here added to a seam line on a foam bug to glue it to a hook. Such CA glues can also be added to the end of a bug body to "wick" along the hook shank when the hook shank is punched through a hole in the bug body.

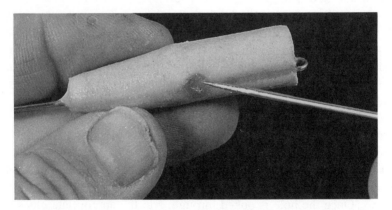

A bodkin points to the enlarged area in a glued foam body where an extension connector has been added to a long shank hook. Note that the new line tie is in line with the hook point and bend—not at right angles to it.

137

waterproof glues. Ethafoam will not glue at all with CA glues and the best results, according to chemist Nick Skirkanish, come with AquaSeal or epoxy.

Where they can be used, the advantage of the CA glues is that they work rapidly and in essence weld the bonding surfaces as well as the hook. One caution: Follow all directions on these and any glues. Cyanoacrylate glues will bond skin in seconds. Use special clamps made from spring clothespins if you have to clamp a bug body while the glue dries.

If working with hard foams (such as those that are molded without the hook in place), use regular epoxies, or the glue recommended by the manufacturer or supplier. Already mentioned was the problem of hard-foam bugs dissolving when using airplane cement instead of epoxy glue.

Making Poppers

Unlike working with cork or balsa, where the slit cut into the bottom of the bug must be as wide as the hook or the wrapping on the hook, the slit for a soft-foam popper is best made with a razor blade. (Do not try to make a wide slit.) With the low-viscosity glues, hold it the hook in position and add a drop of glue to one end to allow the glue to wick through the slit and bond the hook to the foam.

If working with gel glues, spread a small amount of glue onto the hook shank and work it into the slit. Rotate back and forth slightly so the glue is distributed, and then hold tightly until the glue bonds. For glues that need more curing time, including the five-minute epoxies, use clothespin spring clamps.

When making poppers following the EdgeWater technique of gluing the hook into a hole in the foam, first use an awl to make a hole through the foam just under the surface of the center of the belly. While you do not want this hole to break through the surface, the closer you can make it to the surface, the greater the hook gape and the greater the hooking effectiveness. Once the hole is poked through, add the appropriate glues (see gluing suggestions above) and insert the hook. Align the hook properly before the glue sets.

In all cases, make sure the eye of the hook is clear of the popping face for easy tying, and that the bug is left with plenty of gape by gluing the hook shank close to the belly surface. Also, if poking the hook through a hole, use an awl or bodkin to clear any glue from the eye of the hook before the glue sets up.

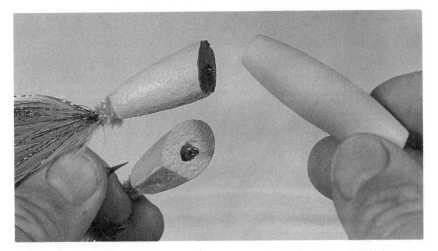

Various types of foam surf flats can be used to slip onto a tail-tied hook to make a simple, tapered body version of Bob's Bangers. The idea is also a variation of the one-half perch float body used years ago in the old Cap Colvin KaBoomBoom bug (which was glued in place).

Here an EdgeWater pre-shaped diving body is made into a completed bug with a simple tail.

Making Sliders

Sliders are nothing more than reversed poppers, in which the rounded or tapered part of the bug is forward, with the larger diameter and squared face against the tail and hackle. The same concerns, glues and gluing methods apply.

Gluing Foam with Tails in Place

The best way to glue foam bodies onto a hook on which the tail is already attached is to follow the above instructions, paying particular attention to the thread wrap that was used to finish the bug. In most cases, this thread wrap will be forward of the hackle or tail, and is designed to be covered and sealed with glue. Thus, you may wish to use a small pin-point routing stone on a Dremel Moto Tool (or similar rotary hobby tool) to rout out a small area in the back of the slit for this thicker thread wrap. Also, as the glue sets, pay particular attention to the rear of the bug body so that the slit does not separate as a result of the thicker thread wrap.

If using gel CA glues or gel epoxy, add a little extra glue to this area to seal in the thread wrap. (This usually is not necessary if poking the hook into a hole in the foam, since the foam will expand and surround the wrap.) Naturally, the tail should be tied so that the extra thread wrapping will be completely covered by the foam body and only the tail will show.

Inserting Materials into Foam Bodies

In addition to the hook, other materials can be added to the foam body using holes routed, drilled, or poked into the foam and using gel CA glues or gel five-minute epoxy. It is possible to glue a hook into a foam body and ream a hole in the body with a small routing bit, fill it with glue, and then add a thread-wrapped tail. The same method can be used to add two frog legs, feather or fur moth wings to the sides of the foam bug, a leather BugSkin or Ultra Suede mouse tail to a mouse-shaped bug, or a series of tail materials around the rear perimeter of a foam cylinder big-game bug. Slits cut into the side can be used to add glue-soaked hackle or marabou fibers for Gerbubble-style bugs.

Here a big-game popper has a fur tail tied onto the hook shank and a marabou feather skirt inserted as a plug into the upper part of the EdgeWater foam body. Small routers are ideal for making such sockets for adding skirt or leg materials.

Slip-On Tube Bug Bodies

Slip-on bug bodies are designed to slip onto the fly leader, with the leader then tied to a hook, dressed hook, or fly, with the previous addition of the floating body making a bug out of the rig. These have generally been used for offshore big-game fishing, where larger cylinders are used for the floating bug portion, and a fly or hook (sometimes two hooks joined by wire or heavy mono) completing the bug. Foam is almost uniformly used for these slip-on bodies, and thus included in this chapter, although cork, balsa, or other materials could be used. That these other materials are not often used is a function of how easy it is to make slip-on bugs of foam, and the fact that the foams are soft and thus feel lifelike to a striking fish. Foam will stand up to hard strikes that might shatter balsa or cork, and thus is the best choice for big game. Years ago I used this same design when making some bass bugs of a slip-on design of cork, and they worked

141

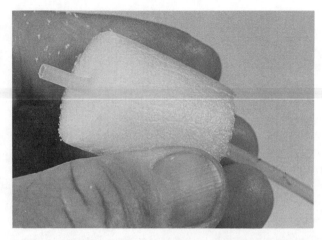

Here a short length of white Ethafoam cylinder from King Neptune
Flies with a central plastic tubing is used to make a salt water
big-game popper.

The Ethafoam popper material can be glued (use epoxies—the CA glues will not work
on this foam) onto a plastic tube on which is tied a tail material to make a completed
tube-type bug.

well, but did not have any real advantage over standard bass bugs other than interchangeable tail/body colors.

While such designs are primarily found on big-game flies, the same basics can be used in smaller sizes for any size or style bug. Use a foam cylinder, through the center of which a stiff plastic tube is inserted as a sleeve for the leader or shock leader. Any plastic tubing will work, but the best stuff is the hard one-eighth-inch diameter Nylaflow tubing. Other possibilities used by anglers include coffee stirrers (a little light) and the blue, hollow plastic tubing used for some cotton swabs, which Jack Samson favors. The tubing is a must on soft bug bodies, since otherwise the bug body may slide down onto the fly and jam the hook—preventing strikes—or tear through the leader. Some of the wicking, thin-viscosity CA glues are effective for gluing the tube in place, although gels and epoxies are also good choices. Depending upon the design, the tube is flush with the rear of the cylinder, or extends slightly (about a quarter of an inch) from the face. If extended, the purpose is to add a short length of larger-diameter, flexible tubing that will fasten (glued) to the stiff tubing and can be formed to slip over the eye of the hook to keep it in place. An additional possibility is to add one or more additional short sleeves of flexible tubing for adding tail materials directly to the bug body. The purpose here is to build up a larger base for adding the materials so that the tail will have more of a bulky look that will match the size and shape of the floating body. Tying materials onto a thin tube, or only on the hook shank, results in an unnatural-looking bug with a large head and a pencil-thin tail.

Another way to build a bulky tail is to use the thin, stiff tubing through the bug body, and then poke or drill holes around the rim of the rear face for gluing in large feathers or bundles of tail material. Use one of the small rotary cutters for a Dremel Moto Tool and drill a recessed socket for inserting tail materials. An advantage here is that a bulky tail like this can completely hide the hook (or hooks). For additional bulk, a hook can be dressed with fur, synthetics, or feathers to create a bulky or two-toned appearance.

An alternative that I like is to use a tubing section about one-half-inch shorter than the length of the bug body and insert it so that the end of the tube is flush with the front of the bug, leaving the back half inch without any tubing insert for jamming onto the hook, as described above, but without the possibility of the body sliding down on the hook and blocking the point.

To make the tail bulky enough to match the body for these combined bugs, tie down and criss-cross some thread on the hook, then thread on a small cylinder of hard foam and glue it in place by wicking CA glue along the hook shank. This cylinder should be about three-quarters the length of the hook shank and about one-half to three-fourths that of the foam body diameter. Then re-tie the thread (or bring it up over the cylinder if still tied in place) and tie down the tail materials in bunches around the perimeter of the cylinder. The tail can be saddle hackle, fur, synthetics, or combinations of these. Tie off when complete. Do not use excessive pressure on this cylinder, since even with firm foam it is possible to compress it with the pressure from the thread.

To complete the tail, coat the wrap with five-minute epoxy or an epoxy rod finish, and rotate the fly on a curing motor. An alternative is to wrap the foam cylinder with material such as chenille, ice chenille, cactus chenille, wool, or tinsel to give it a bulky look.

One big advantage to separate bodies and tails is that you can mix and match colors and styles as you wish on the water to reduce your total bug inventory, yet still be prepared for any bug-fishing situation.

Sigler-Style Bug Bodies

Cam Sigler (address Appendix B) makes and sells big-game bug bodies and tails on tubes, with the bodies different from those already described, but easy to make. These are EVA-type foam heads with snout-like slider heads and round collars at the rear—almost like a Dahlberg Diver shape, if the shape were completely symmetrical. Three holes punched through the collar, equidistant around the edge, make bubbles and foam—prime attractants for big-game fish. Also, some weights glued into the perimeter of the head keep the bug riding correctly so that the eyes are horizontal, although this is probably not necessary.

Such heads are easy to make by carving and sanding down a foam head to shape, and using a small tube cutter to punch holes through the collar. Then add stem-type plastic eyes with CA glue to holes drilled in the forepart of the head. The heads are also drilled through the center and fitted with a tube for sliding onto a leader.

An alternative way to make these is to use a small-diameter, straight cylinder for the snout, with a short quarter-inch section of larger-diameter foam for the collar. Punch the collar to make the holes desired. Glue both sections together and then onto a plastic tube for threading onto the leader.

Adding Materials to Bugs

Materials can be added to bug bodies after they are glued on the hook. The methods for this are no different from those used for any type of bug body. A wrap of thread is started at the rear of the bug body, building up a thread base, and then the materials are added in turn. First tail materials are added using feathers, synthetics, or furs, then a hackle (if desired). Finally, the thread is tied off with half-hitches or a whip-finish, as close to the bug body as possible. Protect the thread wrap with several coats of head cement.

CHAPTER 9

Tying and Finishing Methods for Hard-Bodied Bugs

Tying and adding tails, legs, and hackles to hard-bodied bugs of hard foam, soft foam (PVC and EVA), cork, balsa, and similar materials can be done either before or after the bodies are glued to the hook. There are advantages and disadvantages to each method. If tying to a bare hook shank, you must know the size and shape of the bug to be used so that you can properly position the tail materials. The one advantage is that you can use more of the hook shank to finish off the tie and also seal it completely by gluing it into the bug body. For this, you might have to slightly rout out the rear of the slot in the bug body for the larger diameter created by the additional wraps of thread on the hook shank.

If tying onto a glued and painted bug body, you will have less space to tie off the bug, and must do so carefully between the tail/hackle area and the bug body. The advantage is that it is not necessary to paint the bug with the tail in place, but there are some tips for painting and gluing using both procedures.

Preparing Hooks with Bodies Attached for Tying

Most bugs have the tails tied on after the body is glued in place, painted, and finished with eyes and any clear finishing coats. The advantage is that bugs can be prepared and painted in advance, finishing with the tail and colors when the need arises. One problem is that once the tail is tied tightly against the back of the bug body, it is difficult to add sealer or head cement to protect the wrap from unraveling.

One simple solution is to use a small scrap of plastic bag (size doesn't matter—anything from about one inch to about two inches square is good), and poke it onto the hook point, sliding it as far forward as possible before beginning the tie. If the plastic scrap is too large, it might get in the way of the tying thread, but a simple solution is to use a rubber band or masking tape to hold the plastic body.

The plastic scrap is not used in tying but, when ready to seal the wrap with head cement, it does allow protecting the painted body while pulling the hackle or tail material back to expose the base of the wrap and when tying off. Once the wrap is completely sealed, it is easy to rip off the plastic scrap.

Another possibility is to use the largest Hackle-Back—a cone-shaped plastic shield designed for fly tying, but also useful for shielding hackle and tails when painting bug bodies and sealing tails. A slot in the side allows it to easily slip on and off.

Preparing Hooks for Tying Before Bodies Are Added

It also helps to use a scrap of plastic sheeting or a Hackle-Back between the wrap and bug body when tying the tail before adding the body, but this does not have to be added until the tail and wrap is complete. At that time, it is easy to poke the center of the plastic (or the Hackle-Back) over the hook eye to butt against the thread wrap. This is even more important than the similar technique listed above, since it prevents contact between the tail material and the wet paint of the body while painting and finishing. It is removed once the bug is complete.

Begin tying after noting the position of the rear of the bug body, since the tail materials cannot extend forward of that area. The technique for starting is the same as described above, and the same as that used for fly tying. When tying tails first, it does not hurt (and often helps) to wrap the thread in an up-down spiral from the tail point to the eye, to add surface area and tooth for the later gluing procedure.

Threads

Threads can include any that you currently like for fly tying. Match the thread to the size of the bug, with thread for small bugs something like 2/0 Gudebrod, Thompson Monobond in 3/0, Mono Cord, 3/0 Uni-Thread, or similar sized threads. For larger bugs go with size A Gudebrod, Thompson Super Strength, or other threads. In all cases be sure to use a thread strong enough to securely wrap or spin the tail materials used. The same considerations apply to making legs or tails that are wrapped separately and glued into holes in the bug body. Any color can be used, but I like to at least generally match the color of the tail materials used—white or light with white or light tails, black with very dark or black tails, and middle shades for middle colors.

Bobbins make it easy to wrap, and are particularly good with bugs, since the bobbin shaft allows easily wrapping around the bulky bug body.

Tying Down Tails

Tails are easy to tie down, since the technique is no different from tying down a feather or fur wing on a streamer fly. The one consideration for fur tails (such as bucktail) is to decide if you are going to stack the tail on top of the hook (as you normally would a streamer wing) or allow the fur to wrap around the hook shank. I prefer the latter, since it more completely disguises the hook and, in my opinion, also makes for a better "look" in the finished bug. Both are possible, however, even over the bare shank.

Begin by wrapping the thread around the hook shank to lock the thread in place right in back of the bug body, or where the bug body will be if not yet glued in place. Move the thread to a position about one-eighth- to one-quarter-inch in back of this point. I like the closer position if not adding hackle, and the greater space if adding wound hackle.

Simple steps in tying a bug after it has been painted include tying down the thread as for basic fly-tying procedures.

Here the tail is wrapped in place behind the body.

Select the proper amount of fur and clip close to the skin. The proper amount depends upon the style of bug you are tying, and selection comes with experience. As a general rule, start with a bundle about the diameter of a lead pencil for a saltwater bug (#1/0 to #4/0 hooks), about half that size for a bass bug (#4 to #1 hooks), and about one-fourth that size for a panfish bug (#10 to #6 hooks).

If necessary, place the tapered ends in a hair stacker to adjust the length evenly, or hold the long ends and pull out the shorter ones, overlapping them to match the lengths. Trim the butt ends square. Here you can leave the butt ends long, to be trimmed after the tail is tied down, or trim to the correct length to position the tail directly in back of the bug for wrapping. I prefer this latter method when tying bugs that have the body glued in place. When adding the bug body later, I find no advantage either way.

Hold the tail on top of the hook and bring the thread straight up alongside the butt ends. Pinch with the fingers holding the tail, release some tension, and then bring the thread straight down on the other side. Continue to hold the tail material and pull the thread down. Repeat several times along the length of the butt ends to lock the material in place. Once locked in place so that it will not twist to the far side of the vise, continue wraps to secure it.

If not adding hackle, completely cover the butt ends with thread and then tie off with half-hitches or a whip-finish, completing the bug with several coats of head cement. If tying on a bare hook with the bug body to be added later, delay this step so that you can glue the wrap into the slot in the bug and permanently seal it.

Distributing the fur tail around the hook shank requires a slightly different technique. For this again select the bundle to be used, adjust and trim as outlined above, and hold in place on the hook shank. If possible, work the fur around the shank. Then make two to three loose wraps of thread around the bundle before pulling tight. Pull tight so that the tightening thread wraps will evenly spread the bundle of fur. Hold in place and make more wraps, eventually completely covering the butt ends with a collar of thread.

(If working with large bundles for large bugs, or if you find the above technique difficult, another method for either of the above is to work with smaller bundles, placing each bundle in the desired position, wrapping down, and repeating with another bundle. For wrapping in one spot on top of the hook shank, tie each bundle in the same spot, one on top of each other. For a tail that surrounds the hook shank, place each successive bundle in a different spot around the hook shank to achieve the same effect as above.)

The best feathers for a hackle tail are saddle hackles, since they are longer and fuller for bulk and body. All feathers should be matched by size and shape, although different colors can be used. In all cases, though, the color combinations should match on both sides. Most bugs will require at least two hackles on each side, some will require four or more per side. Several methods of attachment are possible. Traditionally, the hackles are flared or splayed out on the sides (with each side having the concave surface out), with the hackle of each side tied on separately.

To do this, select, match, strip, and trim the hackle butts so those you'll be tying on one side are the same length and size. Then place them along the side of the hook shank and wrap in place with several loose loops of thread, pulled tight to secure the hackle stems without movement or twisting. Then carefully match the other side to the first and wrap in place the same way. Trim the hackle butts and secure both sides with thread. Norm Bartlett likes to seal matching side feathers with his glue gun, position them while the glue is still warm, make any necessary adjustments, and then wrap for security.

An alternative to this is to reverse the flare so that the two concave sides of hackle face each other for a slim, streamlined look. Again, select, match, strip, trim, and tie each side separately. Then trim excess butt fibers and wrap to secure.

A third method is to bundle the hackles in random order and tie in so that they surround the hook shank. To do this, select the predetermined number of hackles. Do not try to match them by the feather curvature, but instead let them fall into random bundles. Select, match, strip, trim, then work the butts in a bundle around the hook shank. Tie using several wraps of loose thread around the bundle, trim any excess butt ends, and wrap securely. The result is a bulkier tail than with either of the other methods, and often one that is especially good for large bugs for pike and salt water fishing.

An occasional method, used primarily for large saltwater bugs or big-game bugs, is to tie some hackles at the sides in a vertical plane, with those on the top or bottom in a horizontal plane. This achieves a bulky look similar to the random method above.

Tying in Synthetics

Using synthetics is not much different from using natural materials. In fact, some synthetics such as FisHair, Fly Fur from Mystic Bay, Gehrke's

The hackle or hackles, if used, are tied down and then wound forward using hackle pliers.

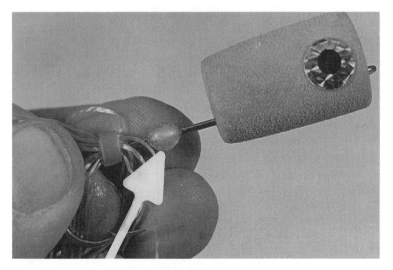

A small bead of epoxy glue added to a bulky wrapping of thread in back of this EdgeWater popping head makes for a stop over which a rubber, silicone or Lumaflex skirt can be added or changed at will—even while fishing.

Fish Fuzz, and craft fur (available from craft and hobby shops) are not much different from real fur. The one difference that I have noted is that there seems to be greater disparity in the length of individual fibers in any bundle you clip, so that you end up using a hair stacker more or pulling and matching lengths. There also seems to be more of an underfur, which can be combed out with a fine comb if desired.

Some synthetics such as Ultra Hair, Dynel, and nylon strands are less compressible than natural materials, so care must be used to get enough pressure to hold the material without breaking the thread. Two solutions are to go to a heavier thread, or to use a sealer or head cement on the tail even before adding wrapped hackle or tying off.

Wound Hackles

If adding wound hackle, select a good saddle hackle, strip the fibers off the butt end, flare out the remaining fibers, and tie the butt end in place at the rear of the tail wrap. Then trim the butt end of the hackle, and wrap forward to further secure it. Use hackle pliers to wrap the hackle around the hook shank, until enough hackle has been added or the hackle used up. At this point, hold the hackle with the hackle pliers and weave the thread through the flared hackle to secure it in place. After several wraps, trim the excess hackle and tie off the thread.

(In some cases, more than one hackle may be used. More than one will be required on big, bulky bugs, and colors can be mixed on any size bug. In these cases, it is best to tie both butt ends down and secure them at the same time, trimming and wrapping in place. Then each hackle can be wound individually, or all of them together. It is usually easier to wrap each individually to prevent any looseness that might result when trying to wrap both at once. In adding additional hackles, just be sure to weave subsequent hackles through the first so as to not mat any fibers.)

Any of these methods of adding wrapped hackle can be used with any type of tail—fur, feathers, or synthetics.

Tying Tails and Hackle Over Tubing

Some bugs are made on plastic tubing so that they can be slipped on to a leader that is then tied to a bare hook, dressed hook, or fly. These are mostly made of foam, although any material, such as cork or balsa, can also be used. The result with any of them is the same—a floating bug

Here a tail or skirt is tied to a tube to be made into a tube-style big game bug. The tail is being tied into the tube using a Perry Designs tube vise, which is ideal for the job.

body forward of a hook. Some of these are made so that the body is bare and the hook contains all the dressing; others include some dressing on the bug body. It is these latter that we are concerned with. In these, the bug is made on a hard plastic tube, as previously described.

The technique is the same as for tying in any tail materials as outlined above, except that you will be tying over a base with a larger diameter, and you must use a tube vise designed to accept the tubing that you are using (or modify a vise to hold the tube-constructed bug). If you lack a tube vise, one easy way to do this is to grip a finishing nail of the right diameter for the tubing in locking pliers (like Vise Grips) and hold the Vise Grips upright in a bench vise. Other than working on such a vise with a large-diameter base, the method of tying on, wrapping materials, and tying off is the same as for any other bug.

Tying Feathered Minnows

Feathered minnows, in the traditional sense, are tied with a feather tail on a slider or bullet head, with the rounded part of the head forward. Once the bushy tail and surrounding flared hackle are tied down, feathers are tied in on the sides of the bug. For this, the bug must be sealed and painted first. It is also a good idea to add a protective finishing coat, even though additional protection will have to be added to the thread wrap.

To tie in the side feathers, first choose the hackle to be used. Regular saddle hackle, guinea fowl hackle, and the short wide hackles from ducks and geese are all suitable. The choice will depend upon the length and colors that you want, although it is possible to stack and layer feathers for a different look or multicolored effect. Thread color can be neutral, or a bright color like red to show and look like flared gills.

Begin by wrapping the thread up over the cork or balsa bullet body, about one-third of the way back from the front. Take care that you wrap evenly so that there is minimal crossing over of threads. Once the thread is locked in place, using the same method as for a bare hook, clip the excess thread and place the prepared hackle or feathers on one side. Try to use a minimal number of wraps to hold the feathers in place, and trim the excess feather from in front of the thread wrap as soon as possible so that the wrap can be kept narrow. Add the feathers to the other side the same way. Follow this same process for more feathers if building up several layers.

Finish by making a careful whip-finish over the wrap, trying to keep each wrap adjacent to the previous one until four or five wraps are complete and the thread pulled through. Trim and then protect the wrap with a clear finish coat. One easy way to do this is to dip the head of the bug into a coat of clear finish just up to the back edge of the wrap to protect the wrap without coating the feathers.

A similar wrap can be made using fur such as bucktail, squirrel tail, or synthetic fur, but the fur must be spread out so that the thread will hold down the individual fibers.

Tying Moth Wings

Tying moth wings is no different from tying the feathers into the feathered minnow, except that the wings are tied on top of the bug and spread out so that they extend out over the body, rather than tied closely along the sides. The techniques of feather selection, tying, and finishing are exactly the same; only the wing location is different.

Wrapping Bodies

While it is seldom done, it is also possible to wrap a bug body with yarn, chenille, or similar materials to give it a fuzzy look. The reason that this is seldom done is that it is more work, often makes a bug waterlogged and thus harder to pick up and cast, and does not seem to have any particular advantage. If you wish to try this, you must have a tapered bug (popper or slider) that has an even or straight taper. Glue the bug body onto the hook, and tie in the tail material. If making a popper, add the body material before tying off. If making a slider, leave a little bare hook shank in back of the eye and tie down body material at this point. Then coat the body with a clear sealer or liquid glue. Begin wrapping spirally around the body, working from the thin end to the thick end. Once you reach the end of the bug, add some extra glue, clip the end of the material, and set the material in place. For additional security, you can also finish later with a thread wrap over the end of the material (around the thick end of the bug), then seal it with paint or head cement. It is also possible to use two different materials to make a variegated pattern; yellow and black chenille to make a wasp or bumblebee pattern, for example.

Adding Rattles

Rattles can be molded in or glued in as described in Chapter 5, or they can be wrapped in while tying in tail materials. See Chapter 10 for details.

Adding Glued-In Legs and Tails

Tails and legs of synthetics, natural fur, rubber strands, formed legs (Fly-craft has some for their foam frogs that can be used, and others are available from fly-tying shops and catalogs), and sections of Ultrasuede or BugSkin or similar materials are all popular and easily added to bugs.

Standard materials such as natural fur (bucktail, kip or impala, other long body fur), or synthetics (Ultra Hair, FisHair, Dynel, nylon) must be wrapped first to insert them into any hole in the bug. To do this, first clip enough material for the leg or tail desired. If using natural fur such as bucktail or a tapered synthetic such as FisHair, use a hair stacker to get the exposed ends even. Then hold the bundle in one hand, secure tying thread with that same hand, and use the other hand to wrap around the bundle a few times, trying to cross over the thread to lock it down. At this point, pinch the exposed end of the bundle with the fingers of the other hand, leaving a one-eighth-inch gap between the fingers of both hands. Then use a rotating motion to rotate the bobbin around the bundle and to wrap the bundle tightly. (You may have to adjust the tension on the bobbin for this. One easy way to do this is to wrap the thread several times around

Making jointed or bent legs for hair-bodied bugs or cork/balsa bugs is easy by wrapping leg material (here deer tail is used) around a stainless-steel pin or length of stiff wire (the stiff wire is not visible, but held in the vise jaws), and then wrapped as a fly wing.

one leg of the bobbin before the thread goes through the bobbin tube.) Make enough turns to securely wrap the bundle with a tight wrap, then finish off the wrap with several half-hitches. A whip-finish is difficult to do with this (nothing is held in a vise) and not necessary, since the bundle will be glued into the bug body. Once finished, clip the thread, and then carefully clip the bundle as close as possible to the end of the thread wrap. Serrated scissors are best for this.

The hole for the inserted legs or tail (usually drilled when the bug is shaped, as described in Chapter 5) must be big enough for the bundle, but should not be any larger than necessary. It should also be deep enough to hide the wrapping, which is why the wrapping should only cover a tiny area of the bundle. Assuming that the bug will be painted at this point (pros and cons are discussed in Chapter 11), soak the bundle thoroughly with glue and use a bodkin to spread some glue in the hole in the bug. Make sure that you use enough glue, but do not use *too* much, since this will make cleanup difficult or could react with the paint used on the bug. Also be sure that you use glues compatible with the bug if working with hard-foam bugs.

Pliers are used to bend the knee joint of the leg before the joint is sealed with fly head cement or paint.

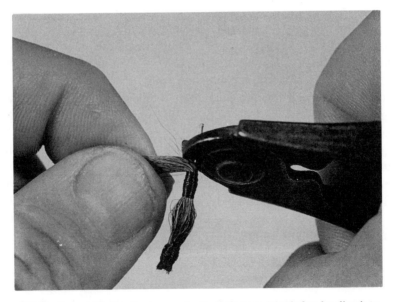

Here, cutters are clipping the excess wire from the knee joint before bending it to shape.

Wrapped legs are inserted into sockets routed into the rear of a frog-pattern bug. They are easily glued in place with five-minute epoxy glue.

A variation of this is to prepare two half-sized bundles of contrasting color, one light for the belly side of the bug, the other darker for the back or top side. Usually this is not necessary, and although it looks more natural to anglers, the fish don't seem to care.

Positions for such bundles include as a tail in skippers for saltwater bugging, as two legs for frog patterns, and into the sides of the bug to make spent "moth" wings.

Cut materials such as Ultrasuede, chamois, leather, BugSkin or similar, mouse tails, mouse legs, and frog legs, are easily added by soaking with glue, spreading glue into the hole in the bug, and inserting the butt end of the leg or tail. Often a bodkin helps to force the butt end all the way into the hole. Scissors or blades (razor blade or X-Acto knife) can be used to cut materials for these inserts.

Making Bugs Weedless

There are many ways to make bugs weedless, and many of them also apply to hair-bodied and soft-foam bugs. Many of these involve gluing or inserting weedguard material into the hard bug body; some involve tying

To add rubber, silicone, or Lumaflex legs to a cork or balsa bug after it is painted, use a bodkin to make a hole through the bug body above the hook shank.

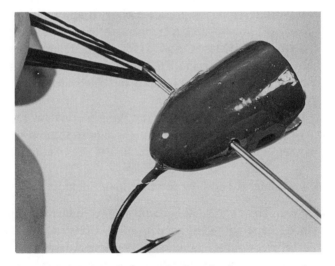

Once the hole is through, insert a large needle, then use a mono loop to thread the legs through the needle eye as shown. Then pull the needle back to pull the legs through.

Completed bug body with rubber legs. For best results, use CA or epoxy glue to hold the legs in place.

methods. Also, the size of the weedguard material (often mono but sometimes wire) will vary with the size and type of bug and where it will be fished. Big bugs fished in heavy grass for big fish will require a heavier weedguard than will small panfish poppers. A good starting point for mono is to use stiff mono (Mason is good) for all weedguards, using about fifteen-pound-test for small bugs to #6, twenty-pound-test for larger bugs to #2/0. Other brands of mono can be used, but check stiffness and pound test before making a lot of bugs.

Also note that some weedguards require tying part of the guard to the hook shank just in back of the eye. This might require some adjustment in gluing bug bodies onto hooks or tying deer hair if you plan to make these styles.

Types of weed guards and how to make them include:

- **Horseshoe**. This weedguard requires only light mono, since the horseshoe shape provides good rigidity. Construction is simple, since it involves only poking or drilling fine holes on two sides of the belly of any hard-bodied bug, cutting the mono to the right length, and gluing the ends into the two holes with cyanoacrylate or thin epoxy glue. For additional durability, sand or roughen the inserted ends of the mono for stronger bonding. These weedguards are possible with any hard-bodied bug of hard foam, soft foam, cork, balsa, or other woods.

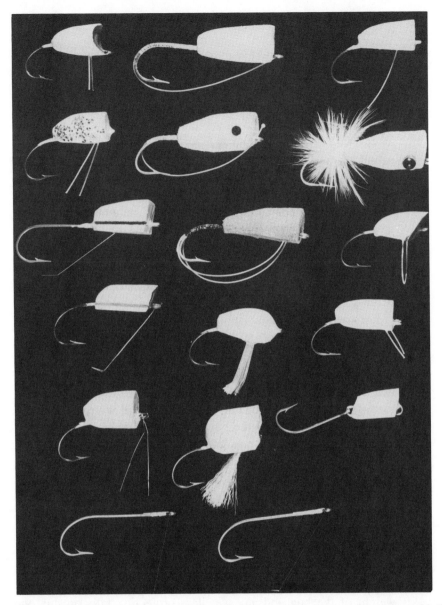

Some methods of making weedless bugs. Bottom two hooks: examples of how a wire weed guard is tied to the hook *(left)* and then cut and bent to shape *(right)*. Left column, top to bottom: Two short mono weed guards glued into the bug body, two long mono weed guards glued into bug body, wire weed guard glued into bug body (or can be tied to hook before gluing body onto the hook), wire weed guard tied to hook shank in back of hook eye, flip-type weed guard that is double pronged and loose on eye. Center column, top to bottom: Mono weed guard tied to bend and eye of the hook (tail must be tied on before this style is finished—tail not included in this photo, for clarity), mono weed guard showing the ball on the end of the mono after tying it in place in back of the eye and before the mono is pulled down to seat the ball against the tying thread, double mono weed guard, double-brush type of weed guard made from jig weed guards and glued into holes drilled in the body, synthetic tail material double weed guard glued into holes in body. Right column, top to bottom: single long mono weed guard, heavy hackle to serve as minimal weed guard, horseshoe or loop-type of weed guard, with both ends glued into body, forward-prong or limb-hopper style of weed guard, upturned jointed hook.

- **Double short prong**. This is like the former, but with two short lengths of mono that extend from the bug body, each glued separately into the body. Usually the exposed length is about equivalent to the gape of the hook and placed forward of the hook point by some distance.

  This can also be done on hair-bodied bugs, by tying a doubled strand of mono over the hook shank where you want the weedguard, figure-eighting under the hook shank so that the strands point down, then finishing the rest of the bug by adding more deer hair. Hold the weedguards while trimming, and then cut the weedguard monos to length.

- **Double long prongs**. These are like the above, glued in the bug body the same way, but usually at more of an angle so that they extend back to fully protect the hook point. The ends are in front of and below the hook points. These are possible on any hard-bodied bug.

  For hair-bodied bugs, tie this in the same as for short double prongs above, but do not trim as short when finished. Because these are longer, heavier mono is often required.

- **Limb-hopper weedguards**. This is a short double prong weedguard that is similar to the above, but with the short prongs extending forward and in front of the bug body. The design is intended to hit a limb or weed and "hop" the bug over the obstruction. This can be used on any hard-bodied bug, but mostly found on long, slim styles.

  These can be tied into hair-bodied bugs, by tying in two short strands of mono on either side of the head before finishing. Tie them so that they angle slightly down. Wrap over the mono, keeping each strand straight on each side, and then whip-finish. Trim the mono to short lengths and seal with head cement.

- **Single long prong**. This is made like the double long prong weedguard, but with one single prong of mono. Often this must be slightly heavier mono than when using two prongs, since the full weight of the bug and any weedless protection falls on this one strand of mono. It is not as effective as the two prongs that bracket on both sides of the hook point. Often the natural curve of the mono (line or leader memory) is used to curve the weedguard in line with the hook point. The same method can be used with a short, single wire as well.

  When tied in at the head of the bug, this is also easy to do with hair-bodied bugs. For this, finish the bug and then tie in the end of a length of mono so that the mono extends in front of the bug. Then build up the head area. (You want this built up so that there will be some taper to the head and thus some angle to the weedguard as you tie it down.) Thread the mono through the eye of the hook and then wrap with thread so that the mono extends down and in front of the hook point. Whip-finish and seal with cement, then adjust and trim the mono weedguard.

- **Single wrapped weedguard**. This is a mono weedguard often seen on bugs, since it can be used on hair-bodied as well as hard-bodied styles. It is wrapped onto the hook shank rather than glued into the body. The method is to wrap a length of mono onto the hook shank before beginning the tasks of gluing or wrapping tails. Once the mono is tied down partway on the bend of the hook, the rest of the bug is tied, or glued and wrapped. The weedguard is completed once the rest of the bug is finished by bringing the mono forward under the hook (which is how it protects hooks from snagging) and then tying it off just behind the eye. Make sure that you have clearance of about one-quarter inch between the hook point and the mono.

  If making hair-bodied bugs, this is easy to do as a part of finishing the head. If making a hard-bodied bug, it adds an additional tying step, in which the thread must be tied down to this small area of the exposed hook shank and then the mono tied in place. One problem is that this end of the mono might pull out from the short wrap at the eye. One solution to this is to determine the length of the mono, add about one-eighth inch, cut the end, and use a lighter or alcohol lamp to form a ball on the end of the mono; the ball will keep it from pulling free, once cooled and tied down. Another alternative for hard-bodied bugs is to glue the forward end into the body as close to the center line as possible.

  This type of weedguard can be made more or less protective by the extent to which it is wrapped on the hook bend. Little wrapping results in less protection—a more collapsible weedguard—than one that is wrapped far down the hook bend. About one-quarter inch space between the hook point and the mono is about right for most bugs.

- **Double wrapped weedguard**. This is like the above, but with two strands of mono used for additional "bracketing" protection for a bug that might lay sideways when skated across heavy weeds. It often requires a lighter mono than that normally used for the single-strand version. To do this, wrap in two strands of mono first, but at the end of the wrap, criss-cross the thread around the hook and each strand of the mono to separate them slightly. This will provide side protection to the hook point. Then complete the bug as above, and bring the two ends forward and wrap as above. A good alternative to this for hard-bodied bugs is to insert and glue the ends into the belly of the bug so that the mono strands are slightly separated for further side protection. This is not possible with hair-bodied bugs.

- **Single wire weedguard**. Wire can be used for weedguards, and several methods of attachment are possible. First, if using light, twisted leader wire, you can make a wire equivalent of the horseshoe and the various double-prong and limb-hopper styles in hard-bodied bugs. It is best, however, to use single-strand wire, with the wire angling down, and bent in front of and in line with the hook point to completely protect it. For this, the weedguard wire can be wrapped and glued to the hook shank before gluing into the bug body, or inserted and glued into the belly of the bug. A surer option that will prevent twisting is to insert a straight, inverted "J"-shaped piece of wire through the top of the bug, as close to the center as possible and at a slight angle so that it will exit the belly close to the center. Bury the short arm of the "J" into the top of the bug and glue in place. Then bend the exposed belly length of wire back parallel to the hook shank and bend the end parallel to the point so that it covers the hook below the point.

  For hair-bodied bugs, wait until the deer hair is about one-quarter-inch from the eye of the hook (this will minimize wrapping around the weedguard wire.) Then wrap the "L"-shaped bend of the wire to the hook shank, with the wire running through the eye of the hook. Complete the bug with more deer hair and finish off. Adjust the position of the wire in front of the hook point. An alternative is to wrap the top of the "L" to the hook shank, then fold the wire under the hook shank and wrap that; finish the bug with more deer hair and then bend the wire down to angle in front of the hook point.

- **Flip-up wire weedguards**. These are double-prong style, like those found on the Arbogast bugs. To make them, bend a length of wire double the length of the single wire guard and fit it over the hook shank just behind the eye. Curve each end of the wire down through the eye and straighten with pliers. Depending upon the wire, you will probably have to straighten the wire after you pull each end through the hook eye. Once you do so, it is easy to spread the ends and adjust the wires so that both sides are equal in slant and length. The advantage is that the wires can spring forward and out of the way on a hit, yet will fold back when the bug slides over weeds. In all honesty, they work fine, but will usually look a little ragged after being straightened, even on a new bug.

- **Jointed-hook bugs.** Jointed-hook bugs are not really a type of weedguard as much as a design of bug that makes the bug weedless. I came up with them after experimenting with other types of bug designs for weedless fishing. The basic design (described in Chapter 10) is that of a slider or popper body built on a wire form, with an eye at one end for a leader tie and at the other end for a hook eye attachment. The hook is a straight-shanked hook, regular length or only 1X or 2X long, and added to the wire form before the form is glued into the bug body. The hook hangs down for good hooking yet, with the point up, it will ride over any weeds to make an almost weedless design.

To tie one of these bugs, the legs, tail material, or fur and/or feathers and hackle (if used) is tied to a straight-shanked hook in a fly-tying vise, just like tying a regular fly. Seal the head with several coats of head cement. (A number of these can be tied up before the next step.) Then attach the hook to a wire form that is made in the shape of an elongated figure-eight, the distance between the eyes that of the length of the bug on which it is to be used. One solution to this is a wire connector link, primarily used for terminal tackle riggings and surf rigs in salt water. Different sizes are available. Standard spinner wire (usually about 0.035-inch diameter) is ideal for making these wire forms also, using round-nose pliers to shape the eyes at each end. Once the wire form is glued in place (make sure that the hook point is up), and the glue cures, the bug can be painted and is ready to use.

This basic design can also be used with hair-bodied bugs, tying the legs or tail to the hook shank and the deer-hair body to a wire form or link. One problem is that any connector link or doubled wire makes it more difficult to spin hair, although stacking usually works well. An alternative is to cut the bend off (carefully!) of a long-shanked straight-eye hook, heat the cut end and form a second eye to which the hook can be added, and tie the deer hair on this double eye connector. Make sure that you tie and trim so that the rear eye is in a vertical plane, to allow the hook trailer to work properly.

Bugs of this basic design can also be made with the hook point down, but there seems to be no real advantage to this, even in open water where weeds are not a problem.

- **Heavy-hackle weedguards**. These are nothing more than exactly what the name says—heavier and sometimes longer-than-normal hackle or fibers, at right angles to the hook, that help to protect the point from snags, while not preventing hooking fish.

  The best hackle or fibers are those that are stiff. For hackle, this means that you will have to use more than normal. Perhaps the best weedguard "hackle" is deer hair, spun on the hook as when making a deer-hair body, but concentrated in one place ahead of the tail and behind the body, then tied off and, if necessary, trimmed to cover the point (without being excessively long). Standard deer-hair spinning procedures are used for this, as outlined in Chapter 3. Realize, however, that heavily hackled bugs are often very air resistant, and so more difficult to cast and turn over.

- **Point-up weedless designs**. Bugs with the point up are generally not satisfactory, since the balance of the bug is upset, and in extreme cases the bug will torque to one side from the high center of gravity caused by the weight of the hook. One exception to this is with the Central Draught hook, such as the Mustad 3777 style. These have a sharp upward bend of the hook shank about one-third of the way back from the eye, so that a popper body can be glued onto this forward portion of the hook shank (wrapped with coarse thread first, since there is no kink), the main part of the hook hanging down in the water. Then insert and glue the tail or legs of the bug into the body or tie them to the angled hook shank. The idea is good, but not as good, or with the balance of, the jointed-hook bugs listed above. It can be used on hair-bodied bugs as well, but has a tendency to roll.

Tying Off—Half-Hitches and Whip-Finishes

Hard-bodied bugs can be finished in one of two ways—with a series of half-hitches or a whip-finish. Even this can be avoided with bugs in which

The bug is completed using a series of half hitches to finish the tying portion.

The finished bug, here with an eye and some glitter on the belly added as a final touch.

the legs or tail are inserted and glued into the body and there is no tying on the hook shank. On most bugs, however, a tail of some sort must be tied to the hook shank, either before or after the bug is glued in place.

In all cases, any finishing ties are done after all materials have been added to the hook shank, although some tyers like to half-hitch each material in place, and sometimes even add head cement or sealer for additional security.

The half-hitch is done just as described for any fly-tying operation—make a loop of the thread, place it around the hook and over the bug body, then pull it tight. To prevent catching hackle fibers, it helps to use a bodkin to hold the loop and guide it into place while pulling it tight.

Several half-hitches are a must, and each should be pulled up tight over or adjacent to the previous hitches. Even this does not guarantee that the final one will not come undone when the thread is cut. One way to help prevent this is to make several half-hitch loops and carefully pull all up at once, then clip and finally secure with several coats of head cement carefully applied to the tie point with a bodkin. While half-hitch tools are made for fly tying, they won't work for hard bugs, since they can only be used to pull the half-hitch loop tight at the eye of the hook—not over the bug body.

A whip-finish is far more secure, since it is like the whip-finish of a rope, or a crude version of the finish of a rod wrap. Whip-finishers are commercially available, but can only be used if they will throw the loop over the bug body. (Some are long and designed for this.) The knots are easy to make by hand, by making a loop of thread with your finger, wrapping it over and around the hook shank and standing thread, and continuing this for several sequential turns in order, finally pulling the loop tight after holding the loop with a bodkin as you pull it up.

Once clipped, it is less likely than a half-hitch to fray, but must be sealed with several coats of head cement or sealer applied with a bodkin.

Hard-Bug Design and Styles

"H ard bugs," as defined in this chapter, include any bugs that are not hair bodied. Thus, the designs and styles are applicable to any of the glue-on or slip-over materials such as cork, balsa, other woods, hard molded foam, and the soft foams such as EVA, PVC, and Ethafoam.

Once the basics of hard-bug construction and tying are understood, there is no end to the variety or types of bugs and the variations of tails and finishing that can be done. Most of these designs simply involve the basics, with perhaps some slight modification that results in an entirely different bug design. Just use common sense for the design and material used.

Hook Sizes and Styles

Hooks for hard bugs are almost always hump-shanked or kink-shanked so that they will not turn in the bug body. See Chapter 5 for details on hooks.

Sizes range from #14 through #2/0 from most manufacturers, and some special hooks are made for the purpose. Mustad makes a 9082S stainless (in #2/0 only) that has an extra-long shank for making the larger pencil poppers and skippers for saltwater fishing. They also make a tinned 32669CT in #1/0, with a single kink, also with a long shank for long bugs. Tiemco has a similar 511S stainless steel hook that is 4X long, 2X wide in #2/0, #1/0, #2, and #6. Mystic Bay has a special 2044SS kink-shanked popper hook in stainless steel in an extra long #2/0 on #1/0 wire.

There appears to be no standard as to the size or shape of the hard body used with any particular size of bug hook. Some attempts have been made, and it is still hard to argue with the guidelines of the late Joe Brooks in his first book, *Bass Bug Fishing* (A. S. Barnes and Company, New York, 1947). He advocated the following:

- $\frac{3}{8}''$ diameter cork body: #2, 3X long hook
- $\frac{7}{16}''$ diameter cork body: #1, 3X long hook
- $\frac{1}{2}''$ diameter cork body: #1/0 or #2/0 hook, standard length
- $\frac{5}{8}''$ diameter cork body: #3/0 hook, standard length

While Brooks dealt mostly with cork, the same would apply to foam, balsa, or other hard materials. A basic guideline that I have always used is to choose a hook with a gape at least as large as the largest diameter of the bug body, be it hard or of deer hair.

Balance

Balance in a bug is most important. With good balance a bug floats correctly, so that strikes are almost always converted into hooked fish. An example of how a bug can be balanced is in the design of the frog Randy Swanberg makes using his Flycraft foam, in which he uses lead wire wrapped and sealed part way around the bend of the hook shank to make the frog float tail down in the water (as does a real frog). Joe Messinger uses the same technique in cocking the legs of his Bucktail Frog up, so that they form a "wing" to help the fly land properly and also float with the hook down.

An example of poor balance can be found in some caterpillars that I made once (only a few—check your prototypes before making a gross of anything!), in which I cut a wide slot in a foam cylinder for better gluing with a chenille-wrapped hook. The removal of the foam caused the cater-pillar to float head down—my design fault, not the fault of the foam. (To correct, it was easy to use only a wrapped hook with the hook glued into a slot, or to slightly extend the forward part of the caterpillar foam for additional forward flotation.)

Balance esentially involves positioning the hook in the bug body, using the proper size and length hook for the bug, the angle of the hook in the bug, and the way the resulting bug floats. There are several basic "don'ts" to all of this:

- Don't use too small a hook for the bug body. Check above for some suggestions on hook and bug sizes.

- Don't use a hook with too short a shank and be particularly careful with long bugs like pencil poppers, pencil minnows, and saltwater skipping bugs. For these it may be necessary to extend the hook length, to be described shortly.

- Don't use a hook with an upturned eye on a hard bug. This can cause the bug to angle down at the moment of pick-up, causing the bug face of a popper to catch in the water and making pick-up difficult. The one exception to this might be the few bug styles that are made on a Central Draught hook like the Mustad 3777 (odd size numbers available, but the best for bugs would be about #22 through #32, or about #4/0 through #6 in conventional sizes). The bug is made with the hook point up, the body high on the forward bend of the hook, and the tail glued into the bug body.

- Don't bury the hook shank in the bug body, since this will reduce the gape of the hook and make hooking fish more difficult. Keep the hook shank close to the belly surface of the bug when gluing it in place, and do not cut the slot through the center of the bug.

- Don't angle the hook up at the rear, since this will also reduce the hook gape and also make the bug very unstable at rest. If you position the hook at any angle at all, make it an angle with the hook down at the rear, the shank just clearing the belly surface at the rear, but with the hook eye close to the center of the bug in the front. Tom McNally, quoted by A.D. Livingston in his *Tying Bugs and Flies for Bass*, suggests a rear-downward angle of almost forty degrees. This is perhaps extreme, with photos of his frog bug show-ing perhaps a twenty-degree angle, which is plenty for good hook gape and bite. Extreme angles can be obtained, if desired, with Mustad Central Draught hooks using a point-up design, and with double-bent shank worm hooks.

- Make sure you have enough flotation to keep the bug floating properly.
- Check all bugs for general appearance, and test completed bugs in a water bath for flotation. Cast prototypes with a fly rod to see if they will land right side up, or roll over immediately to float properly. Things like this can only be checked on the water under casting and fishing conditions.

Poppers

Poppers are basically bullet-shaped hard bugs with the flat or cupped face toward the front so that any twitch or jerk of the bug makes a popping, gurgling, bubbling, or splashing sound, usually with some water splashed

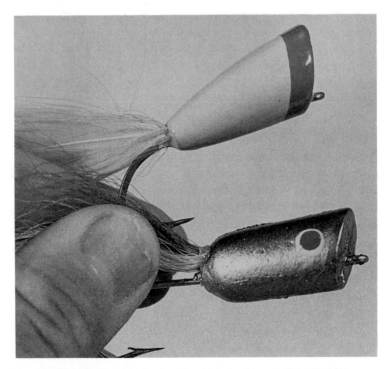

Examples of salt water skipping bugs in which the skirt or tail is glued into a socket in the back of the bug.

174

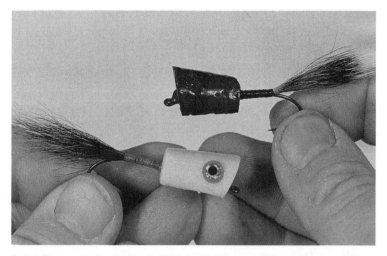

Lefty's Popper, designed by Lefty Kreh for the Potomac River, utilizes a simple tapered cork head and squirrel tail with no hackle. *Top,* an original; *bottom,* one molded in hard foam.

Examples of sliders made of cork *(top)* multicolored foam *(center)* and solid color foam *(bottom).*

175

with each movement of the bug. In this sense, they are the opposite of sliders, which can be made with the same type of bug body placed on the hook in reverse so that the rounded bullet head is toward the front. There are some variations, such as skippers and spouters, to be covered shortly.

Sliders

Sliders are nearly silent when fished. They will make a wake (as will anything in the surface film that is moved), but they will not pop. They are made with popping-style or bullet-shaped bodies, but with the rounded end toward the front. Unlike most feather minnows, they have the hackle and tail tied to the hook shank, rather than to the body of the bug. They are very effective, particularly when fish are skittish or when fishing very shallow water.

One problem with some sliders is that the bullet head/slim tail makes for an unnatural appearance. A solution is to make the bug body with a rounded "collar" at the rear, around which the thread is secured and the tail wrapped. The result is a larger, bulkier tail without using any more materials, and one in which the tail more closely matches the bulk of the bullet head for a more lifelike silhouette.

A bug variation called the spider developed by the author; it combines a slider and spider appearance. The bodies can be shaped of foam, cork, or balsa, though these are hard foam walleye lure floats, slotted and glued into place, then wrapped.

Since this collar is covered by the tail, long bullet shapes are easy to cut to this collar shape using files, sanders, or rotary hobby tools. A rough finish will not hurt, since the tail materials cover this area.

Spliders

This is a term for a type of bug that I developed using a hard foam bait float (often called a walleye float), although any rounded body or slider body can be used. These floats come in different sizes and colors, and, while hard, can be slotted with a saw and glued onto a hook using epoxy. Glue them so that there is a short length of hook shank between the front of the bug and the eye. When the glue is cured, tie on a short tail, and then a very wide hackle in back of the body. Add a second large hackle wrapped around the hook shank in front of the body, tie off, and seal. The result is a rounded "slider" body, with larger-than-normal hackle (like spiders and skaters used for trout fishing) to make a splider.

Skippers

Skippers are basically specialized saltwater popping bugs, but the design can be used on any fish. The main difference is that skippers have a slightly longer body than freshwater bugs, and a flat face that is far more angled than those typically used. They are usually made in large sizes for saltwater fishing.

Gerbubble Bug

The original Gerbubble Bug was originated by Tom Loving, an early innovative fly tyer in the Chesapeake Bay region. The Gerbubble Bug was tied with a cork or balsa body with an unusual shape, and side feathers. The bug used a very long-shanked hook, and special hooks for this were not available when this design was developed. The bug was built on an extra-long-shanked hook to which a small piece of metal paper clip was soldered in the plane with the hook bend. Methods of extending the hook shank (covered later in this chapter) make this easier today.

The bug body was flattened and squared, with a square front, sides, top, and bottom, and a tapered rear section. After the body was slotted and glued on the hook, it was painted, the splayed tail feather of saddle hackle tied on, and then the side feathers added. In the original design, the side feathers were also saddle hackle, and were added by slitting each side of the body with a razor blade, then working glue into the slit, folding lengthwise the saddle hackle, and then working it into the slit with a back-and-forth sawing motion. The ends were clipped and the feathers held in by means of a vertical pin in each end of each side to prevent the hackle ends from working loose. Joe Brooks, who knew Loving, does not describe specifically how to make the Gerbubble Bug, but does describe the dimensions in his book *Bass Bug Fishing*. It was, according to Brooks, tied on a #2/0 hook with a cork body of nine-sixteenths-inch high, eleven-sixteenths wide, and seven-eighths long. The popularized "Gerbubble Bugs" of today tied with hair bodies are variations of this original design.

Fly tyer Norm Bartlett came up with a variation of this by using marabou for the tail and side feathers in place of the standard hackle. His differs in construction by using a wide slot along the sides (marabou center quills are thick and would not fit into a razor slit), stripping the feathers from one side of the marabou, and taking pains to find matching feathers for the two sides. After gluing the feathers in place, the ends are trimmed with a razor blade. Another variation is to use thin rabbit fur strips (like Zonker strips) that are tied in at the rear and then pulled forward through glued slots and tied at the front, or just glued in slots and trimmed.

Frogs

Frogs can be made any size and in a number of styles, depending upon the complexity that you want and the work you are willing to put into the finished product. Since a real frog has both front and back legs, one of the features of a "frog" pattern is the presence of at least two hind legs, and sometimes the addition of two front legs as well. Often the back legs are nothing more than divided hackle or a fur tail, and the front legs nothing more than a few strands of rubber leg material threaded through the body.

Frogs can be made in several ways, but they involve either tying the rear legs on the hook shank or inserting them into the rear of the bug body. Among the basics are those that are made with the tail material tied onto the bug after the bug body is glued to the hook, with the tail material then divided or splayed into two separate "legs." The same thing can be done with four to eight saddle hackle feathers, the hackles divided into two bundles and tied in place so that the hackle flares out and is further splayed by criss-crossing the thread to divide them.

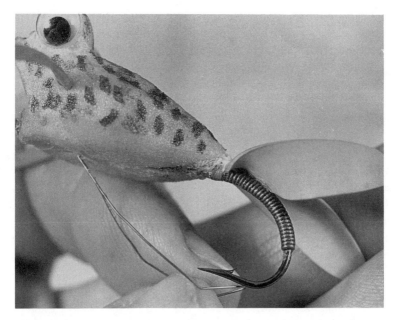

Balance of all bugs is important. Randy Swanberg of Flycraft balances his foam frogs with lead wire so that the tail hangs low in the water for better hook-ups. Also note the wire weedguard.

Another method is to glue the bug onto the hook, and drill or grind two holes at angles in the tail of the bug so that the legs will be slightly above the hook shank. With the hook shank at a slight angle in the bug body, this also helps to stabilize the bug, keep the hook point down for better hooking, and make for a more lifelike appearance. Paint the bug body (but do not paint the holes—leave them bare for a better gluing bond with the leg bundles).

Divide the leg material (fur or synthetic) into two equal bundles and wrap as outlined in Chapter 9. Soak with epoxy or waterproof glue and insert into the hole in the bug body. Repeat with the other leg. If desired, these can be made more lifelike (and get a little more complicated) by making the legs two-tone, with a white or yellow material on one side (for the bottom of the bug) and green or brown on the other side (for the top of the bug).

For additional touches, you can make legs with a bent joint so that the lower part of the hind legs will bend forward to look like a kicking frog.

For details on this, follow the method of Joe Messinger, covered in Chapter 3.

A further refinement is to wrap both the butt end of the leg and the joint over a single wire. When finished, push the two wraps slightly together so that you get a bulky look to the upper leg.

Another way to do this is with thread (Joe Messinger style), wrapping both joints around a heavy thread and then pushing the "knee" joint along the thread while you maintain tension to bulk-up the upper leg. Clip the excess wire and thread when this is completed, coat with finish, and glue in place. This adjustment of the leg can also be done after the butts are glued into the body.

In addition, frogs can be made with two jointed "tail" sections to simulate legs and allow more movement.

Frogs are typically tied on a popper-style bug body, but any style can be used, including skipper, slider, and spouter styles.

Snakes

Snakes are best made with hair bodies, with complete descriptions in Chapter 4. They can be made using cork, balsa, or foam, using a long tail and slider head to simulate a snake.

Feather Minnows

Feather minnows come in two styles. One is like the slider that we are familiar with today, with a bullet head, hackle tail, and heavy hackle wrapping around the hook in back of the body. The other type has feathers wrapped to the body. These are an old style of bug, tied on a slider style of bug body (reversed popper), painted after the bug is glued to the hook, and then the body wrapped with thread around the cork or balsa head. The usual tie includes a layer of bucktail or synthetic tail material, covered by body feathers such as those from a guinea fowl or hen mallard. Several different feathers of different lengths can be used for a layered or mottled effect. The bug is finished with painted eyes on the rounded, hard-body head.

The other old style, with the feather tail and thick hackle, were once sold as the Wilder-Dilg bugs from Heddon and similar Feath-Oreno bugs from South Bend, as well as from other companies.

Here a plastic tubing body is sealed and combined with a Zonker-like rabbit strip tail to make an unusual bug.

Moths

Moths are made the same way as feather minnows in which wing materials are tied to the body. For these, the bug is glued to the hook, painted, a short tail tied on, and feather or fur wings tied to the body. Unlike feather minnows, in which the feather and fur additions are tied close to the body, moth patterns are tied so that the feathers or fur that make up the wing are fanned out and extend on both sides of the bug body to make a moth-like silhouette. Heddon Bass Bug Spooks and Heddon Fuzzi-Bugs were tied this way, as were South Bend Cal-Mac bass bugs.

Spouters

Spouters are typically made with the face of the bug shaped like the prow of a ship so that it will throw water to both sides when twitched on retrieve. They can be made tapered (like a slider), although too much of a

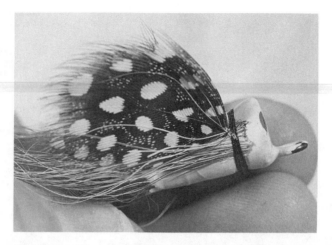

This moth pattern was tied by Matt Hodgson. This closely resembles those bugs of the past that used separate ties around the head end to hold wing materials.

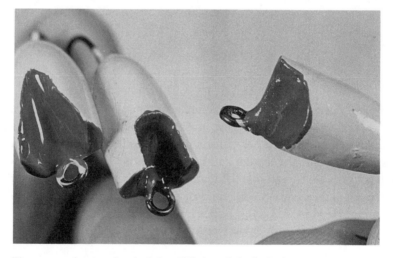

Three types of spouter heads. Left, a "V" shaped slot in the head; center, a squared, ramplike slot in the bug face; and right, a more traditional boat-prowlike spouter face.

taper will ruin the spouter effect and just cause the bug to dive under the surface. A face at right angles to the hook shank is more typical and usually better.

There are other ways to make spouters. One is to take a regular flat-faced popping body and cut a small angled ramp or slope in the front center. Thus, the sides of the bug are still popper style, with the center a ramp that will throw water up over the bug. A small grinding wheel in a Dremel Moto-Tool makes this easy. A flat wheel can be used to cut a right-angled corner "U"-shaped slot; a rotary bit in line with the hook will cut a rounder "U"-shaped ramp. (The edge of a flat file also works to make this ramp.) This can also be reversed, with a central popping face, but with the sides cut back and at a slight upward angle to throw water up when popped.

Another method is to use a fine-toothed saw blade or razor to cut a small, tapered "V" in the front of the bug. The effect is similar to the above, but with a "V" instead of a squared "U" shape. Still another possibility is to use a regular flat or concave-faced popping bug body, and use a small rotary grinder bit or drill bit to cut a hole at an upward angle from the front of the face. Usually this is best done before gluing the hook to the body, to prevent the possibility of the hook eye from interfering with this operation. With experiments that I have done, all methods work well, but there seems to be no advantage to this "drilled hole" model—and some disadvantages, primarily in painting and durability.

Divers

Hard bugs can be made to dive just like the hair-bug Dahlberg Divers. To do this, use a cork, balsa, or foam cylinder or popper heads, but cut them so that they have a sloping or diving face that will dive when pulled into the water. The methods of gluing and tying are the same as for any bug previously described. They do require care when picking up the line for a new cast, since the wrong pick-up can pull the fly underwater, where it will grab before popping out of the water, making backcasts difficult. See Chapter 13 for details.

Extending Hooks

Sometimes hooks have to be made longer for a certain style of bug. This is most frequently required with the slim pencil poppers and pencil minnows, various slab-side minnows, and saltwater skippers. There are several ways to do this. An easy way is with a connecting link, similar to that typically used in saltwater bottom rigs. The size #1 is about three-quarters of an inch long, the size #2 about one inch long. Connecting links are easy and secure to use; since a sliding band holds them closed, but allows you to open them to slip on the hook eye. It isn't a problem, but connecting links will change the hook eye from a horizontal to vertical alignment.

Tiemco also has a hook extension twelve millimeters (about half an inch) long, designed for their nymph hook, but in many cases this could be used on bass-bug hooks also. The open eye on one end allows adding a hook eye.

Another method is to make your own extension with spinner (or similar) single-strand wire. The easiest way is to form a wrapped eye in one end of the wire (just as you would for a spinner) and then begin a second eye at the desired length of the extension. Add the hook eye and complete the wire wrap. Note that you can make the final eye in the bug a vertical or horizontal alignment, depending upon how you position the two eyes in the wire.

Heavy mono (twenty- to thirty-pound test) can also be used by wrapping a double strand (to form a loop) on the hook shank. Wrap securely; for big bugs, consider forming a ball at the end of the doubled mono loop first to prevent the mono from being pulled under the wrapping threads. While this latter method works, however, it is not as good as any of the previously listed methods.

Note that in using any of these methods, the position of the hump or kink in the shank is not changed, and thus might be too far back in the final design and interfere with the tie. If this occurs, you can usually use straight-shanked hooks, since the eye of the hook will be glued into the body and will help stabilize the hook shank and prevent it from turning.

Another possibility is to connect two hooks, using the methods listed below, or to heat one hook, cut off the point, and form a "J"-shaped loop to connect it to the eye of the main hook as an extension.

Pencil Poppers

Pencil poppers are nothing more than very long, very slim poppers that look like the fly-rod equivalent of long, conventional-tackle saltwater chuggers. Often they have to be made with wire extensions added to the hook to get the proper length for the hook size. As a result of this joint of the hook eye to the wire extension, they sometimes require a wider slot for gluing in the hook or a slight widening in the area of this joint.

Pencil Minnows

Pencil minnows are almost identical to pencil poppers, except that the body is slim—like a Rapala plug—and they do not have a popping face. The result is a silent bug that simulates a minnow on the surface, or an injured minnow with a damaged swim bladder, making it unable to dive. These can be made with standard gluing and painting methods with a short tail of fur, feathers, or synthetics. They can also be made by sliding Mylar tubing over round foam rod, or a shaped cork or balsa body, tying it down at the front and rear in separate operations, and tying on a tail at the same time the rear is tied down. Coat with a clear finish and then turn on a curing motor for a very durable, good-looking bug.

Bob's Bangers

This design, from Bob Popovics, utilizes a long-shanked hook on which a foam Live Body head is added (and interchanged if desired). Bob ties in bucktail at the bend of the hook, adds a wrap of Estaz or Ice chenille to cover the wrap, then wraps forward to make a slightly tapered thread wrap on the forward part of the hook shank. (This is to aid in keeping the head firmly in place when inserted on the hook.)

The head is made from a foam cylinder that is long enough to butt up against the chenille, yet allow the hook eye to project from the cylinder. Poke a heated bodkin through the center to form the hole for the hook shank. Then wrap the body with a piece of prism tape (Phantom) whose length is one-and-a-half times the circumference of the body (so that the tape will overlap and thus properly adhere). One tip from fly tyer Bob Clouser is to lightly pinch the foam cylinder at the point where the overlap begins so that there is tension on the tape when pressure is released. The one-half circumference overlap keeps the tape in place; the tension keeps it from coming loose.

Surf Float Bangers

A variation of the above (one I learned from mid-Atlantic fly-rodders Walter Knapp and Lou Caronna) is to use the slim, football-shaped foam floats designed to suspend baits when surf fishing. Cut each float in half

An awl is used to make a hole in a Live Body foam cylinder for making a foil-wrapped Bob's Banger (from Bob Popovics) that can be added to any color tail tied to a hook shank (shown to the left).

at an angle (the angle will determine whether it will be a skipper or popper), then sand the cut end and sand flat what will become the bottom of the bug.

Tie the bucktail tail in the middle of a long-shanked hook, then wrap the forward part of the hook shank with chenille to build this up to a size that will allow for a snug fit of the large hole in the foam float. Check for fit, then tie off the chenille. The foam float can be painted or left as is, since most come in bright colors. As with the Bob's Banger, it must be made so that the hook eye is exposed at the front of the popper.

Jointed-Hook Bugs

Bugs can be jointed between the body and the hook. The rationale for this is not so much to make a "different" bug, but to solve one of the problems of making bugs weedless. There are methods of tying weedless bugs (see Chapter 9), but many are not entirely effective. One method that I came up with is to use a regular-shanked hook (not kink-shanked) and to join this to a connector link or wire form that is then glued into the bug body. The two are joined with the hook point up. Bugs have been tied on hooks with the point up, but this usually creates balance problems as the weight of the hook torques to one side to unbalance the bug. With the jointed-hook bug, the hook hangs down when the bug is at rest so that balance is not compromised, yet the hook shank rides up and slides over most weeds, and the hook point avoids weeds and snags. I first tried these in some weedy, milfoil-laced water and found that I hung up on only about one of twenty retrieves. Nothing is perfect, but this seems acceptable. I have since discovered some older ties with jointed hooks, although they don't seem to be made with this purpose in mind. (Many had the hook point down.) Also, some new ties have jointed hooks, but often with the hook point down, and with little advantage over a fixed hook.

As with any bug, the tail can be tied to the hook shank (right behind the eye in this case), or plugged into the body (as with some popping bugs and frog legs). This design can be used with sliders, poppers, skippers, frogs, or almost any other design of bug.

Jointed-Leg or Tail Bugs

Jointed-leg bugs can be used for frogs, sliders, poppers, skippers, or any bug design. One way is to make a wire form from spinner wire or fine #2 (twenty-seven-pound-test) or #4 (thirty-eight-pound-test) single-strand fishing wire. This wire form can be of several shapes but must be suitable for wrapping onto the hook shank, easily inserted into the bug through slots cut into the body, and have two loops or eyes to hold the legs. A commercial variation of this is dressmakers' "T" pins. Cut off most of the shank, use an awl to open up the bent ends of the "T" to make eyes to hold the leg loops, and tie the pin shank to the hook shank. Once you've made the wire form and glued it into the bug body, paint the bug and add the legs: a doubled-fine wire loop through the wire loop eye in the bug, trim the butt ends of the leg material, place them around the doubled wire, and wrap with thread as above. A knee joint, if desired, can be formed the same way. If using synthetic material, an alternative is to make the synthetic strands twice as long as the desired leg, run them through the loop in the body, and then wrap the strands. The same can be done with other materials, such as thin rods of balsa (for legs), tubular rubber, or foam such as that from Clemen's (Live Body), Flycraft, and Rainy's (Float

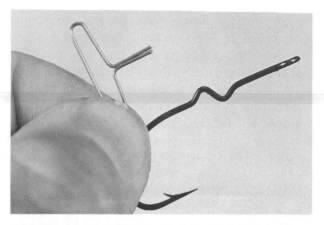

Jointed leg or tail bug can be made using a wire form tied to the
hook shank to hold the jointed part. Here a form to hold two legs is
shown with the hook to which it will be added.

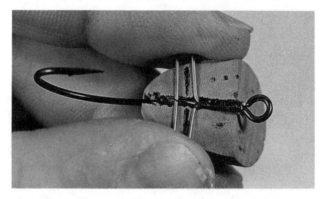

This cork body has been slotted for the hook and marked for slotting
for the transverse wire form to hold the jointed legs.

The wire forms on which the legs are wrapped are held in a fly-tying vise after being added to the finished cork body with wire form. This method of tying is not as awkward or difficult as it looks. An alternative method of making jointed legs or tails is to tie the legs to the small omega-shaped wire forms that have been attached to a hook eye, then clip the hook bend and glue the hook shank into the bug body for the joint.

Foam). In these cases, the wire can be run through the leg material or just glued into one end. There is no tension on these as there is on a hook connection, so glued-in wires are usually sufficient.

Another variation is to mount the bug on a hook with the wire form to hold the legs, and use two straight-eye hooks with material tied streamer-wing-style around the shank as a leg. The resultant bug then has three hooks, and the wire form must be securely fastened should a fish hit one of the legs.

Jointed-Body Bugs

Bugs can be made with jointed bodies, although this is best with large, long-bodied bugs, such as those used for largemouth, saltwater fish, or pike. The usual method is to first decide on a bug shape and length, make

Here an unfinished jointed body bug is made by using two cork bodies and a connector (the same used for hook extensions) attached to a hump-shank hook. The bug can be painted and finished as desired.

that body, then cut it in half for jointing. Glue the forward part to a wire form or connector link that has previously been joined to a hump-shanked hook. Then glue the rear part to the hook, first making sure that the two body parts have some clearance for movement and a side-to-side wiggle. Make sure that you have good round eyes in the wire form (which is why commercial connector links are good) for maximum movement.

Double- or Multiple-Hook Designs

Double hooks in bugs are not new, and can be achieved in several ways. One way is to make a long-bodied bug—like a pencil popper or pencil minnow—from two hooks joined together, hook points down and glued into the bug body. If the rear hook has a down eye, this generally works better. These can be joined by threading the point of one hook through the eye of the rear hook, or snelling or tying the two hooks together before gluing both hook shanks into the slot in the bug body. Also, hook "legs" can be used when making frogs, as described above.

Big-Game Poppers and Sliders

A second way to make double-hook bugs is to use a method used for big-game poppers. This is simply a big salt-water fly with a forward hook one size larger than the rear, the two snelled together with heavy mono, or wire and leader sleeves. Usually heavy mono (one-hundred- or eighty-pound-test) or wire is used, with the rear hook often a #3/0 or #4/0, the forward hook one size larger. Both hooks can be snelled, looped with knots, or wire looped with crimping sleeves (which is better). If looping with crimping sleeves, the two hooks are looped eye-to-eye, and the leader laid along the forward hook shank and wrapped down with the body or tail materials.

These are flies, and become poppers for big game such as sailfish and marlin only with the introduction of slide-on popping heads that are

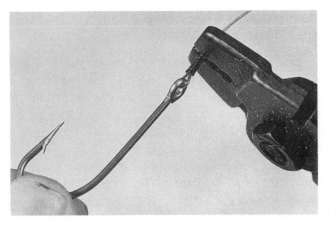

Leader sleeves and the proper crimping pliers are ideal for making single- or double-hook big-game poppers and sliders.

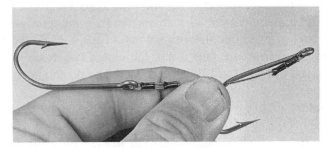

A short length or stranded wire leader and leader sleeves make up the basis for a two-hook big-game popper. Note that one hook points up, the other down. While shown bare for clarity, a skirt can be tied to the tail hook first, and then tied over the hook shank and leader of the forward hook to end in the popper or slider.

jammed onto the forward hook eye. The rear hook can be pointed up or down. Jack Samson, fly-fishing writer and record holder, likes the rear hook at one hundred eighty or ninety degrees to the main, point-down hook of such poppers. Billy Pate, holder of many big-game fly-rod records, likes his two-hook bugs with the hooks ninety degrees apart. The technique for working with the foam is covered in Chapter 8.

Of course, any bug can be made into a double-hook bug by first snelling a suitable hook (point up or down) onto the hump-shanked hook so that the rear hook extends into and is hidden by the tail. This is done before the forward hook is glued in place.

Slip-on Popping Heads— Big-Game Poppers

Slip-on popping heads can be used with any bug size or style, but are mostly used in big-game saltwater poppers. And while any material— cork, balsa, hard foam, soft foam, or wood—can be used for these sliding popping heads, a firm, soft foam (such as EVA or PVC) is most common and durable, although Ethafoam heads are also commonly used. The technique for this is covered in Chapter 8.

While these bug bodies are large, this same concept can be used with foam cylinders for bugs for largemouth, stripers, panfish, pike, or any species that will take a surface lure. The tubing is generally one-eighth-inch in diameter, and stiff plastic, but to attach the hook eye to the bug, add a short sleeve of larger-diameter tubing. You can even add a second sleeve to make the diameter even larger, and for building up the tail material tied to this tube. See Chapter 9 for details.

Another possibility for jamming the head onto the hook is to use a length of tubing about one-half-inch shorter than the length of the bug body, the tubing glued into the forward part of the bug and the hook eye fitted into the rear of the bug where the closed-cell foam will hold it through friction. It still can't slide down on the hook, and holds the fly as well.

A variation of big-game poppers, reported to me by Scott Fine of *Saltwater Fly Fishing Magazine* and one used by some Australian anglers, is made with an Ethafoam slip-on popper head, with a slit cut into the bottom so that it "blows off" of the tube when the fish hits. The foam head is lost, but is easily replaced.

Examples of salt water bugs. Top to bottom, a bug tied with an Edgewater popping head, a fly to which a popping head can be added to make a popper, a second skirt to which a popping head can be added, a foil-covered cylinder that can be combined with a fly to make a popper, and a Live Body cylinder with UltraHair glued-in skirt material and a central tube for slipping over a leader.

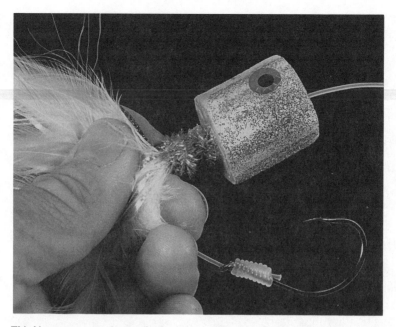

This big-game popper is completely tied on a tube with the big-game hook separately snelled to the heavy wire leader.

A completed big-game popper.

Slip-on Bug Tails

Just as bugs can be built on tubing, using a tube vise, so tails can also be tied on short tubes. One result is a bug that is completely interchangeable, from the hook size and style, to the tail, to the bug body. The method of rigging is to run the leader first through the bug body, then through the tail or tails desired, and then tie the leader to the desired hook. The best hooks are short-shanked, since the tail or bug is not mounted on the hook as with standard bugs.

The method of tying is to use as short a length of tube (usually Nylaflow or similar tubing) in a tube vise and tie down the tail materials desired. Tie off, seal with head cement or epoxy, and you are ready to fish.

Slip-on Complete Bugs

A variation of the two above ideas combined is to use a length of tubing longer than the bug-body cylinder so that the tubing extends beyond the rear of the bug body. First, slip the head on the tubing. Then add larger diameters of tubing to build up the diameter at the rear, and to this larger tubing tie in the tail materials. Then remove the head, slightly rout out the rear around the hole, add some glue (type depending upon the head material), and jam the head back on the tubing so that the head covers the wrapped head where the tail materials were tied off. Then this whole body-and-tail combination can be slipped onto a leader, used with a hook of your choice to make a finished bug.

Adding Rattles

Rattles can add a whole new dimension to bug fishing. They help add noise, and while their use might be questioned by some anglers, they certainly can't hurt. After all, most bugs are built with the premise of noise, and water disturbance and displacement, to attract attention. Rattles are available in glass, plastic, and aluminum. Each creates a different noise. In many cases, the serious bass shops may carry more styles and selections than fly shops. There are a number of different ways by which rattles can be added.

- **Molded-in rattles**. See Chapter 7 for details on incorporating rattles into molded bug bodies.
- **Glued-in rattles**. With any hard-bodied bug, rattles can be glued into holes drilled in the bug material. This is possible with cork,

195

balsa, other woods, or foam bodies. I like to use thin bits, followed by larger ones, to prevent chewing up the material, or the small grinder bits on a rotary hobby tool like the Dremel Moto Tool. Holes can be drilled straight into the bug body from the front in line with the hook, at an upward angle in line with the hook, from the rear in line with the hook, and crosswise through the body at right angles to the hook.

For bugs that will wobble from side to side, the crosswise hook placement is good; for all others I like the upward angle position (going toward the rear). This tends to throw the rattle back to the rear to make a noise with each twitch of the bug, something not always possible with an in-line rattle.

Glue the rattle in with an epoxy or epoxy/material-dust mixture (the dust of the bug material—cork, balsa, or foam) to serve as a filler. Overfill slightly to allow for glue shrinkage during curing. Once cured, sand smooth with the bug surface and paint.

- **Rattle wrapped on hook**. Rattles can be wrapped onto the hook shank and then glued into place with the hook, although a wider slot to accommodate the rattles will be necessary for this operation. The hook must be built up to prevent the rattle from sliding off to the side from the position of the hump or kink in the shank. As a result, this method is usually the least effective and hardest to do— and offers no advantages over others.

- **Attached to tail**. Rattles can be easily attached to the tail of any bug—hard-bodied or hair-bodied. For this, buy shrink tubing just larger than the size of the rattle, cut pieces about two times the length of the rattle, and place the rattle inside close to one end. (Shrink tubing is used to insulate electrical connections and is available in electrical, electronics, and hobby shops.) Heat, and once the tubing shrinks around the tubing, run the hook through the inside of the wall of the non-rattle end of the tube. Continue to run the tubing up onto the hook shank, then secure the wrapping thread on the hook shank, position the tubing in line with the hook shank, and wrap in place. After the tubing is wrapped down, add the tail materials (feathers or fur) and any hackle. The tubing is thin enough to cover easily with these materials and also helps to completely hide the rattle.

Examples of rattles in bugs. Here, glass and plastic worm rattles are glued in clear-plastic straws and shrink tubing and tied into the back of a bug body under the tail material.

An alternative is to use thin plastic straws the diameter of the rattle, glue the rattle in place, then cut half of the wall of the remaining straw at an angle. This leaves about half an inch of cut straw wall, which is easy to wrap to the hook shank, then cover with tail materials.

- **Tying bubble rattles.** While most rattles are cylinders about half an inch long, Lonnie Stanley (Stanley Jigs) makes a bubble-shaped rattle (called Stanley Pro-Rattler) with a small button attached that is designed to fit into "button holes" punched into plastic spinner-bait skirts, pork rind, and Stanley's Pro-Trailer. This button also makes it easy to tie these rattles onto any bug as a finishing touch after all other tail and hackle materials are tied down. To do this, first make and paint the bug body, then tie down all the materials; finally, hold the Pro-Rattler in place over the end of the bug body, bringing the thread over the small button molding. This secures the rattle in place on top of the bug (underneath might create hook gape

197

Here a Stanley Jig button-style rattle has been tied to the top of a popping bug. On large bugs like this, the rattle does not upset the balance of the bug in the water.

problems). Wrap several times until the rattle is secure, then tie off with a whip-finish and coat with head cement or other sealer. If you wish, you can delay painting until this point, mask off the tail materials, and paint the rattle and bug body at the same time. In large bugs (bass and saltwater), this will not upset the bug balance at all.

Adding Weights

Just as rattles can be added in several ways, the same is true with adding weight to a bug. Weight is added for several reasons. It will help large bugs to float lower in the water and thus plow through the water better. This often creates more pop, surface disturbance, and splash, which is particularly good for larger saltwater bugs. It also helps keep the bug from bouncing around in a chop (common in saltwater fly fishing) and catching the leader or shock tippet. Another reason is that it will help in turning over large, air-resistant bugs. (This air-resistance/weight ratio is important in fly fishing. Too little air resistance from feathers and fur, and a bug can cast like a bullet on the end of a line; too much air resistance and the bug will not turn over properly, as the air resistance keeps it from moving forward on the end of the cast.)

There are several ways to add weight to a bug. In all cases, it must be added to the hook shank, near the hook shank, or low in the bug body, and it must be centered to maintain the proper balance of the bug. Since there is no way to figure formulas for hook size/body size/body material/wraps of lead wire/wire size, experimentation is the key. Make only a few bugs with a certain type of weighting. Keep notes as to the methods of adding weight and the wire size, number and position of wraps, etc., before making up a gross of bugs this way. Ways to add weight include:

- **Wrap lead wire on the hook shank.** Lead wire used for fly tying is typically in sizes from 0.015 to 0.130 inches in diameter, and all can be used with bugs. To use wire, wrap the hook shanks first, just as you would normally prepare the bug for gluing into a hard body. Then wrap on the wire, making note of the size and number of wraps. Usually the wire should be wrapped evenly along the hook shank, but if this is not possible, weighting toward the rear of the bug is best to keep the hook low for better striking. Note that you will have to follow the kink or bend in the hook shank. Wrap over the wire to secure it and then glue the hook into the bug body. Note that you will need a wider slot for the hook as a result of the wire— use multi-blade saws as previously described for this.

- **Molding in weight.** Roy Hilts of Hilts Molds alerted me to this— see Chapter 7 for details.

- **Using lead eyes.** Lead eyes, typically used on streamer flies and available in many sizes, can also be used for weight, but it is more of a nuisance than other methods. For this, you wrap the hook shank with thread, then tie down the eyes in the middle of the hook shank in typical crosswise fashion. Once the eyes are secured, cut the slot for the hook shank and measure and cut a wider crosswise slot for the insertion of the eyes. Glue in place, cover both slots with glue or filler, and allow to cure before sanding to shape.

CHAPTER 11

Painting and Finishing Bugs

Painting is not required on a bug, but most of us do it and it is a nice touch. It isn't necessary to catch fish. My fishing buddy Norm Bartlett, who always gets down to the basics in his fishing and fly tying (a glue gun is his most important fly-tying tool) no longer finishes any of his cork or balsa bugs, and he catches just as many or more fish than the rest of us.

Examples of bodies not needing painting would be bug bodies of colored foam (either hard, non-compressible or soft foams), and terrestrial patterns in which the bug color is determined by the color foam used. And hair-bodied bugs are seldom painted, although they can be painted to make a hard popping lip on the front of a bug or colored with felt-tip markers over light or white hair.

Paints vary widely, but as with any paint job, be sure to use paints compatible with the bug and with your various sealers and finishing coats. For example, acrylic latex paints are recommended for hard-foam bodies such as those sold by Wapsi. Hilts Molds recommends epoxy paints (they also sell their Roy's Benchmark epoxy paint set) for their polyurethane foam bugs.

Using the wrong paint over a sealer or the wrong clear finish over paint can result in a crazing, bubbling, shrinking, or running of the finish, ruining the bug. Check first to be sure, or try the combination on a scrap piece of cork or foam.

While a variety of methods is described for painting and finishing, realize that often the best bugs are those that are simple, and that the basic design, tail materials, and retrieve of the bug are what seem to attract fish and provoke strikes. This is not to eschew the beautiful paint jobs that some like on bugs, but only to put it in its proper perspective in relation to the additional time and care required. Fish will certainly see the bellies of bugs, and might see the sides, but they'll seldom if ever see the back of a bug. Thus, bugs that have light bellies, medium-color or scale-finish sides, and dark backs might be overkill, though they are necessary to sell bugs (although it's not the intent of this book to examine the bug market).

When painting, an assembly-line process is best. It is not cost effective in paint or disposable brushes to paint only a few bugs at a time. The best procedure is to tie up or make a number of bugs, then paint them all with a sealer, follow later with a base coat of white, and then follow up with each color in turn using the colors, shades, and designs you wish for the finished product. Once complete, all the bugs can be coated at the same time with a clear finish coat or two.

Paints and Sealers

Sealers are just what their name indicates—they seal the surface of the item so that subsequent layers of paint will be smooth and professional. A base coat or two of paint—usually white—can often be substituted for a sealer. Special sealers are made for balsa and cork, and some paint systems include sealers that are designed to fill small holes or soak into end grain to provide a base for painting. Duco cement thinned with acetone to a brushable liquid works well as a sealer.

Paints can include epoxies, lacquers, enamels, and acrylics. While there are differences between them, the basics are that the epoxies are two-part mixes and often must be used within a short time after they are mixed. Sometimes this can be extended by keeping the mixed paint in a refrigerator or freezer, but it is best to mix only small quantities and use all at once. A good epoxy paint designed specifically for lures and bugs is Roy's Benchmark Paint Set, which includes the basic epoxy mix and a number of colors.

Lacquers and enamels are similar in that, unlike epoxies, they do not require mixing of two parts, and they are readily available in small hobby-size containers. Vinyls are a little thicker and more rubbery, but work equally well. All are available from tackle and fly shops, mail-order supply houses, and hobby shops. All are suitable for brushing or dipping.

Aerosol cans are available for sprayed finishes, or you can buy an inexpensive air-brush kit. Spray paint is ideal for making patterns, designs, and scale finishes on bugs.

You can also experiment with other paints. Recently, I have been trying several brands of craft paints sold as "fabric writers" or "dimensional fabric and craft paint." Some popular brands are Tulip, Scribbles, Jones Tones, and Polymark. These are the thick paints used for three-dimensional writing and designs on T-shirts and sweat shirts. They don't give a smooth finish even when brushed on (they are lumpy and thick if

Fabric paint is about the only paint that will stick to the soft Ethafoam used for many salt-water and big-game bugs. Many colors, finishes, and glitter types are available.

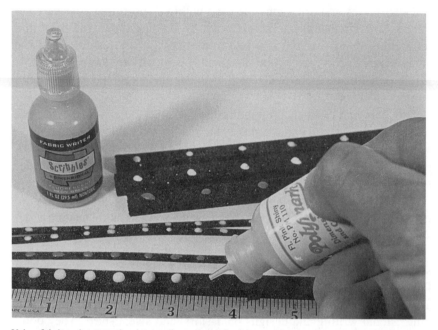

Using fabric paint to make dots on foam strips for later cutting into lengths for making beetles and ants with visible spots for quicker striking.

A simple wire form like this (made from spinner wire) can be used to hold jointed bugs such as this weedless style with jointed hook developed by the author. Such wire forms are handy when painting as shown here.

just squeezed out of the bottle), but can be used for accent or design patterns on bugs. They are bulky when cured, will cure overnight, and hold up well in water. If used in very cold water, they do have a tendency to crack. Both these and the dimensional "puff" paints that puff up when heat is applied (use a hair dryer) are also ok for making the bright dots used as visual keys on the backs of foam terrestrials.

Clear finishes will protect bugs, and most paint manufacturers supply a clear finish coat in addition to base coats, sealers, and standard and fluorescent colors. In many cases the thin epoxy finishes for rods (some manufacturers make "light" finishes for fly rods that are also ideal for bugs, and thinner can sometimes be used to thin standard epoxy rod finishes) are also ideal. Avoid too many coats, however, since this will add to the weight of the bug and sometimes affect performance.

Tools and Brushes

For brushing paint, I like inexpensive disposable brushes. If using latex, or some acrylic, paints, they can be washed out, but they're cheap enough to discard if painting a number of bugs at one time. The best of these seem to be those available from Flex Coat (more widely known for rod-building finishes and supplies).

If the paint bottle is too small for dipping (most are), use a small plastic container. Unless working with very large bugs, plastic thirty-five-millimeter film canisters are ideal, and they include a tight snap-on lid that allows saving the paint for later use.

A slow-turning curing motor is ideal (see Chapter 1) since this allows slowly rotating the bug body to eliminate sags and runs in each coat of paint.

Painting Preparation

Before painting, bugs must be checked thoroughly. Be sure that any large holes in cork, or flaws in other materials, have been filled. For cork or balsa, plastic wood is best for this, although a mixture of balsa dust or cork granules mixed with a waterproof carpenter's glue will also work well. Sand smooth any rough or glued surfaces. Areas that require particular attention include the slot area where the hook is glued in place, and each end of the slot (hook shank and hook eye), where glue can ooze out. Remove it with a file or emery board before proceeding.

Once the bug body is smooth, apply a sealer or base coat, followed by the finishing coats and any scale markings or design patterns.

Paint Before or After Tying Tails?

As previously mentioned, the tails and hackles of bugs can be tied on before or after the bug is painted. There are pros and cons to each method. One advantage to painting a simple bug like Lefty's Potomac River Popper is that the paint can be used to seal the thread wraps. This bug has a simple bottle-cork body and straight fur tail (no hackle) so that it is easy to brush or dip the bug body to coat the tail wrap at the same time. This also makes a more uniform color, as there is no thread-wrap color as would occur if it were tied on after painting. Also, if tied after painting, the thread must be protected in some way, with the possibility that any head cement or clear finish on the thread could react adversely with the paint. This is not a problem with bugs designed so that the bug body added after tying will cover the thread wrap, since the glue to hold the bug on the hook will seal and hide the thread wrap.

Conversely, if tying a bug with a bushy hackle, it is difficult to paint by brushing or dipping and avoid getting paint on the hackle or tail fibers. One solution to this is to place a small square cut from a plastic bag on the hook as a "hackle guard" before tying the tail (or use a Hackle-Back cone), to pull the hackle back and separate it from the bug body, but even this is a risk since the paint could "wick" along the hackle and tail and stain them.

My solution is to examine each bug type and to paint first those bugs on which it will be difficult or impossible to do a good job after the tail is tied, and to paint *afterward* those that will be easy to do without harming the tail or hackle. Those that are tied as moths or feathered minnows in the older styles (with wings tied to the body) must be painted first and then finished with the thread wrap to hold the wings in place on the cork or balsa. Naturally, if you are spraying, you must mask the entire tail and hackle area to protect it when painting.

Painting Methods—Dipping

Dipping can be done in any small container. I like thirty-five-millimeter film cans, since they can also be sealed with the snap-on lid so the paint can be used later. I usually do not dip when using epoxy paints, since their life span is short and dipping can thus waste a lot of paint.

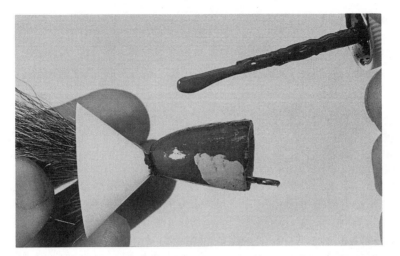

The Hackle-Back, while designed for tying off heads of bushy flies and bugs, works equally well for painting bugs after the tail, skirt, and hackle material has been added. The Hackle-Back makes it easy to paint without touching the fur or feathers.

One disadvantage of dipping is that it will coat the hook eye, although this is easily punched out later. One advantage, if tying a tail without hackle (such as a Lefty's Bug), with the tail tied on after the bug body is glued in place, is that the dipping procedure can be used to coat the thread wrapping as well. This eliminates the necessity of coating the thread with head cement. In fact, if doing this, you should not use any coating prior to the paint, since this could provoke a chemical reaction. This also gives the thread wraps the same color as the bug body, making for a more "color-coordinated" appearance.

The secret of a good paint job when dipping is to use thin paint. Lower the bug body into the paint slowly, to avoid bubbles or pockets, and remove it slowly to allow the paint to sheet off as you pull the bug out of the paint. Allow to drip into the paint can for a minute or two when removed, and then place on a slow-turning curing motor to prevent sagging.

Painting Methods—Spraying

Spraying is great for picnic tables, but it can waste a lot of paint when doing anything as small as bugs. Also, since spray is broadcast widely, it is best for bug bodies before they are tied; otherwise a mask of some sort must be used to protect the tail and hackle. While paint cost is seldom a big concern in making bugs, waste is still a concern. The solution is to spray a number of bug bodies at once. One way to do this is to spray each in turn in rapid order, hanging up the bug as soon as it is finished. Another way is to fasten a series of alligator clamps to a board (like teeth in a comb) and then fasten each bug by the hook in each alligator clamp. One swipe up and down with the spray can will coat all the bug bodies, reducing paint waste. To protect the hook points from paint, cover them with a strip of masking tape.

If making bugs with sides, back, and belly of different colors, it is possible to line up the bugs in order, with the side to be painted facing up, and paint with one swipe of the paint can. One easy way to do this is with double-sided carpet tape taped to a board, with the bugs stuck to the exposed tape. Naturally, new tape will be needed for each set of bugs or different paint, since the paint will cover the tape between the bugs. This must be done in several steps, since the paint must cure before the bug is repositioned and painted again. Position the bugs belly up and first paint the belly color, allow to cure, and then place the bug on one side and paint that side. Allow that to cure, reverse, and paint the other side, then position the bug back up and paint the dark back color. (An alternative to this when painting the sides is to hold the bugs in the alligator clamp-board and paint both sides at once, then allow to cure.)

Painting Methods—Spraying Scale Finishes or Designs

Scale finishes are done on the sides of bugs to simulate scales of fish. As a result, they are more often seen on sliders, which retrieve more like an injured minnow than do poppers. Scale finishes are easily done with fine netting (sold in tackle shops and mail-order catalogs for the purpose, and also available from fabric and sewing shops). The best way is to stretch the netting in a frame (embroidery hoops are ideal for this), and then press the netting over the bug body (already painted with a base coat) and spray through the netting.

To make maximum use of the netting, paint spray, and time, it is best to include several or more bugs on their side under the netting. Don't include too many, though, or use too big a frame, since this makes direct contact of the netting with the bugs in the center difficult; it is direct contact that makes for a clear scale pattern.

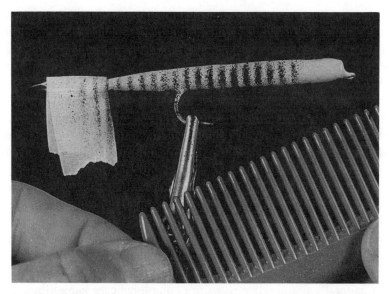

A comb with large teeth can be used as a template to spray paint bars and stripes on bugs as shown. Note that the tail has been protected by covering it with masking tape.

An alternative method is to secure the framed netting vertically in a vise and, using long-nose pliers, hold the hook of each bug up against the netting where you can hit it with the spray paint.

For the scale finish to show, the final coat of paint must contrast with the base paint. There are two ways to do this—a dark paint over a light base coat to make light scale lines, or a light paint over a dark base coat to make dark scale lines. Either will work, and any combination of colors can be used.

Templates can be made or bought for spraying designs onto a bug, although this is used less frequently than on plugs, due to the smaller size and increased difficulty of applying the finish. Templates can be made of cardboard or plastic, the bug held in back of the template and sprayed from the front.

Painting Methods—Brushing

One of the advantages of brushing is that you can coat the entire bug with paint and yet avoid coating the eye—one of the problems with dipping. I find that brushing is best with a small disposable brush such as the type sold by Flex Coat or available in hobby shops. A quarter-inch width is good for most bugs. Do not load the brush with too much paint, and work from the tail to the head, and carefully around the hook eye.

While you can use the fabric paints directly from the bottle for foam bugs (most have a squeeze tip), this will result in a thick line or blob of paint. I prefer to brush out the paint, working with a clean brush from paint squeezed directly onto the bug, or onto a base from which it can be brushed onto the bug. In any case, you will not get the smooth finish possible with standard paints; fabric paint is thick and will not level out even when the bug is placed on a curing motor.

If painting bugs that have a bushy hackle directly behind the body, use a shield to protect the hackle and pull it back and away from the bug body during painting. You can make your own from a square of plastic (scraps cut from plastic milk and drink containers work fine), but it is easier to use a cone-shaped Hackle-Back, slipped over the bug between the body and hackle or tail.

It is generally not possible to paint two colors at the same time, since liquid paints will mix and mar the finish. One exception: if painting the face of a popper a different color than the body, you can first brush the face with the desired color, making sure that you stop precisely at the edges of the face and do not overlap onto the body. Then paint the body a different color, working from the tail toward the head, but not overlapping onto the face. Only brush from the tail forward at this point—brushing in the reverse direction will pick up paint from the face and smear the bug.

If painting two colors with a brush, paint the lighter color first. Dark paints will cover light, but light will not usually cover dark paints.

While brushing two or more colors is fine, realize that you will not get the same professional results and feathered finishes that you can by spraying, or that you will find on commercial bugs. The fish won't mind, and in fact the sharp contrast of the two colors—even though slightly crude looking—has often been cited as a good trigger for flies or lures.

It is also possible to paint some surfaces of hair-bodied bugs. Back in the 1950's I began tying hair-bodied bugs in which the hair was tied on, pulled forward, and then tied again to flare and make a popping face when trimmed. To increase this effect, I painted the front "popping" surface. Today, you would probably use epoxy, which was not available then. The result is a soft, hair-bodied, frog-style bug with a hard popping face.

Clear Coat Finishes

Often bugs will have the best look and last the longest if they are also protected with a clear coat after the paint, foil, glitter, eyes, and other extras are added. Clear protective finishes are available for any type paint. Be sure to use one that is compatible with the paint used on the bug. Clear-coat after all finishing steps, since the clear coat will help to hold in place any applied glitter, foil strips, or decal eyes.

Curing

Paints can be cured in one of several ways. One is to hang the bug on a rack and let it dry overnight. Racks are easily made using bead chain strung between simple wood supports.

This will work if brushing controlled amounts of paint or spraying carefully. But too much paint by these methods, or by dipping, will result in sags. To prevent this, build a curing motor (see Chapter 1) that will turn the bugs slowly so that the paint never gets a chance to sag in one spot.

For the best finish, paint in the evening so that the bugs can cure overnight when family traffic won't stir up dust. As an alternative, place an open box over the drying rack or curing motor.

Adding Glitter

Glitter is available in many colors and different sizes. Recently, I have seen craft-store displays of "micro-glitter"—smaller particles of glitter, similar in size to that used for the highly reflective finishes seen on some crankbaits and plugs, and more compatible with the size of fly-fishing bugs.

The easiest way to add glitter is to sprinkle a little on the bug when the final coat of paint (not the clear finish coat) is still wet. You can do this all over or selectively, such as on the belly or on the sides. If sprinkling, sprinkle over a clean sheet of paper that you have previously folded in half and then opened up. Then when finished, fold the paper in half to carefully funnel the unused glitter back into the container.

For thicker, more concentrated glitter, pour a layer of glitter on a sheet of paper, then lightly roll the wet bug in the glitter. Tap the hook lightly to knock off any loose glitter and allow the wet paint to cure.

After adding glitter, protect it by coating the bug with a clear finish coat or two.

Adding Foil, Decals, and Other Coverings

Self-adhesive foil from Phantom, and other makers can be cut into strips and attached to any bug. For best results, use on bugs that do not have complex curves. (It is far easier to attach a strip of foil to a straight cylinder than to a bullet-head popper or slider.) Straight cylinders, such as those used in tube flies, also lend themselves to being completely covered with tape, overlapping the tape to secure it. Round the corners of the overlapping end to prevent possible separation.

Some tapes, such as those of bright-colored self-adhesive vinyl from J and L Tool Company, are made for use with bugs and plugs.

Decals are different, since they require soaking in warm water and then sliding the decal off of the paper backing and onto the bug body. Since they are thinner and more fragile, they are best used on smoothly finished bugs as opposed to those of coarse, closed-cell foam such as Ethafoam. In all cases, decals and some tapes should be protected with a clear-coat finish.

A different process is possible with other materials, such as Bug Skin, which I've found effective as a covering for surface bugs. This material, developed by Chuck Furimsky and Phil Camera, is a thin-cut lambskin—printed and colored—and originally designed for making underwater flies such as nymph patterns and crayfish. But it can be used on straight-taper-body sliders and poppers as well. (The straight taper is best, since it makes it easier for the BugSkin to adhere to the surface of the bug. BugSkin can be stretched to conform to slight curves, but not to severe curvatures on a bug body.)

The technique developed by Furimsky is to first cut out small pieces—one to fit on the flat bottom surface of the bug, the second to cover the rest of the bug body, with a slight overlap over the bottom piece. He uses barge cement (although probably any good waterproof cement will work), coats the surface of the bug, and then places the bottom strip in place, followed by the top covering, finally gluing the overlapping edges (about one-sixteenth to one-eighth of an inch overlap) to the bottom. Any excess along the front or back can be trimmed off once the glue is cured.

BugSkin has been used as a finishing material over sliders, as Chuck Furimsky did here with this and several other patterns.

An alternative method is to use a strip that will cover the entire bug, keeping the seam of the two edges along the top of the bug. This won't be as attractive to the fisherman, but will look better to the fish, and the lack of seam lines on the bottom might make for a more durable bug.

Another suggestion when making sliders is to cut the covering Bug Skin so that it has a small projection from the top front center, this projection tied down with thread in back of the eye. This will produce a more durable bug, with less possibility of the covering peeling back during fishing or from water resistance.

Furimsky also uses his BugSkin to make tails for long, snake-like bugs, cutting strips (almost like you would cut a strip for a Zonker, but in the width desired) and tying them down as tails. These are usually mixed in with other materials such as bucktail, Flashabou, Ultra Hair, and Lumaflex.

Covered bugs like this can be made with the tail tied on first and the bug glued over the thread wrapping, or the tail tied on after the bug is completed with the covering. The exposed surfaces of the rest of the bug (back on sliders and the popping face on poppers) should be coated with paint or epoxy finish. It is also possible to coat the entire bug body with a clear, light epoxy or vinyl finish.

Other Finishing Methods

Bug bodies can be finished in ways other than painting. For example, A. J. Hand recently wrote in *Fly Fisherman* about using aluminum foil wrapped on a bug body and then protected with a covering of cut strips of clear vinyl (PVC), shrink-style temporary storm-window sheeting. The technique, while different and updated with technology, is not new. A similar method (using foil transfers) was described almost fifty years ago by George Leonard Herter, who sold the materials in his catalog.

Hand's method is to rub the foil on a file to give it a simulated scale finish, then coat the dull side with rubber cement (although other cements can be used) and wrap carefully around the bug body, cutting and shaping where necessary to fit the foil to the bug shape. Avoid handling the foil too much, as it could smooth out the simulated scales. When dry, cover with thin (three-eighths-inch) strips cut from PVC window sheeting that will shrink when dry. Tie in at the tail, and wrap around the body to the head and then back down again to the tail to tie off. Warm with a hair dryer to shrink the film so that it conforms to the body shape and protects the aluminum foil. Shrink tape for this purpose is also available from hardware, electric, and electronic firms, although it is usually available in three-quarter-inch widths (though it can be cut in half) and in relatively expensive one-hundred-foot rolls.

Another way of finishing is to wrap fly-tying body material over the bug body. See Chapter 9 for instructions in this method, since it is more one of wrapping and tying than of finishing, even though the wrap becomes the exterior of the bug. Any type of chenille, yarn, or tinsel chenille can be used for this.

In either of these finishing methods, eyes can be added using most of the same methods used for more traditional bugs.

Using Felt-Tip Markers

Permanent felt-tip markers can be used to color hair-bodied and solid-bodied bugs. Different sizes and brands of permanent markers are available, with Pantone a popular brand for fly tyers and bug makers. For best results, these should be used over white-dyed deer hair or bug bodies painted white. White foam also provides a good base for artistic designs with felt tips.

Examples of bug with different coverings. The top bug has a wrapping of tinsel chenille to make a bright shiny finish. The bug was coated with glue and then the material wrapped around and secured. The lower bug was coated with glue and then covered with synthetic dunning material to make for a fuzzy-bodied bug.

Felt tip markers can be used for marking bugs, as Randy Swanberg did here on a foam frog from his Flycraft products.

Adding Eyes

Eyes have proven to be extremely important in fishing lures and flies. Fortunately, there are a number of ways in which eyes can be added to bugs. Almost always, eyes are added after the bug is painted, but before the clear finish coat is added to protect the bug body.

When painting eyes, hold the bug by the hook so that you can look at the end of the bug and get a good idea of the proper position for the eye on each side of the body. If desired, use a soft pencil to make a small mark to indicate eye placement. In most cases, you will be adding two eyes. Often it helps to place them so that they are looking slightly "down," and hence more visible to the fish. Another alternative is to use only one eye, placed on the head but directly on the bottom in line with the hook as if the bug is an injured minnow, lying on its side. Painted, doll's, decal, and tape eyes can be added this way, but stemmed eyes (plastic or wire) cannot, since the stem would run into the hook shank.

In some cases, eyes are difficult to handle and position properly, particularly if they lack a stem or other way to hold them. This is not a small problem, since proper, clean mounting of the eyes will do much to make or break the appearance of the finished bug. One way to do this is to moisten your finger and touch it to the exterior surface of the eye, and then quickly move the eye to the bug body where glue has already been applied.

A second way is to add glue to the bug body at the exact spot for the eye, then touch this part of the bug to the eye, which is lying with the exterior side down. With either of these methods, you don't risk getting glue on the eye or your fingers.

Possibilities for adding eyes include:

- **Painted Eyes**. The best way to paint eyes is to make painting tools in different sizes. Nails, tacks, pins, and other headed parts can be stuck into the end of a length of dowel to make a tool for this. Thus, tools of different sizes can be used to make the eye and pupil (two different sizes), or eye outline, eye color, and pupil (three different sizes). The secret of using these is to not submerge the nail or tack head into the paint, but to touch it lightly to the paint and then touch it to the bug body. A good way to do this is to use the cap of a paint bottle (they must be shaken anyway, so paint gets on the inside of the lid), and use this as the paint supply. Also, do touch the paint to the bug body, but do not press so that you make hard contact of the

Examples of eyes that can be used on bugs, here shown on a block of foam. Left to right, top to bottom: four sizes of the movable pupil doll eyes, a half bead (they are sold that way), dress makers pin, plastic stem eye (two of them in different sizes and colors), prism sequins (two styles) tape prism eye (Phantom and Palsa have these) and a vinyl eye.

Painted eyes are easy to add; use different sizes of nail heads or similar tools, which can be dotted into paints and onto bugs. Two sizes of such tools are shown. The eye on this bug has a rim of red, an eye of white and a black pupil, using three different-size tools.

tool with the bug, since this will spread the paint and also prevent a solid coating. Repeat once the paint is dry with a smaller tool to make the pupil.

While this method is used primarily for eyes, it can be used to make bugs with a spotted coat using any size tool and color of paint.

The thick fabric paints in squeeze bottles allow squeezing the paint out to form an eye, followed by a small dot of contrasting color for the pupil.

- **Decal Eyes**. These are available on sheets. Cut two from the sheet and soak them in warm water. After a minute to two, check to see if they can be moved, and then slide them gently onto the bug body. Check for position and then blot dry and allow to dry overnight. Finish with a clear coat.

- **Tape Eyes**. These are usually bright, reflective eyes, available in many colors and sizes. They come on self-adhesive backs so they can be carefully peeled off and then positioned on the bug body. If possible, cover with a clear coating.

- **Doll Eyes**. This is a common term for eyes with moving pupils; they are available from craft shops and increasingly from fly shops and suppliers. Most have black pupils, but I have found some with pink, blue, yellow, and green pupils. Red would be a nice touch, but I have not yet found them. I have also found some elliptically shaped. They are available in sizes from three millimeters up to too large to use for any type of bug (over one inch in diameter). They are easily glued to a bug body using hobby cement, epoxy, or CA glues, using due care to match the glue with the body material.

  One completely different application, used by Chris Helm, involves the use of doll eyes on hair-bodied frogs. For this, glue two eyes back-to-back. Then use pointed scissors to cut out one half of the clear eye shield of one eye and remove the black pupil. Then trim the frog so that there are two slight "tufts" of deer hair extending up where the eyes will be located. Add glue to the opening cut into the double eyes and slip over the tufts of hair. The result is a very bug-eyed-looking frog.

- **Plastic-Stem Doll Eyes**. Solid half-round doll eyes on plastic stems are also available, and are ideal for bugs. I have found that it is sometimes difficult to find them in small sizes (although some mail-order companies carry them), and they are never available in sizes as small as the glue-on eyes with moving pupils. The eyes are available in different eye colors, including blue, yellow, red, and black, all with a black pupil. Depending upon the position of the eye and the size of the bug, you may have to cut the stem off or cut it back slightly. Wire cutters are ideal for this.

Depending upon the material used for the bug, use an awl to poke a hole in the bug body (foam) or drill a hole (cork and balsa) using a drill bit the diameter of the stem. Add a small amount of glue and insert the stem in place.

- **Map Tacks and Dressmaker's Pins.** These are discussed together, because they are similar in construction. The map tacks are on short stems, the dressmaker's pins on long-shanked pins, but both have round plastic heads. Map tacks are available in colors (usually sold in multicolored or single-colored packs), while dressmaker's pins are usually white or black. In both cases, cut the stem off to about one-quarter-inch length (or appropriate for the bug size) and stick into the bug body at the proper position. Before pushing the tack into final position, place a small dot of glue on the stem and then shove it into place. The glue will hold the eye on. If desired, you can countersink or drill a very shallow hole at the eye position to keep the pins from creating too much of a "bug-eyed" look, which will occur if the entire round pin head is exposed. If drilling or countersinking, however, plan for this and do this when making the bug, not after painting.

- **Half-round Beads.** These are half-round beads that can be glued right on the bug body to make an eye. Thus, they resemble dressmaker's pins or map tacks when the eye is countersunk. I find that the best way to mount these is to add a small dot of glue to the right spot on the bug body and then pick up the eye and seat it in place, or touch the bug to the eye, which is lying flat side up.

- **Monofilament Eyes.** For very small bugs, you can make pupils by heating a piece of monofilament with a flame to form a small black or brown ball on the eye. Do not touch the eye when it's hot, as it will stick to your fingers. Make up a number of these and, when needed, clip to length to insert into a hole in the bug (or to be tied to the hook shank in the case of soft foam or hair-bodied bugs). Use mono appropriate for the bug size—about twelve-pound-test for small bugs and proportionately heavier for larger bugs, to about fifty-pound-test for large saltwater bugs.

Example of an EdgeWater slider with large plastic bead (like bead chain, only plastic for light weight) added to the head.

- **Bead Eyes**. Plastic or glass beads of any size and color can be glued onto monofilament, or threaded onto mono with balled ends (to keep the bead from sliding off), and then tied to the hook shank of hair-bodied bugs. Plastic beads can also be glued onto a hard bug body or into countersunk or shallow holes as described for the eyes of map tack and dressmaker's pins.

- **Strung Bead Eyes**. Beads come strung on cord, so that you can cut off two and figure eight them to the front of a slider for a look similar to that of metal bead chain, but in lightweight plastic.

- **Molded Plastic Eyes**. One different method of making eyes is used by Joe Messinger, Jr., for making his hair-bodied bugs. See Chapter 3 for details on this special method.

- **Combination Eyes**. I have also made eyes using combinations of the above. I have used a painted background under a bulky fabric paint eye, with a half-round plastic bead pupil. Other possible combinations include fabric paint with map tacks, paint and half-round beads, and sequins (available from craft shops) used as a background color with a map tack or dressmaker's pin through the hole in the center of the sequin.

CHAPTER 12

Rigging Bugs and Bug-Fishing Tackle

S ome years ago I wrote an article on choosing fly tackle. The premise was that we often pick tackle in the reverse order of what is sensible or practical. Thus, we pick the rod and reel, then the line to match the rod and reel, and finally the leader and the fly. The size of the fly needed to take the fish, the size of the fish sought, and whether or not the line and leader combination will properly turn over the required fly is left to last. Nowhere is this more true than in bug fishing, since surface bugs are bulky and air resistant, and are heavier than most flies used with the same basic tackle. With this in mind, we'll approach tackle discussion from the fly to the rod, in that order.

Leaders

Leaders are a must between the fly line and the bug. With bugs, the leader should be as short as is practical, and with a straight taper that will allow the best possible turnover of the bug. Too short a leader can often cause a bug to splat on the surface (although such a splat can be an attractant to "call" in fish).

As a general rule, the tippet size must be matched to the bug size, often referred to by hook size. Thus the following is a starting point, a suggestion as to matching hook and tippet sizes, since bugs vary widely in their mass, air resistance, and size. A slim Lefty's Popper reacts far differently in the air than a fluffy, marabou-hackle Gerbubble Bug or a hair-bodied frog.

TABLE 12.1

Hook Sizes/Tippet Diameters			
Hook size	Leader diameter (inches)	Leader size (tippet)	Leader test (pound test—will vary with maker)
to 18	0.004	7X	1 to 2
16 to 14	0.006	5X	3 to 4
12 to 10	0.008	3X	5 to 6
8 to 6	0.009	2X	6 to 7
4 to 1/0	0.011	0X	10
2/0 to 4/0	0.014	7/5	15
5/0 and larger	0.017	4/5	20

Note that these are approximations only—you may be able to use larger or smaller tippets with bugs of these hook sizes depending upon the bug design, weight, and air resistance.

Leader lengths also vary with the bug used, line, fish species, and fishing situation. A long leader of nine to twelve feet might be a must on some limestone trout streams where jassids, crickets, hoppers, beetles, and ants are mainstay patterns. A short leader of four or five feet or even less would be the best choice when fishing sinking lines, making it easier to pull a bug under in a floating/diving retrieve. Since bugs are heavy, generally the shorter the leader (consistent with the fish and fishing requirements), the better the control and easier the casting.

Note that if you are fishing for records you must use tippets that conform in length and pound test to International Game Fish Association or National Fresh Water Fishing Hall of Fame standards. Consult the Appendix for the address of these groups for more information. Basically, both require fish to be caught using "class line or tippets," which means that the tippet must be non-metallic and test *under* the pound test of the line class. Tippets must be of a certain length—fifteen inches in the case of IGFA, with a shock tippet of up to twelve inches also allowed.

Lines

Lines should match the leaders; thus light lines can be used with light tippets and smaller bug sizes, but would not carry heavier bugs and leaders. In all cases, weight-forward tapers are best for bugs, since they allow shooting line for long casts and loading the rod with only a short length of line out of the rod tip. Within the weight-forward line category, there are different tapers, such as the so-called "bug tapers" and "saltwater tapers" with shorter bellies than standard weight-forward lines. They will more easily cast and turn over the air-resistant bugs.

A specialty line for very long casts is the shooting taper, which is a short belly to which is attached a long, narrow, running line. In most cases, these are not necessary or even wise for bug fishing, and these lines are used primarily when fishing wet flies and streamers in Western steelhead and salmon rivers. They will work once you get the hang of casting a shooting taper, but the standard bug tapers are preferred where possible.

Generally lines should be floating, but there are applications for neutral-density lines, and sometimes even sinking lines. Neutral-density lines are good for fishing in saltwater, where during a fast retrieve the resistance of the line in the water will help to keep the leader down and overcome any tendency of the bug to bounce out of the water and catch the leader or line.

Sinking lines allow bugs to be fished as floater/divers, using either the popular Dahlberg Diver, or any popper or slider. A short leader is a must for these, to help pull the bug under the water before allowing it to pop back up to the surface.

TABLE 12.2

	Fly Line Sizes	
Bug Size	Leader Tippet Test (pound test)	Line Size
to #14	to 3 or 4	3 and 4
#12 to #8	5 or 6	5
#6 to #1	6 or 8	6 and 7
#1/0 to #3/0	10 or 12	8 and 9
#4/0 and larger	15 to 20	10 to 12 and larger

Reels

Because fly fishing with surface bugs can vary from trout to tarpon, bluegills to billfish, the reels will vary widely. For fishing terrestrials for trout, any light fly reel suitable for holding a 3-, 4-, or 5-weight line and a little backing is certainly adequate. For billfish, you will need the best possible machined aluminum bar stock reel filled with perhaps two hundred yards of Dacron backing, some mono as a shock absorber, and a full-weight forward fly line sized to cast the big bugs or cylinder head/fly combination used. In between these extremes, there is a lot of room for reels in various sizes for bass, panfish, pike, bluefish, stripers, cobia, redfish, walleye, and any other species that will hit on the surface.

I like single-action reels for most fishing, direct-drive for light fishing, and direct-drive or anti-reverse for bigger fish. Most of the fish you catch with lighter rigs will not run far enough to make direct-drive a problem in banging knuckles, and the direct contact makes it easier to know exactly the amount of pressure you are putting on the tippet. For larger freshwater and small saltwater fish, I like multiplying reels that retrieve several turns of the spool with each turn of the handle. There used to be more of these around than there are now, but they are still available from Martin (three models available for 6- through 9-weight lines), all with a 3:1 gear ratio for rapid retrieve. Orvis also sells a 2:1 gear multiplier in their D-XR Multiplying models, in both 7/8 and 9/10 sizes.

The advantage of multipliers is most evident when casting varying distances, such as when wading large rivers where targets might vary from twenty to eighty feet away, or similar boat fishing along shorelines, and to specific targets in fresh and salt water. They allow retrieving excess line to keep it from piling up on a deck (or in the water, if wading). Any bug reel should be of a size to hold a full weight-forward line or shooting taper and enough backing for the fish you are seeking. Also, all reels should be filled (but not overfilled) so that you retrieve the maximum amount of line with each turn of the handle.

Rods

Rods must be matched to the line size, since it is the line weight that we are casting. I strongly believe in cork grips for all fly rods since the current foams do not have the same feel or allow the same "punch" when delivering a cast. I also strongly believe that the best handle shape is a half Wells or full Wells, but with the half Wells put on correctly, not reversed as some companies are currently doing. The reversed half Wells does not provide a swelled forward portion for pushing the rod on the forward cast, as does the half Wells or a full Wells.

I also like uplocking reel seats, since the threaded barrel at the bottom of the reel seat makes a mini-extension butt and helps to separate the turning reel from the body when you are fighting a big fish and the rod is pressed against your chest or stomach. If you do go with an extension butt, the best are those that slip in via "O" rings, rather than screwing in (hard to do when you are fighting a fish and need the extension). They are also best if kept as short as possible, with two inches about the best length.

Since you will be casting long distances and usually shooting line on each cast, it helps to have large guides and a larger tip-top for maximum line flow.

Accessories

Some accessories are obvious. For example, you will need fly or bug boxes. Many options are available, but since bugs are bigger than most flies, be sure that you buy those that have large compartments that will hold the bugs you are using. Similarly, be sure that they are deep enough for your bugs. Often the best have long compartments in which bugs can be placed full length, so the long tails are not bent or damaged. Often boxes that will hold bugs are larger than those used for flies, so be sure to pick a vest compatible with the size of the bug boxes (or vice versa). Most terrestrials will fit into standard fly boxes, so these are less of a problem for trout anglers than the bugs used by others.

A good bug box will be like the one shown in which the compartments are adjustable or long for holding the long tails found on most bugs. Bug tails should not be bent or crimped by too short a compartment.

Fly-fishing vests number in the hundreds if you consider all the options —number of pockets, shorties versus regular lengths, colors or types of fabric, and types of speciality pockets (leader tippets, sunglasses, thermometers, etc.). Buy the style that you prefer and find best for your bug fishing, with particular attention to pocket size to hold the large bug boxes.

Another option is the over-the-shoulders carrier, in which large front and back bags are connected by shoulder straps. Often the rear bag is one large compartment, with the front made of multiple compartments for fly boxes and accessories. These ride high and are often good for the few boxes and accessories required to fish bugs. They are particularly good for wet-wading streams and rivers, and when fishing in and out of a canoe or small boat.

Other accessories for bug fishing depend on your personal preferences more than anything. I always carry a pair or two of pliers, on a belt sheath or in a fishing vest. Hook honers are very important, and I especially like the Diamond Machining Technology Ocean Pointer. This a diamond hone that is ideal for small and large hooks, although for very large hooks a coarser hone or file is also good for rough shaping of the hook point. The Ocean Pointer has a plastic handle that makes it easy to use, although I cut off about one inch of it to make it easier to pack and handle.

A hook disgorger, such as the Gaines BugOut, is good, as are nail or line clippers, spare tippet material, a small scale if you wish to weigh fish, and a foam patch on your vest or shoulder bag for drying out used bugs. Polarized sunglasses to help you spot fish and bottom structure are a must, as is a good high-number sun block to prevent skin damage.

One "must" accessory for bug fishing is an awl or pin to poke paint and finish out of hook eyes left from dipping or sloppy painting. Special tools for this are available commercially, but a simple solution is a large safety pin fastened to your fishing vest or bag. I keep a couple on each vest and carry-all just for this purpose.

Proper gape clearance is important for any fishing. As a general rule, I like a bug that has a hook gape approximately the diameter of the bug body at its largest dimension. Assuming that, there are some generalities as to the best hook size for various species of fish.

Tandem Rigs

Bugs can be fished in tandem rigs, usually with a fly as the second offering, sometimes with a bug. The most typical of these would be a bug in which a fly is used as a trailer, tied to the hook bend of the bug with about two feet of mono. Usually it is best to use slightly lighter mono on this trailer, so only one fly is lost should the fish break off from too much pressure.

A second arrangement could be a fly as a dropper on the line forward of the bug, with the dropper tied far enough up the leader so that the fly is about one to two feet ahead of the bug. In both of these rigs, often a popper is used, under the theory that the noise and disturbance of the popper will attract fish and that the fly might take those that refuse the popper.

A final possibility would be to fish a minnow-like bug as a trailer behind a popper or slider. Both will float, but will have a different appearance in the water. One might attract fish that would ignore the other bug.

Rigging Slip-on Bugs

Big-game bug fishing is often done with bugs in which the floating body is separate from the tail, with the body slid on the leader and the tail tied to

TABLE 12.3 Hook Sizes

Freshwater Species		
Species	*Hook Sizes*	*Comments*
Trout, streams	#20 to #2	hook size depends upon fish size and food
Trout, rivers, & lakes	#8 to #1/0	larger hooks for larger fish
Smallmouth bass	#12 to #1	smaller fish will take trout-sized bugs and terrestrials
Largemouth bass	#6 to #3/0	hook based on bass size, conditions
Walleye	#6 to #1/0	finding them in shallow water, often at night, is a must
Sunfish	#12 to #6	can include any of the many species in this category
Pike, muskie	#1 to #5/0	long-shanked hooks best

Saltwater Species		
Species	*Hook Sizes*	*Comments*
Bluefish	#1 to #3/0	heavy-wire hooks a must
Striped bass	#4 to #3/0	
Weakfish	#2 to #2/0	
Redfish	#1 to #3/0	
Shark	#1 to #5/0	
Amberjack	#1 to #4/0	
Cobia	#1/0 to #4/0	
Billfish	#1/0 to #9/0 (#3/0 to #5/0 typical)	often double-hook bugs are used
Sailfish	#3/0 to #6/0	
Tarpon	#1 to #4/0	size depends upon size of tarpon; surface bugs not the best, since big tarpon tend to push them away when striking.
Dolphin	#2 to #4/0	
Snook	#2 to #3/0	
Roosterfish	#1 to #4/0	

the hook. In essence, these are really big flies with a large, cylindrical popping head or slider added. While these are often made so that they will friction-fit onto the eye of the hook (see Chapter 8), the pressure of the water as the fish runs with the hook can slide the bug body up the leader. The danger is that other fish might see this bug body in the middle of a fight, bite the bug, and cut off the quarry. Lefty Kreh described his first billfish hit this way, and the loss of that fish persuaded him to lash the bug to the hook on all future bugs. Since most of these big-game bugs are designed so that the hook eye is hidden in the body, this lashing is only possible after rigging the leader or shock trippet to the fly. The easiest way to do this is to use Dacron line, wrap once completely around the shock leader in front of the bug placed on the hook, then criss-cross the lines over the body of the bug and wrap again completely around the hook shank immediately in back of the bug body, finishing with a square knot. If working with a Bob's Banger or a similar surface bug, in which the body slides completely onto the hook shank to expose the eye, it is possible to make the same wrap, beginning just in back of the eye, wrapping around and over the body, and securing around the hook shank. However, if the fit is snug—as it should be—these bodies will usually stay on the hook.

Billy Pate, a master angler with fly-rod records for big game, likes to position his bug bodies slightly up the leader for maximum hook gape and clearance for a striking fish. For this, he uses several methods. One is a figure-eight knot in the one-hundred-pound mono shock leader, about two inches above the fly, with the bug body above that. A second method is to use a star bead as a stop for the bug body, with the bead held in place with a wrap of thirty-pound-test (a nail knot will do) super glued on the one-hundred-pound shock leader. Bug bodies can also be toothpick-pegged in place. See Chapter 13 for information on fishing these large poppers.

Bug-to-Leader Attachment and Knots

Proper attachment of the bug to the leader is a must. Usually, the best hooks for any surface bugs are those with a straight eye; those with turned up (especially bad) or turned down eyes are not as good, since any pickup with the fly line will not pull the bug in a direct line with the hook shank.

Since fly-rod bugs and bug fishing can involve such a wide range of tackle, and fish species and sizes, the appropriate connections can vary widely. Here are some typical possibilities:

- **Small bugs and terrestrials to light tippet.** Here, the best leader-to-bug knot is an improved clinch, palomar, Trilene, or similar high-strength terminal knot. Since the leader tippets are low test and thin, there is no need for a loop knot.

- **Medium bugs to medium-light leader tippet.** The same knots listed above are ideal in most cases. In most cases a loop knot is not required.

- **Medium and large bugs to heavy leader or shock tippet.** To keep the bug working naturally in the water, a loop knot will be required for bugs tied to heavy leaders or shock tippets; a tight knot will deaden any action of the bug. A good loop knot is the Homer Rhode loop knot. It is not strong, but with a heavy shock leader this is not important. Test strength is about fifty percent of the line strength, but with a shock leader at least two times the strength of the tippet, this knot will do fine. A Rapala loop knot, tied like a reversed improved clinch on the line, is also good, as is a uni-knot loop (Duncan loop). Both are difficult to tie in heavy leader material, but both are stronger than a Homer Rhode loop knot.

  For large big-game bugs, a favorite method is to use mono or braided wire with leader sleeves, and crimp a loop in the leader.

- **Medium and large bugs to wire leader or wire shock tippet.** Wire presents special problems, since most wire (there are exceptions) will not pull up into a knot when standard knots are used. One simple solution is a figure-eight knot, pulled up tight. While it does not look strong or secure, it works fine for all wire-to-terminal-tackle applications. A better solution is to use the appropriate leader sleeve and leader crimping pliers to lock the wire leader onto the bug. Make the loop reasonably small.

Proper knots for making leaders and for leader-to-line connections are no different from those for any other form of fly fishing. Nail knots and needle nail knots are preferred for the leader butt-to-line connection; blood knots for the sections of leader when making up your own. A variation of this is to use loop connections at various points in the leader.

Most anglers will use a loop at the end of the fly line, connecting to a loop in the end of the leader.

The leader loops are easy; use a perfection loop or surgeon's loop. For the fly line there are several choices, including lashing in a loop of mono, doubling and lashing the fly line to form a loop, and doubling the end of the fly line, which is then secured with two nail knots tied in series and clipped.

I feel that a knot that I developed is better and quicker than any of these, since it results in a mono loop at the end of the fly line. To make this loop knot, double a length of twenty- or thirty-pound mono, hold the loop very close to the end of the fly line, and then use the double ends to make a standard nail knot. Make sure that the doubled strands stay parallel, and use only five to seven wraps, since the line will be doubled (making ten to fourteen wraps of mono). Tuck the end through the tube (as with a standard nail knot) and pull tight. Keep all the wraps tight to keep the resulting loop as small as possible.

Some anglers like loop connections in the leader for adding prepared shock leaders already secured to the bug. For these, a mono loop (perfection, surgeon's, uni-knot loop, or other loop connection) works fine, with a similar loop in the shock leader. If you plan to keep the bug attached to the shock leader, one of the two connection loops must be large enough to pass the bug through it to make the interlocking loop connection.

Storing Prepared Bug/Leader Rigs

Some anglers, particularly those who pursue toothy fish and big game, like to tie up bugs to shock leaders so that the shock leader can be tied or looped instantly to the end of their leader. Their are some commercial tackle storage systems for this; an example is the Stu Apte system by McKenzie, which allows hooking the fly on one side and stretching and securing the leader on the other side of a wide, shallow box. Similar methods of clamping (clothespin or banker clip) the leader end and hooking the bug (rubber bands or bungee cord) in a made-up box also work well. A system that I like for short shock leaders is to use a surf angler's snelled hook holder that holds the bug at one end and secures the leader by means of a slit in a rubber ring at the other. They will hold up to sixteen bugs and come in two sizes: seven-and-one-half inches and fourteen inches between the attachment points.

One way to store bugs on which wire or heavy mono leaders have been permanently attached is to use a surf leader holder like the enclosed. Two lengths are available and the bug can be slipped into the slots at one end, the leader end held by the rubber bumper at the other end. Similar rigs for holding tarpon flies and big game flies are also commercially available.

Storage of Leader Materials

Even if not using the above, it is important to keep the heavy diameters of shock mono straight. For this, dip the mono in very hot water, and stretch or hang weights from it until cool to make straight sections. Cut these sections into the lengths that you want (usually eighteen inches) and store in a one-half-inch-diameter PVC pipe (available at hardware or plumbing stores), with one end cap glued on, the other a friction fit. If storing mono of different pound tests, use a felt-tip marker to label each tube.

Lighter leader material can be stored on the spools that it comes on, or transferred to larger spools or one of the leader boxes that separately store large-diameter spools, the mono dispensed through small holes.

Sharpening Bug Hooks

As with any lure or fly, bug hooks must be sharp. Among serious anglers of any style of fishing, a sharp hook is one of the first things on their minds when questioned about tackle and lures. The methods for sharpening bug hooks are no different from those for any lure or fly, with triangulating the best method. This involves using a file or hone to form the hook point into a rough triangle (in cross section), sharpening along the point at two angles to make a knife edge, then slightly flattening the outside base of the point to make a triangle.

Any favorite hook-sharpening tool can be used for this, provided that it has the right grit or cutting surface for the size of the hook. I like a diamond hone such as the Ocean Pointer from Diamond Machining Technology, but hook sharpeners by many other companies are also fine.

Unlike sharpening bare hooks, you must take care when running the sharpener along the hook point that you do not cut into the body or tail of the bug. Often it helps to hold the bug by or near the bend of the hook to protect this area from the hook hone.

CHAPTER 13

Fishing Methods, Retrieves, and Manipulation of Bugs

H ow you fish bugs is often the biggest factor in how many fish you unhook. There are many variations in bug "action." The terrestrials covered in Chapter 2, for instance, are imitative patterns and styles designed to simulate a given insect, and thus can be effective fished dead drift, as well as with little twitches to simulate a kicking insect. Bugs such as those for bass, panfish, pike, and saltwater species such as bluefish, stripers, snook, and such are more often attractors. While they're suggestive of an easy meal, it is often more the movement they make and splashing water they create that gives them the appearance of something edible. In short, they are the piscatorial equivalent of the military's MRE's (Meals Ready to Eat).

How you fish such bugs—how fast, what retrieve, the mix of pauses, twitches, pops, skips, jerks, and swimming motions—can often make the difference in the number of strikes or fish logged at the end of the day.

Casting and Line Pick-Up

Basic fly casting is a skill that must be mastered to fish bugs effectively. This doesn't mean that you have to cast one-hundred feet (in fact, short casts allow surer strikes and less line stretch when striking a fish, and so better hook-ups), but that you must have loop control, accuracy, and consistency at reasonable distances. Casting bugs is often slightly different from casting flies, in that bugs' air resistance will slightly slow down the line movement, so that timing is slightly slower. Often, watching the forward cast and backcast helps in adjusting to this.

Picking the bug up off the water is difficult if done wrong, easy if done right. Basically, you can't be as cavalier about the pickup as you can when fishing smaller flies. The resistance of the bug can "catch" in the surface tension and throw off casting timing. The right technique is to lower the rod when almost ready to pick up the line (this is best anyway, for sure striking of fish), to point the rod tip at the bug, and to remove any loops or curves from the line by retrieving straight back. Then lift the rod firmly, but without angling it back, until the line and leader are off of the water and the bug is ready to pop free of the surface. At that point, it is easy to flick the rod back in an arc in the beginning part of the backcast, pulling the bug from the water and throwing the line back into a tight loop. Follow through with the rest of the cast as you would normally, adjusting for the slightly slower timing required by some bugs. Note that this pick-up system is still a smooth, continuous pickup; it is most important with poppers of any type that have a face that will "grab" the water. (It is less important with small bugs and with slider styles.) If you don't follow the above, the bug will tend to pop out of the water in the middle of a backcast, killing some of the energy that goes into it and making it difficult to recover and complete a forward cast.

This system is also important with a sink-tip fly line (sometimes used for bug fishing), since a fairly fast retrieve is a must to get the sinking tip to "plane" on top of the water for easy pickup. If using a long sink-tip, you might want to consider retrieving in most of the line, bringing the rod back as for a roll cast, then making an upward-angled aerial roll cast to pull the sink-tip and the bug from the water and to throw it into the air where an ordinary backcast can be accomplished.

Neutral-Density and Sinking Lines

One of the more unusual methods of fishing surface bugs—mostly poppers—is to fish them with a sink-tip fly line and short leader which, on a long, sustained retrieve, will pull the bug underwater and swim it along several feet down. Just how deep they go depends upon a number of variables such as the size (flotation) of the bug, type of bug (slider or popper), length of leader (short will take them deeper than long), and weight and length of the sink-tip section of the line. These lines can also be used for fishing various divers, such as the Dahlberg Diver and Pop Lips.

Fishing Still Water

Still water generally requires a slower retrieve than does fast water. Among warm-water species of freshwater fish, still water implies large-mouth bass; fast or running water implies smallmouth bass.

One of the traditional ways of fishing a bug (or a topwater plug) in still water is to cast the bug or lure, light up a cigarette, and when it is finished, make the first jerk of the bug. While perhaps an exaggeration, and while smoking is not socially correct any more in many circles, the long pauses and slow retrieves are still effective.

The result is that each retrieve takes far longer to accomplish than a retrieve in fast water. Often how you retrieve will depend upon water depth and the type of surface bug used. Poppers are noisy and thus can scare some fish in shallow water. In such situations, use long pauses, gentle pops, and some twitching and gurgling retrieves to avoid spooking fish. In deeper water, use a more vigorous retrieve to make more pops and more noise more frequently. The trick here is to make as much noise as possible with the popper to bring fish up from deep water, almost like a plug fishermen using a big chugger or Zara Spook to bring fish to the surface.

Sliders are ideal for quiet, shallow water, since they have more of a swimming motion and create less water disturbance than poppers. Since they often imitate a swimming or injured minnow, they are best fished with small twitches, slow swimming retrieves, and short jerks to simulate an injured baitfish.

Fishing Running Water

Running water—any type of current or flow—usually requires a faster retrieve than does slow or still water. There are exceptions to this. One is when fishing terrestrials, in which a terrestrial can be fished dead-drift through a feeding lane in a trout stream, or fished in a feeding lane, but with small twitches to cause the terrestrial to kick and jerk (but remaining in the same current or feeding lane). Here, the best cast is often upstream or quartering upstream, often with a long leader and long tippet, so that the terrestrial will float drag-free through the current for as long as possible. Using a long rod to get some "reach" out over the water to prevent drag, and mending with upstream loops of line to prevent bellying in the current, help in getting the longest drift.

One method of enhancing such presentations (if not prohibited by law) is to "chum" with live insects matching the imitation you plan to cast (or more properly, picking an imitation that will match in size, color, and species those most commonly falling into the water). For this, throw insects, one at a time, into the feeding lane of the trout (other fish—smallmouth, for example—will react and can be chummed the same way), getting the fish to take several live insects before getting into a downstream position for casting. Often the best days for fishing terrestrials are those in which there is a major "hatch" of the land-borne insects, and/or a slight breeze to cause some of them to fall into the current. Many terrestrials, such as hoppers and beetles, fly, and can be thrown into the water by a gust of wind. Others, such as ants and termites, are often swept into trout streams under high water that will flood out their nests and float them into the stream. Thus right after a storm is almost always an ideal time to fish, since the waters are often filled with floating meals that have been swept in by the weather.

Bugs—such as sliders, poppers, skippers, pencil poppers, frogs, and mice—whether of cork, balsa, foam, or deer hair, can be fished in a variety of ways for smallmouth, pike in running water, panfish, and perch. One technique is similar to that for fishing terrestrials for trout. Make an upstream or quartering upstream cast, cast some lazy "S" curves into the line to prevent drag, and float the bug in a drag-free drift through a likely current or feeding zone. A variation of this is to make the same cast, but then twitch the rod to cause erratic movement of the bug. A third method is to make a cross-stream cast, and immediately upon the bug's landing, begin by making a series of short, repeated jerks with the line hand, following the course of the line and bug with the tip of the rod. This will retrieve the bug in a slightly diagonal course to the flow of the current, with the bug usually ending up almost straight downstream, at which point it can be picked up for another cast or retrieved some more before being picked up for a cast.

Using this method, it is possible to vary cast lengths along with your movement straight downstream to completely criss-cross the water and cover it like a grid. Several casts from one position at varying distances can be followed by moving downstream several steps, then repeating the casts.

Another effective retrieve used when the bug is straight downstream is to "mend" the cast by throwing line first to one side, then to the other, to cause the bug to swing erratically back and forth in the current. The effect on the bug is like snapping a whip. It is also possible to float a bug downstream at the end of a cast, then retrieve back again, then float the fly downstream again, and repeat as desired. This is best if the direction of the cast is close to and parallel to good structure—the edge of a grass bed, a rock shelf, a submerged boulder, a bridge piling, a log jam, a dock, or a duck blind.

Structure is always good in any fishing, and especially so in running water. Fish hide in front of, to the sides of, and behind any sizeable structure such as a rock, boulder, log jam, downed tree, bridge support, or dock piling. Casting all around such structure is always worth the effort. Be particularly careful when casting upstream or upcurrent of any above-surface structure, since any miscalculation of the current can wash the bug right into the structure, possibly hooking it. If you are upstream of the snag, sometimes you can snake out line to form a belly, pull hard against the belly, and pull the bug downstream and off the snag. Sometimes a fast, hard roll cast will get a bug free, while holding the line above water with the rod and twitching rapidly also works. Other times you just have to wade in or boat in to get the bug back, or break off and start over.

Reading the currents can often help prevent such problems. Look for eddies, or differences in the speed of debris floating downstream. Fishing around the junction of two currents—one fast and one slow—can produce good results. Different anglers refer to these spots by different terms—"current breaklines" and "edges" are just two terms used.

Fishing Tidal and Salt Water

Tides create varying currents in salt water; they vary as to the time of day (there is a slack tide between high and low tides) and force of current. The latter will vary with the degree of tide (distance between normal high and low tides), and the location.

Another factor in salt-water fishing is the water's chop, which is often far rougher than in any freshwater fishing. Much of this is a result of shallow, inshore waters, combined with continuous boat traffic and the unprotected expanses exposed to the wind. The result is that you often need slightly larger, heavier surface bugs (usually poppers, but some sliders also). Larger bugs will hold in a chop better than will lighter, fluffier bugs and will not bounce or skip around on the surface as would a light freshwater popper.

The faster retrieves used in river fishing are also necessary for several reasons. First, the fast current allows you to keep the bug in a strike zone longer, instead of being carried downcurrent, as would happen with a slow retrieve. Second, there is less structure in salt water for baitfish to hide in, and their one escape is speed. As a result, saltwater gamefish will often slam a bug much faster and far harder than will any freshwater gamefish. The same techniques used in fishing running water (see above) apply to saltwater fishing. The same fan-casting at varying distances to cover all the water applies, as does the same casting around structure. The only difference is that the structure in salt water will be different—pilings, jetties, bridge supports, rock piles, dock and pier pilings, and sunken boats. Unfortunately, all of these structures will likely be covered with mussels or barnacles, so a snag on these will be even more difficult to extricate—and the sharp shells are also more likely to cut the leader!

While reading the water is important in any fishing, it is often easier in salt water, as a result of tide lines that show up as wavy, watery lines of algae, foam, and flotsam. Other clues to good spots are obvious differences in the speed of adjacent currents. Big fish will often hide out in the slow current, or downtide of a structure, and slash out to take something swimming or drifting by in the fast current. As with river currents, fish can be in front, alongside, or downstream of any structure that will block the current and protect the fish. Just realize that if fishing "downcurrent," this will change during the day as the tide changes. The protected area will be on one side during an outgoing tide, and on the opposite side during an incoming tide. There will be no or little movement during high tide and low tide, and fishing is seldom as good at these periods as during running water.

Fishing Big Game

We all thrill at the television shows and videos that vicariously bring us the sights of big game—marlin, sailfish, dolphin, and other species—caught on the fly. Often they are caught on a form of popping bug, although to be honest, the split-second timing required of this fishing does not always make a floating surface bug a necessity. The advantage of a floating surface bug—a popper of some type, in most cases—is that it allows the offering to stay on the surface where the fish expects it, should the fish not hit immediately.

The technique for this is one of complete cooperation between the fly fisherman, mate or assistant, and boat captain. It can be practiced on relatively small boats (twenty-footers) or with large big-game sportfishing groups. The method is not one of trolling a fly (which any serious fly rodder would abhor, and which would be illegal under the standards of the IGFA), but rather one of casting to a specific fish from a "dead" (not in gear or moving) boat.

The basic technique is to use teasers (lures without hooks) to attract the fish into the wake of the boat. Generally outriggers are not in fishing position, since this would interfere with casting the fly rod. Thus, teasers are generally trolled from rods, or from one outrigger on the opposite side of the boat from where the fly caster will cast.

Pulling the hookless lure or teaser away and out of the fish's mouth often infuriates the fish more and makes it easier for the fly fisherman. If the fish follows and is attracted to a teaser or lure rigged to a rod (some teasers are used on dummy lines tied to a boat cleat), the technique is to gradually retrieve the lure so that the fish is in the boat wake, with the boat still moving, and the fish within a short cast of the boat.

With the fish within a cast's length, the fly caster gets into a position into one rear corner in the cockpit. At a predetermined signal, the captain takes the boat out of gear, fulfilling the requirements of the IGFA and most tournaments to fish from a dead boat. At the same time, the assistant handling the teaser or hookless lure jerks it out of the water and away from the fish, while the angler makes one false cast and slaps the surface bug on the water in front of the fish. Usually the fish is so infuriated by the teaser's being taken away that it will hit the bug as soon as it strikes the water.

There are variations and nuances to this. While you want the fish to see the bug when it hits, some anglers are fearful of the forward movement of the fish toward the boat once it is hooked. As a result, some recommend slapping the popper down to the side or even behind the fish. Sharply striking the water with these big poppers will make a noise, and the fish will usually turn to the side (or one hundred-eighty degrees), so that when it takes the bug it is going away from the boat.

The bugs for such fish are usually poppers, often cylinders of foam. The EVA from EdgeWater, Ethafoam from King Neptune or from packing materials, Live Body in large (to three-quarter-inch) sizes from Dale Clemens, and cylinders cored from PVC and similar foam lobster and crab pot floats are typically used.

These are typically bug bodies punched with a hole to slide over the leader, fitted with a tube for durability, and slid up to a large, multi-hackled fly to make a bug. Often they are lashed together (see Chapter 12) so that the bug body will not slide up the leader during the fight where another fish can hit it and cut the leader.

Once the fish is hooked, the main task is to make sure that the line clears the deck and through the guides without tangles so that the fish can be fought from the reel. After that, it is strictly a function of the sturdiness of the reel, the efficiency of the drag, and the skill of the angler to bring the fish to the boat for gaffing or billing and release.

Retrieves for Bugs

Retrieves for bugs are not unlike those for any surface lure, and vary with the type of bug, the fish species, and the type of water being fished. Some general rules are:

1. Poppers require short twitches or jerks to make them pop, gurgle, and throw water.
2. Sliders and silent bugs are designed to move water and make a wake, rather than to pop. Thus, light twitches and short swimming retrieves interspersed with pauses are best.
3. Still waters require a slower retrieve than running water, such as currents or tides. Fish expect food to move little in still water and to move constantly with the current in running waters.
4. Different fish are attracted to different retrieves. Smallmouth generally like faster, noisier retrieves than do largemouth. Billfish

TABLE 13.1

Bug Shapes and Actions	
Bug Shape	***Bug Action***
Popper	Will pop and gurgle, often throw water in front of the bug, can sometimes create bubbles.
Skipper	Has a sharply angled face, so that it will tend to ride high on jerking retrieves, often hopping out of the water (skipping), and thus resembling a fleeing baitfish. Often good when fishing schooling, feeding, or breaking fish.
Spouter	The side-angled face will not throw as much water as a popper, but will throw water to both sides.
Slider	More of a "waking" bug, as some call it, since it will not pop and has a swimming or gliding motion in the water that creates a wake. Often best for fish in shallow water, where a popper might frighten them.
Feather minnow	Like a slider, but with a more bullet-shaped head for more water movement and more wake.
Quill or tube minnow	Often has even less of a wake than a slider or feather minnow, as a result of the thin profile. Ideal for situations when fish are feeding on any type of slim baitfish.
Hair popper	Like a regular popper, yet will sit lower in the water than one of cork, balsa, or foam. The coated face allows it to pop.
Hair slider	Like a regular slider, but sitting lower in the water, creating a wake when retrieved.
Pencil popper	A long popper body; otherwise similar to a standard popper in action.
Pencil minnow	More like a slider or quill minnow, in that it does not have a popping face and thus will make a slight wake, simulating a minnow or baitfish.
Dahlberg diver	A hair-bodied bug that floats at rest, but with a diving collar that causes it to dive on retrieve. Ideal for when fish are not feeding exclusively on the surface.
Siliclone	A bug of silicone-coated fleece that resembles a slim surface minnow. Like a slider in that it makes a wake, but will not pop.
Pop Lips	Another diving bug, this one silicone coated, and with a lip in front (in contrast to the rear diving collar of the Dahlberg).
Frog	Generally sitting low in the water, and low at the back to resemble the natural posture of a frog in the water; can be slider or popper style, in hair or hard materials.
Mouse	Mostly hair-bodied styles, like a slider, and sitting low in the water to create a wake.

basically have to have the bug thrown in their direction after being teased into casting range. Snook react like largemouth bass, and like slow retrieves, pops, and lots of noise.

The basis for any retrieve is a series of erratic movements that will simulate a baitfish, frog, minnow, surface insect, or other form of food that in turn will cause a fish to hit the lure or bug. Just throwing a bug out and retrieving evenly back for a second cast might catch a fish, but it will definitely catch far fewer than an erratic retrieve. These movements break down as follows:

- Pauses of varying lengths of time in which the bug is not moved at all by the angler (although it might be swept along with a current). Pauses can be of short, medium, or long duration.

- Twitches in which motion is created through a sharp action with the rod or line hand, but with minimal forward movement. A twitch will cause a slight pop in a popper, only a quiver in a slider.

- Jerks, which are stronger than twitches and which do cause notice-able forward movement of the bug. These can be light, medium, or strong, depending upon the bug, the action, or the water displace-ment and forward movement desired. A jerk, depending upon how strong, will pop any popper, but will only cause a noisy wake and forward movement with a slider.

- Swims in which the bug is moved forward, but with the jerking or twitching motions previously described. These can be for short, medium, or long distances.

Combining all of these in erratic ways will make the retrieve simulate a living creature and provoke strikes. Also, with practice it is easy to get into a rhythm of such movements, even though each one is different. The best possible retrieve in most situations is one that will mix up these movements as much as possible; the worst is one that will repeat the same action throughout the retrieve. The exception to this is in some running water situations, where a repeated twitch or jerk throughout the retrieve is best.

Some possibilities for bug retrieves are as follows:

1. Smallmouth in fast current; striper behind piling in tidal flow; bluefish in running tide; big trout in dam outflow section of river: short pause/jerk/short pause/jerk/short pause/jerk (repeated until pickup).

2. Smallmouth in fast current; striper behind piling in tidal flow; bluefish in running tide; big trout in dam outflow section of river: short pause/jerk/short pause/twitch/medium pause/twitch/short pause/jerk/long swim/medium pause/twitch/short jerk/short pause.

3. Largemouth in quiet, shallow, still water; snook in mangroves; trout in quiet pool; panfish along shoreline; redfish on flat; striper along mud bank: long pause/short jerk/long pause/twitch/twitch/ medium pause/short jerk/short pause/twitch/long pause.

4. Pike in slough; bass along shoreline or rip rap; trout along shore or rock shelf: short pause/long swim/short pause/long swim/short pause/twitch/short pause/medium swim/short pause/medium jerk/ short pause/long swim.

5. Feeding, breaking, or schooling fish of any species: medium jerk (no pause when the bug lands)/long jerk/medium jerk/twitch. (Virtually no pause at all, but repeated jerks and twitches throughout the retrieve to simulate scurrying baitfish.)

Understand that in all of the above, you do not have to exactly repeat the actions listed or memorize their order, only get into a regular rhythm of similar actions that will provoke strikes, and to modify these retrieves as conditions and experience dictate.

Removing Bugs from Fish

Use care when removing bugs from fish. Quick and careful extraction will prevent injury to the fish if you plan to release it. And too much twisting when holding the bug by the body might loosen the hook in the body and ruin the bug. My buddy Chuck Edghill uses hemostats to hold the hook by the bend when removing bugs from smallmouth. Locking long-nose pliers (such as those by Vise Grips) are ideal for larger bugs (and larger fish). Gaines makes a simple plastic, forked-end hook disgorger specifically for bugs, although any similar hook disgorger can also be used. While I don't generally like hook disgorgers, I do like them for bugs, since often a fish will be lightly hooked yet hooked deep. A straight, forked disgorger, such as the type that Gaines sells, is ideal for backing up the hook to loosen it, and the bend of the hook will stay in the fork of the disgorger while you remove the bug from the fish's mouth.

Suppliers

M any materials and tools necessary for making bugs are available
from your local tackle shop or fly-fishing store. The following are
companies that publish catalogs, price lists, or other literature containing
materials and tools for bug making. In addition, check the ads in fly-
fishing and fly-tying magazines such as *Fly Fisherman; American Angler; Saltwater Fly Fishing; Fly Rod & Reel; Flyfishing; Trout; Salm-
on/Trout/Steelheader; The Flyfisher;* and *Fly Fishing News, Views and
Reviews.*

Good mail-order supply houses to check for fly-tying and bug-making
materials include:

• Angler's Workshop, Box 1044, Woodland, WA 98674. Supplier of fly-tying
materials and tools.

- Bass Pond, Box 82, Littleton, CO 80160.

- Bass Pro Shops, 1935 S. Campbell, Springfield, MO 65898. Suppliers of foam, tools, and other supplies for making bugs, in a huge catalog of other fishing equipment.

- Bill Skilton's USA Flies, Box 64, Boiling Springs, PA 17007. Suppliers of foam products and other fly tying materials.

- Bob Marriott's Flyfishing Store, 2700 W. Orangethorpe Ave., Fullerton, CA 92633. Supplier of fly tying and bug making tools and materials.

- Beaverkill Angler, Stewart Ave., P.O. Box 198, Roscoe, NY 12776. Supplier of FTM Wing Cutters, ideal for cutting foam sheeting.

- Cabela's, 812 13th Ave., Sidney, NE 69160. Suppliers of materials and tools for making bugs, along with other fishing and hunting equipment.

- Cold Spring Anglers, 419 E. High St., Suite A, Carlisle, PA 17013. Suppliers of fly-tying and bug-making tools and materials.

- Clouser's Fly Shop, 101 Ulrich St., Middletown, PA 17057.

- Corkers, William S. McIntyre, 106 White Gate Rd., Pittsburgh, PA 15238. Cork bodies of various shapes for making cork bugs.

- Dale Clemens Custom Tackle, 444 Schantz Rd., Allentown, PA 18104. Suppliers of rod-making, lure-making, and fly-tying materials, including Live Body foam for making bugs.

- Dan Bailey's Fly Shop, P.O. Box 1019, Livingston, MT 59047. Manufacturers and suppliers of fly-tying tools and materials.

- Doug Swisher, 790 Bobcat Lane, Hamilton, MT 59840. Supplier of fly-tying and bug-making materials.

- Feather-Craft Fly Fishing, 8307 Manchester Rd., P.O. Box 19904, St. Louis, MO 63144. Mail-order supplier of fly-tying and bug-making tools, materials, and supplies.

- Fly-Rite, 7421 S. Beyer, Frankenmuth, MI 48734. Supplier of fly-tying supplies and tools.

- The Fly Shop, 4140 Churn Creek Road, Redding, CA 96002. Supplier of fly-tying and bug-making tools and materials.

- The Gaines Company, Box 35, Route 349, Gaines, PA 16921. Manufacturers of cork components for making bugs.

- E. Hille (The Angler's Supply House, Inc.) Box 996, Williamsport, PA 17703. Fly-tying and bug-making supplies.

- Hilts Molds, 1461 E. Lake Mead Dr., Henderson, NV 89015. Manufacturers of quality molds and supplies for making molded foam bug bodies. Also make molds for lead lures and jigs.

- Hook & Hackle, 7 Kaycee Loop Rd., Plattsburgh, NY 12901.
- Hunter's Angling Supplies, Central Square, Box 300, New Boston, NH 03070. Suppliers of bug-making and fly-tying materials and fly-fishing supplies.
- Jann's, Box 4315, Toledo, OH 43609. Supplier of fly-tying and bug-making tools and materials.
- Jerry's Tackle Shop, 604 12th St., Highland, IL 62249-1820. Supplier of fly-tying materials and tools.
- Kaufmann's Streamborn, 8861 S.W. Commercial St., Tigard, OR 97223. Suppliers of fly-tying and bug-making materials.
- King Neptune's Flies, P.O. Box 67101, Phoenix, AZ 85082. Suppliers of Ethafoam closed-cell foam popper heads and cylinder rods, and other materials for saltwater flies.
- L. L. Bean, Freeport, ME 04033. Supplier of fly-tying materials and tools.
- Madison River Fishing Company, Box 627, 109 Main St., Ennis, MT 59729. Supplier of fly-tying materials.
- Midland Tackle Company, 66 Route 17, Sloatsburg, NY 10974-2399. Supplier of tools and materials for fly tying.
- Murray's Fly Shop, Box 156, Edinburg, VA 22824. Fly tying supplies.
- Needles & Fins, 35 Robin Lane, Cheshire, CT 06410. Supplier of tubing cutters for cutting out foam and also electric trimmers for trimming deer hair and silicone fleece flies.
- Netcraft Fishing Tackle, 2800 Tremainsville Rd., Toledo, OH 43613. Supplier of fly-tying and bug-making tools and materials.
- On The Fly, 3628 Sage Rd., Rockford, IL 61114. Supplier of fly-tying materials and tools.
- The Orvis Company, 10 River Rd., Manchester, VT 05254-0798. Suppliers of fly-tying and bug-making materials and tools.
- Pennsylvania Outdoor Warehouse, 1508 Memorial Avenue, Williamsport, PA 17703. Fly tying supplies.
- The Practical Fly Shop. 43-18 Little Neck Parkway, Little Neck, NY 11362 Supplier of fly tying and bug making supplies.
- Rainy's Flies and Supplies, 690 N. 100 E. Logan, UT 84321. Suppliers of foam rod for tying terrestrials and other floating bugs.
- Rod Yerger, Quality Fishing Flies, Box 294, Lawrence, PA 15055. Supplier of finished flies and tying components for terrestrials.

- Tackle-Craft, Box 280, Chippewa Falls, WI 54729-0280. Fly tying supplies.
- The Urban Angler, 118 E. 25th St., New York, NY 10010. Suppliers of fly-tying and bug-making materials.
- Vigor Company, 1218 Six Flags Rd., Austell, GA 30001-7599. Distributors and retailers of Aron Alpha CA glues for foam.
- Whitetail Fly Tieing Supplies, 6179 Barnstable, Toledo, OH 43613. Supplier of materials for tying hair-bodied bugs.

Manufacturers & Distributors

T he following do not sell direct to the consumer (the exception are also listed in Appendix A). Most do have catalogs or can refer you to mail-order suppliers or tackle and fly shops in your area that carry their products.

- Cam Sigler, P.O. Box 656, Vashon Island, WA 98070. Manufacturer of specialty saltwater and big-game poppers and supplies.
- Cork Specialties, 1454 N.W. 78th Ave., Miami, FL 33126. Manufacturer of cork products, including cork bodies.
- Daiichi Hooks/Angler Sport Group, 6619 Oak Orchard Rd., Elba, NY 14058 Importers of fly hooks.
- Dan Bailey's Fly Shop, P.O. Box 1019, Livingston, MT 59047. Manufacturers and suppliers of fly-tying tools and materials.

- Danville Chenille Company, Inc., Box 1000, Rt 111A, Danville, NH 03819. Manufacturer of chenilles and threads.
- Dr. Slick Instruments for Anglers, 114 S. Pacific, Dillon, MT 59725. Manufacturers of fly-tying tools and accessories.
- D. H. Thompson, 11 N. Union St., Elgin, IL 60123. Manufacturers of fly-tying vises, tools, and materials.
- DuPont, 6236 Brandywine Bldg., Wilmington, DE 19898. Manufacturer of Lumaflex skirt and leg material.
- Eagle Claw, Box 16011, Denver, CO 80216. Manufacturer of hooks for bug making and fly tying.
- EdgeWater, 35 N. 1000 W., Clearfield, UT 84015. Manufacturers of closed-cell foam bodies and parts for freshwater and saltwater bugs.
- Flex Coat Co., Box 190, Driftwood, TX 78619. Manufacturers of rod-building components—including epoxy finishes—and a curing motor for bug making.
- Fly Dyes, P.O. Box 14258, E. Providence, RI 02914. Manufacturers of dyes for coloring fly materials.
- Flycraft, Box 582, Greendale Station, Worcester, MA 01606. Manufacturers of die-cut closed-cell foam in various sizes and colors, for making all terrestrials, frogs, and surface bugs.
- The Gaines Company, Box 35, Route 349, Gaines, PA 16921. Manufacturers of cork components for bugs.
- Griffin Enterprises, P.O. Box 754, Bonner, MT 59823. Manufacturers of fly-tying vises and tools.
- Gudebrod, Inc., P.O. Box 357, Pottstown, PA 19464-0357. Manufacturers of threads, materials, and tools for fly tying.
- Hareline Dubbin, Inc., 26781 Patterson Dr., Monroe, OR 97456. Manufacturers and suppliers of fly-tying materials and tools.
- Hedron, Inc., 402 N. Main St., Stillwater, MN 55082. Manufacturers of Flashabou.
- Hobb's Feather Co., Inc., P.O. Box 187, W. Liberty, IA 52776. Manufacturers and suppliers of feathers and other materials for fly tying.
- Hoffman Hackle, Whiting Farms, Inc., P.O. Box 784, Delta, CO 81416. Suppliers of genetic hackle.
- Hilts Molds, 1461 E. Lake Mead Dr., Henderson, NV 89015. Manufacturers of quality molds and supplies for making molded-foam bug bodies. Also make molds for lead lures and jigs.
- Kreinik Mfg. Co., Inc., 9199 Reisterstown Rd., Suite 209B, Owings Mills, MD 21117. Manufacturers of threads, braided body materials, and stranded materials for fly tying and bug making.

- Lagartun, 16741 S. Old Sonoita Hwy., Vail, AZ 85641. Manufacturers and importers of stranded materials for fly tying.

- Larva Lace/Phil's Tackle, P.O. Box 4031, Woodland Park, CO 80866. Manufacturers of materials and tools for fly tying and bug making.

- Metz Hatchery, P.O. Box 5666, Belleville, PA 17004. Suppliers of genetic hackle.

- Mystic Bay Flies, Box 602, Green's Farm, CT 06436. Manufacturers of saltwater popper bodies molded on hooks.

- Norlander Company, P.O. Box 486, Puyallup, WA 98371. Manufacturers of rotary vise and bobbin.

- O. Mustad & Son (USA) Inc., P.O. Box 838, Auburn, NY 13021. Manufacturers of fly-tying, bug-making (kinked-shank), and other hooks.

- Orvis Services, Inc., Historic Rte. 7A, Manchester, VT 05254. Suppliers of fly-tying tools and materials.

- Pace Industries, P.O. Box 5127, Fort Lauderdale, FL 33310. Importers of cork products, including cork bug bodies.

- Perry Design, 7401 Zircon Dr., S.W., Tacoma, WA 98498. Manufacturer of tube vise for tying tube in big game bugs, and also other fly-tying and rod-building tools.

- Rainy's Flies and Supplies, 690 N. 100 E., Logan, UT. 84321. Manufacturers of closed-cell foam for terrestrials, and other supplies.

- Raymond C. Rumpf & Son, P.O. Box 319, Sellersville, PA 18960. Suppliers of fly-tying tools, materials, and supplies.

- Regal Engineering, RFD 2, Tully Rd., Orange, MA 01364.

- Renzetti, Inc., 1901 W. Strasburg Rd., Coatesville, PA 19320. Manufacturers of rotary vises.

- Rocky Mountain Dubbing, 2012 E. Monroe St., Riverton, WY 82501. Suppliers of fly-tying materials.

- Satellite City, P.O. Box 836, Simi Valley, CA 93062. Manufacturers of CA glues used for foam bugs.

- Spencer's Hackles, 100 Deemer Creek Rd., Plains, MT 59859. Suppliers of genetic hackle.

- Thomason Products, Box 750573, Petaluma, CA 94975-0573. Manufacturer of the Hackle-Back guard for tying off and painting.

- Tiemco Hooks/Umpqua Feather Merchants, P.O. Box 700, Glide, OR 97443. Hooks for bug making, including kinked-shanked models.

- Umpqua Feather Merchants, P.O. Box 700, Glide, OR 97443. Suppliers of fly-tying tools and materials.

- Universal Vise Corporation, 16 Union Ave., Westfield, MA 01085.
- Vigor Company, 1218 Six Flags Rd., Austell, GA 30001-7599. Distributors and retailers of Aron Alpha CA glues (made by Borden, Inc.), used for foam bugs.
- Wapsi Fly, Inc., Route 5, Box 57E, Mountain Home, AR 72653. Manufacturers and distributors of fly-tying tools and materials, including popping bug bodies.

Bibliography

There have been no books—prior to this one—that specifically and exclusively covered the tying of floating bugs of all types that can be cast with a fly rod. However, most fly-tying books treat (in some fashion) hair-bodied, cork, or foam bugs, and additional tips can be gleaned from these sources. Some books have more closely covered some types of bugs—most often those used for bass and panfish, although there is a recent and increasing awareness of bugs for saltwater fly fishing. The following do not cover the waterfront on bug making and tying, but do provide additional information on the subject.

Almy, Gerald. *Tying and Fishing Terrestrials*. Harrisburg, PA: Stackpole Books, 1978. 238 pages. Excellent on patterns and fishing techniques.

Bay, Kenneth E. *Salt Water Flies*. New York: Lippincott, 1972. 150 pages. Basic tying methods, including some basics on bugs, with a dictionary of flies, including some bugs.

Bergman, Ray. *Fresh-water Bass*. New York: Wm. Penn Publishing Co., 1942. 436 pages. A dated, but still excellent, book on bass, with lots on bugs and bug fishing of the period.

Brooks, Joe. *Bass Bug Fishing*. New York: Barnes Sports Library, 1947. 72 pages. The first book just on fishing bugs with the fly rod.

Camera, Phil. *Fly Tying with Synthetics*. Minneapolis, MN: Voyageur Press, 1992. 192 pages. Mostly on synthetics for flies, but useful information for bugs as well.

Eggler, Tom. "Fishing Popping Bugs" (booklet). Gaines, PA: The Gaines Co., 1987. 28 pages. A small booklet on important facts about fishing bugs.

Herter, George Leonard. *Professional Fly Tying and Tackle Making Manual and Manufacturing Guide*. Waseca, MN: Brown Publishing Company, 1953 (or any other edition). 424 pages. An excellent, almost encyclopedic, source of information (for its time) on all aspects of fly tying and bug making that is seldom given the credit it deserves for fostering fly tying, bug making, and lure making among a lot of anglers in the 1940's and 1950's.

Keith, Tom. *Fly Tying and Fishing For Panfish & Bass*. Portland, OR: Frank Amato Publications, 1989. 192 pages. Excellent on both flies and bugs, but brief on bug making and fishing.

Koch, Ed. *Terrestrial Fishing*. Harrisburg, PA: Stackpole Books, 1990. 176 pages. Mostly on the designs and history of terrestrials.

Knight, John Alden. *Black Bass*. New York: G. P. Putnam's Sons, 1949. 200 pages. On all types of bass fishing, with a lot on fly-rod and fly-bug designs.

Kreh, Lefty. *Fly Fishing in Salt Water*. New York: Lyons and Burford, 1986. 242 pages. An excellent source of information on the subject, with a lot on bugs and bug fishing.

Kreh, Lefty. *Salt Water Fly Patterns*. Los Angeles, CA: Maral, Inc., 1989. 70 pages. Color photos and a dictionary of saltwater patterns, including many bug styles.

Kreh, Lefty and Sosin, Mark. *Practical Fishing Knots II*. New York: Lyons & Burford, 1991. 144 pages. Excellent source of information on knots, including those for fly fishing.

Livingston, A. D. *Tying Bugs and Flies for Bass*. New York: Lippincott, 1977. 144 pages. Brief, but good on tying bugs.

McClane, A. J. *McClane's New Standard Fishing Encyclopedia and International Angling Guide*. New York: Holt, Rinehart and Winston, 1974. 1,160 pages.

An immensely valuable treatise on all aspects of fishing, including bass bugs and other surface bugs for freshwater and saltwater.

Muma, John R. *Old Flyrod Lures*. Lubbock, TX: Nature Child Publisher, 1991. 152 pages. If you like old fly-rod lures, flies, and bugs, this is the book to check. Some lures that do not fit the format of this book, but lots on old bug designs.

Murray, Harry. *Fly Fishing for Smallmouth Bass*. New York: Lyons & Burford, 1989. 192 pages. Some on bugs with a fly rod for river smallmouth.

Pfeiffer, C. Boyd. *Modern Tackle Craft*. New York: Lyons & Burford, 1993. 544 pages. An encyclopedic work on making all types of lures and tackle. Does not cover fly tying or bug making, but does include information on basic lure construction methods.

Pfeiffer, C. Boyd. *Tackle Craft*. New York: Crown Publishers, 1974. 338 pages. An earlier version of the above work.

Samson, Jack. *Saltwater Fly Fishing*. Harrisburg, PA: Stackpole Books, 1991. 212 pages. Fishing experiences for a variety of saltwater game fish, including big game.

Stewart, Dick. *Bass Flies*. Intervale, NH: Northland Press, Inc., 1989. 48 pages. Brief on flies and bugs, with excellent illustrations.

Stewart, Dick. *Fly-Tying Tips*. Intervale, NH: Northland Press, Inc., 1990. 96 pages. Tips on fly tying, including bugs.

Stewart, Dick and Allen, Farrow. *Flies for Bass & Panfish*. Intervale, NH: Northland Press, Inc., 1992. 80 pages. A color dictionary on flies and bugs for panfish and bass. Lots of bug designs.

Stewart, Dick and Allen, Farrow. *Flies for Saltwater*. Intervale, NH: Northland Press, Inc., 1992. 80 pages. A color dictionary on saltwater flies, including much on bugs.

Tabory, Lou. *Inshore Fly Fishing*. New York: Lyons & Burford, 1992. 312 pages. An excellent treatise on inshore fishing methods, with some on bugs and bug fishing.

Talleur, Dick. *The Versatile Fly Tyer*. New York: Lyons & Burford, 1990. 336 pages. Includes an excellent chapter on working with Flycraft foam.

Waterman, Charles F. *Fly Rodding for Bass*. New York: Lyons & Burford, Cortland Library, 1989. 91 pages. Good, basic book on fly fishing for bass, including with bugs.

Wentink, Frank. *Saltwater Fly Tying*. New York: Lyons & Burford, 1991. 169 pages. A good, basic book on standard saltwater fly-tying methods, including bugs.

Whitlock, Dave. *L. L. Bean Fly Fishing for Bass Handbook*. New York: Lyons & Burford, 1988. 158 pages. Basic book on fly fishing for bass, including new bug designs and bugs modified by Whitlock from older, standard patterns.

Videos on Bug Making

Helm, Chris. *Hooked on Fly Tying–Spinning Deer Hair*. Available from *Fly Fishing Video* Magazine, 13410 S.E. 32nd, Bellevue, WA 98005. $19.95.

Messinger, Joe, Jr. *Tying the Bucktail Frog With Joe Messinger*. Available from Joe Messinger, Jr., Rt. 9, Box 119-M, Morgantown, WV 26505. $39.95 plus shipping and handling.

Mickievicz, Jack. *Tying with Live Body*. Available from Dale Clemens Custom Tackle. (Address in Appendix A), $24.95.

Riding, Rainy. *Tying with Rainy's Float Foam*. Available from Rainy's Flies & Supplies. (Address in Appendix A). $19.95.

Record-Keeping Organizations

For more information on fly-rod records, contact:

International Game Fish Association, 1301 E. Atlantic Blvd., Pompano Beach, FL 33060; (305) 941-3474.

National Fresh Water Fishing Hall of Fame, Box 33, Hall of Fame Dr., Hayward, WI 54843; (715) 634-4440.

Tips on Fly Tying and Using Foam

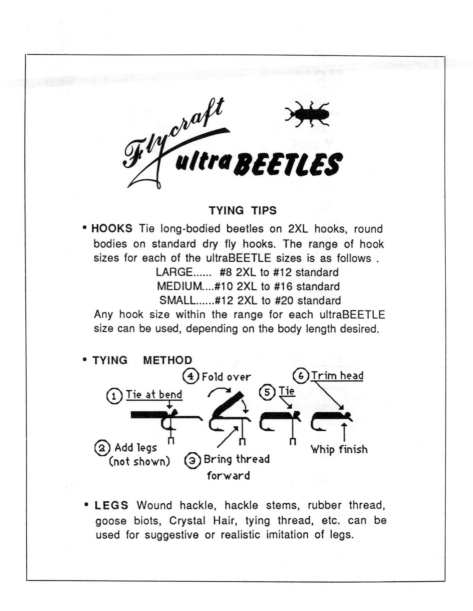

Flycraft ultra**BEETLES**

TYING TIPS

- **HOOKS** Tie long-bodied beetles on 2XL hooks, round bodies on standard dry fly hooks. The range of hook sizes for each of the ultraBEETLE sizes is as follows .

  LARGE...... #8 2XL to #12 standard
  MEDIUM....#10 2XL to #16 standard
  SMALL......#12 2XL to #20 standard

  Any hook size within the range for each ultraBEETLE size can be used, depending on the body length desired.

- **TYING METHOD**

  ① Tie at bend
  ② Add legs (not shown)
  ③ Bring thread forward
  ④ Fold over
  ⑤ Tie
  ⑥ Trim head
  Whip finish

- **LEGS** Wound hackle, hackle stems, rubber thread, goose biots, Crystal Hair, tying thread, etc. can be used for suggestive or realistic imitation of legs.

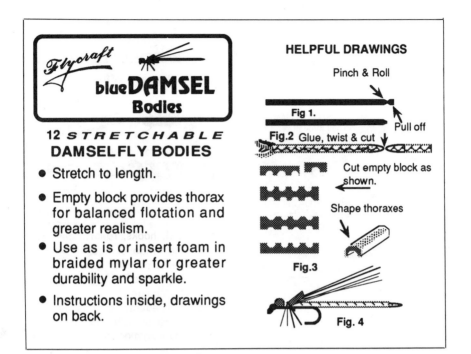

blueDAMSEL Bodies

12 *STRETCHABLE* DAMSELFLY BODIES

- Stretch to length.

- Empty block provides thorax for balanced flotation and greater realism.

- Use as is or insert foam in braided mylar for greater durability and sparkle.

- Instructions inside, drawings on back.

HELPFUL DRAWINGS

Pinch & Roll

Fig 1.

Pull off

Fig.2 Glue, twist & cut

Cut empty block as shown.

Shape thoraxes

Fig.3

Fig. 4

easyHOPPER

ABOUT easyHOPPER BODIES

easyHOPPER bodies eliminate tedious body construction methods while providing superior flotation and durability. Combine them with any of the natural or synthetic materials commonly used for wings and legs. Almost any hopper pattern or style will benefit.

A few suggested tying styles are shown in the silhouettes below.

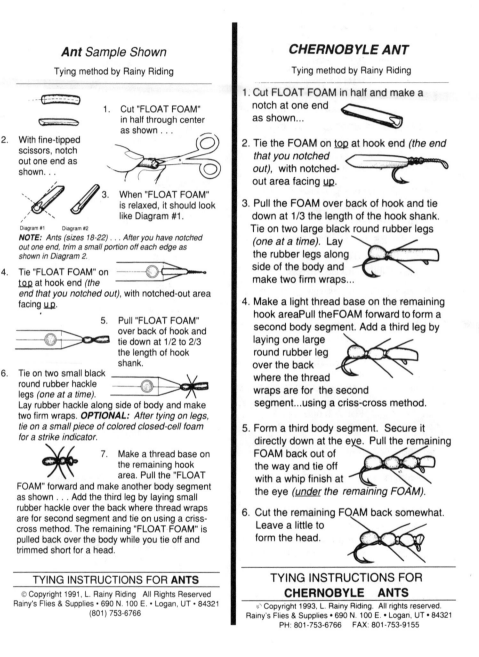

Ant *Sample Shown*

Tying method by Rainy Riding

1. Cut "FLOAT FOAM" in half through center as shown . . .

2. With fine-tipped scissors, notch out one end as shown. . .

3. When "FLOAT FOAM" is relaxed, it should look like Diagram #1.

Diagram #1   Diagram #2

NOTE: *Ants (sizes 18-22) . . . After you have notched out one end, trim a small portion off each edge as shown in Diagram 2.*

4. Tie "FLOAT FOAM" on top at hook end *(the end that you notched out)*, with notched-out area facing up.

5. Pull "FLOAT FOAM" over back of hook and tie down at 1/2 to 2/3 the length of hook shank.

6. Tie on two small black round rubber hackle legs *(one at a time).* Lay rubber hackle along side of body and make two firm wraps. **OPTIONAL:** *After tying on legs, tie on a small piece of colored closed-cell foam for a strike indicator.*

7. Make a thread base on the remaining hook area. Pull the "FLOAT FOAM" forward and make another body segment as shown . . . Add the third leg by laying small rubber hackle over the back where thread wraps are for second segment and tie on using a criss-cross method. The remaining "FLOAT FOAM" is pulled back over the body while you tie off and trimmed short for a head.

TYING INSTRUCTIONS FOR **ANTS**

CHERNOBYLE ANT

Tying method by Rainy Riding

1. Cut FLOAT FOAM in half and make a notch at one end as shown...

2. Tie the FOAM on top at hook end *(the end that you notched out),* with notched-out area facing up.

3. Pull the FOAM over back of hook and tie down at 1/3 the length of the hook shank. Tie on two large black round rubber legs *(one at a time).* Lay the rubber legs along side of the body and make two firm wraps...

4. Make a light thread base on the remaining hook areaPull theFOAM forward to form a second body segment. Add a third leg by laying one large round rubber leg over the back where the thread wraps are for the second segment...using a criss-cross method.

5. Form a third body segment. Secure it directly down at the eye. Pull the remaining FOAM back out of the way and tie off with a whip finish at the eye *(under the remaining FOAM).*

6. Cut the remaining FOAM back somewhat. Leave a little to form the head.

TYING INSTRUCTIONS FOR **CHERNOBYLE   ANTS**

IMPROVED Hopper

Tying method by Rainy Riding

1. Cut FLOAT FOAM in half and then make a "V" cut at one end as shown...

2. Tie in a bright red hackle fiber tail. Lay the FOAM directly on top of hook, securing it by tying three equal portions - starting at the bend and moving toward the eye...

TOP VIEW   SIDE VIEW

3. Flatten the third segment with thread...

TOP VIEW   SIDE VIEW

4. At the base of the flattened area, add an underwing of crystal flash ,over-wing of red squirl tail and knotted quill or pheasant tail legs (*tying in on each side*).

5. Tie in a deer hair collar as shown...

6. Trim deer hair collar ends short to the hook as shown...

7. Pull FOAM over the back to the base of the deer hair collar. "Hand" whip finish... then firmly pull and stretch the FOAM left and cut short as shown.

TYING INSTRUCTIONS FOR "IMPROVED" HOPPERS

Hopper, Cricket & Salmon Fly

Tying method by Rainy Riding

1. Cut "FLOAT FOAM" to desired length, then cut piece at an angle with sharp scissors as shown. . .

2. *(OPTIONAL)* Singe the long end with lighter and rub on cloth to remove any residue

3. *(OPTIONAL)* Pinch "FLOAT FOAM" while still warm to round the edges.

4. Cut with a razor 1/2 to 3/4 through the "FLOAT FOAM" as shown . . .

5. Make a thread base on hook and coat with Quick Gel no-run super glue. Then place the cut over the shank of the hook and tie down the short tip end. Loosely wrap back over the whole body with the thread only long enough for the glue to set *(just a few seconds)*, then unwind.

6. Complete fly as desired *(i.e.: add wings, legs, bullet head, etc.)*

TYING INSTRUCTIONS FOR HOPPERS, CRICKETS & SALMON FLIES

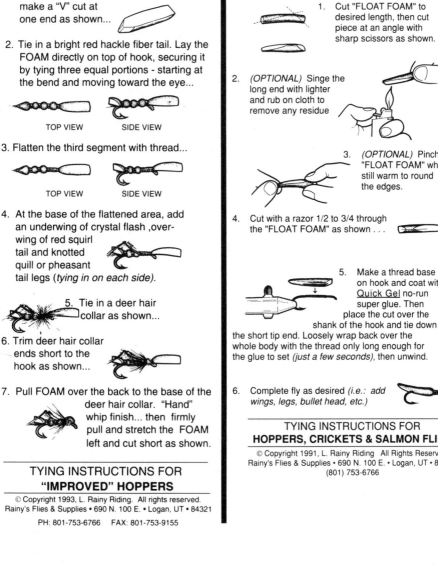

Index

The following is meant as an aid to guiding you through this book, but is not an expansive or cross-indexed reference. As noted from the Table of Contents, the book follows a logical progression and each chapter treats a specific subject—either a bug type or construction and tying method. These chapters and their subheadings make it easy to locate the contents of each chapter. The following is meant to point you to a specific page for a specific process or bug-making tool, procedure, or design.

Balance of bugs, 172–74
Balsa bodies, 15
Balsa bugs, construction, 101–105
    design, 105–108; designs, long sliders,
    108; designs, pencil minnows, 105;
    designs, pencil poppers, 105; designs,
    slab-sided minnows, 105–107

Bobbins, 3
Bodkins, 4

Clamps, 14
Closed cell foam, 15, 16
Cork bodies, 15
Cork bugs, carved heads, 89, 90

construction, 85–88; drilling, 91, 92; gluing hook, 95–97; hook preparation, 94, 95 sanding, sealing, 97, 98; shaping, 88, 89; slotting, 91, 92
Cork, cutting and shaping, 28
Curing motor, 12
Cylinder cutters, 8–10

Deer Hair, 17, 18
Designs, ants, 30–36
balsa bodies, 25, 26; bees, yellow jackets, 36; beetles, 40, 42, 43; big game, 190–192; Bob's Banger, 185; caterpillars, 45–47; cork bodies, 25, 26; crickets, hoppers, 37, 40; cutting, 26; divers, 183; double hook, 190; dragonfly, damselfly, 47, 48; extended-hook styles, 183, 184; feather minnows, 155, 156, 180; foams, 24, 25; frogs, 178–180; Gerbubble bug, 177, 178; hooks, 26; inchworm, 40, 41; jassids, 43; jointed bodies, 189, 190; jointed hook bugs, 186, 181; jointed legs/tails, 187–189; lady bugs, 43; leafhoppers, tree hoppers, 43; moths, 181; other, 18; pencil minnows, 185; pencil popper, 184, 185; skippers, 177; sliders, 176, 177; slip-on bodies, 195; slip-on popper, 192–194; slip-on tails, 195; snakes, 180; spiders, 36, 37; spliders, 177; spouters, 181, 182; surf foam Bangers, 185, 186; termites, 36

Eyes, 18, 216–220
bead, 220; combination, 220; decal, 218; doll, 218; dressmaker pins, 219; half beads, 219; map tack, 219; molded plastic, 220; monofilament, 219; painted, 216; stem-doll, 218, 219; strung bead, 220; tape, 218

Fishing bugs, big game, 241, 242
retrieves, 242–245; running water, 238, 239; still water, 237; tidal and salt water, 239, 240
Foam shapers, 10, 11
Fur, 17

Glues, 13, 14
Gluing, legs and tails, 157, 160

Hackle, 16, 17
Hackle Pliers, 5
Hair-bodied bugs, adding rubber legs, 61, 64
basic spinning, 53–58; basic stacking, 58, 60–63; basic tying, 52; combination, 84; cutting, trimming, 66–68; Dahlberg diver, 82, 83; Designs, basic, 77
frogs, 79, 80; frogs, folded hair, 80; Gerbubble bug, 81; mice, 80; moths, 81; poppers, 78; sliders, 78, 79; snakes, 80, 81
folded hair, 65, 66; Henshall bug, 82; Henshall method, 72–74; legs, jointed, 75; legs, standard, 75; Messinger method, 68–72; muddlers, 83; popping faces, 74, 75
Hair-bodied bugs, preparing hooks, 51, 52
tools, materials, 51, 52
Hair packers, 4, 5
Hair stackers, 5
Half-hitch tools, 4
Hook size chart, 228
Hooks, 21, 26
Hooks, sharpening, 232, 233
Hooks, sizes and styles, 171, 172

Leaders, 222–227
Leaders, attachments and knots, 229, 231
Leaders, storing, 231, 232
Lines, 223, 237

Materials, balsa bodies, 15
closed-cell foam, 15, 16; cork bodies, 15; deer hair, other hair, 17, 18; eyes, 18; fur, 17; glues, 13, 14; hackle, 16, 17; other, 18; synthetic, 18; synthetics, 18; thread, 14, 15
Molded bodies, 22
Molded bugs, coloring, 126
costs, 128, 129; finishing, 125, 126; foam, 121, 122; hooks, 121; others

available, 129, 130; steps in making, 122–125; types, 119, 120; variations, 127, 128

Painting, brushing, 209, 210
clear coat, 211; curing, 211; dipping, 206, 207; felt-tip marker, 214, 215; foil, decals, 212, 213; glitter, 211, 212; paints and sealers, 202–205; preparation, 205, 206; spraying, 207, 208; spraying, scale finishes, 208, 209; tools and brushes, 205

Power tools, 11, 12

Quill bugs, construction, 110, 111

Rasps, files, 6
Rattles, attached to tail, 196, 197
bubble style, 197, 198; glued-in, 195, 196; molded-in, 127; wrapped hook, 196
Reels, 224, 225
Retrieves, bugs, 242–245
Rigs, slip-on bugs, 227–229
Rigs, tandem, 227
Rods, 225

Sanders, 6
Sandpaper, 6
Saws, 5
Scissors, 3, 4
Shaping and sawing jigs, 6–8
Silicone bugs, construction, 111–117
Soft-foam bugs, cutting methods, 133, 134; designs, poppers, 139
Sigler style, 144; sliders, 140; slip-on tubing bugs, 141–144
foams, 131, 133; gluing tails, 140; hook gluing, 136–138; inserting materials, 140
Soft foam bugs, prepare hooks, 148, 149

shaping methods, 134, 135; threads, 149; tying synthetics, 152–154; tying tails, 149–152; wound hackle, 154
Synthetic materials, 18

Tackle accessories, 222–225
Terrestrials, ants, 30–36
balsa bodies, 25, 26; bees, yellow jackets, 36; beetles, 40, 42, 43; caterpillars, 45–47; cork bodies, 25, 26; crickets, hoppers, 37, 40; cutting, 26; dragonfly, damselfly, 47, 48; foams, 24, 25; hooks, 26; inchworm, 40, 41; jassids, 43; lady bugs, 43; leafhoppers, tree hoppers, 43; other, 18; painting, 28, 29; spiders, 36, 37
Terrestrials, termites, 36
tying, 30–48
Thread, 14, 15
Tools, clamps, 14
curing motor, 12; cylinder cutters, 8–10; hackle pliers, 5; hair packers, 4, 5; hair stackers, 5; power, 11, 12; rasps, files, 6; sanders, 6; sandpaper, 6; saws, 5; shaping and sawing jigs, 6–8; power, 11, 12; bobbins, 3; bodkins, 4; half-hitch tools, 4; scissors, 3, 4; vises, 1, 2; whip finishers, 4
Tubing bugs, construction, 110–111
Tubing, slip-on bugs, 141–144
tying tails, 154, 155
Tying, moth wings, 156
Tying-off thread, 168–170
Tying, wrapping bodies, 156

Unhooking bugs, 245

Vises, 1, 2

Weedless designs, 160–168
Weight, molded-in, 127, 128
Weight, tied on, 198, 199
Whip finishers, 4

ML

D/03